PRIMAL SENSUALITY

PRIMAL SENSUALITY

NEW HORIZONS AND EXPLORATIONS FOR LOVERS

by Paula Newhorn

G. P. PUTNAM'S SONS  *New York*

*To Ed, to all our family
and the late Fritz Perls
who, for so many of us,
is still here-and-now*

Contents

INTRODUCTION

THIS BOOK is a map. It directs you to certain experiences. It is a how-to book—not theoretical conjecture.

Achieving orgasm is not its theme; the ultimate experience is not orgasm *per se.*

First is the experience. Words are oceans removed—like the difference between locating the Grand Canyon on the map and actually gazing at its beauty.

If you and your lover follow the spirit and guidelines of my map, you will reach your destination together, exploring the multicolored canyons and peaks of your joint sensuality. To repeat: The ultimate experience is not necessarily orgasm.

The explorations in this book have introduced new peak experiences to adults of all ages and life-styles—adventurous, growing, aware people who attended seminars in primal sensuality* presented by me at various West Coast growth centers during the past several years.

It is through our senses that we experience the consciousness of life. The keener our senses, the more alive we feel; the more joy, grief, pain, ecstasy—the continuum of life.

Our senses have been *flattened* in the crush of a society still suffering the effects of obsolete Victorian moral codes and the grinding dehumanization of a runaway, irresponsible technology.

* I employ the word, "primal," in this book in the sense of the *original state,* not in relation to Dr. Janov's Primal Therapy as enunciated in his books and teachings.

In growing up I was subjected to the same sort of societal devaluation of the senses as most of my contemporaries. I have spent most of my life as a writer, making my living in the world of words and ideas; I expressed my sensual self mainly through dance (studying and performing). My first brief marriage found me abysmally ignorant of sexuality and sensuality. Divorce was the beginning of my journey-still-in-progress toward self-actualization.

In 1963 I became involved in the human potential movement, the "third force" of humanistic psychology, and sensuality. At Esalen Institute and other California growth centers, I learned from the movement's pioneer leaders. Through these and other direct learning experiences I eventually discovered important sensual and sexual potentials.

When sensuality was taught in the form of sensory awareness, it was accepted or tolerated because it was specifically separated from sexuality (which is one aspect of sensuality). Like love and sex, one can sometimes be mistaken for the other, so when we learn to tell them apart, we can do a better job of combining them.

Bernard Gunther has effectively spread the message of sensory awareness. Others have popularized sexuality with a touch of sensuality. My purpose is to unite the two. And to de-emphasize the orgasm concept for women, opening up the immense potentials in primal sensuality.

A great many married women have expressed to me the hurt and frustration they feel because their husbands will not engage in the kind of sensual-sexual foreplay that pleases and excites them. These husbands have their minds on the *fore* instead of the *play*. Women today are seeking not only to please but to be pleased. Those husbands who take their wives for granted and will not open themselves up to the joy that comes from *giving* pleasure to another are sending them into the arms of others, male or female, who understand and care.

At the same time there are many women who are too passive (unsophisticated sensually) to make love to their men. Their idea of being female is the stereotyped one of submission, leaving the responsibility to the man. This type of woman or girl has to be seduced and frequently doesn't protect herself from pregnancy because precautions would be admitting it was as much her idea as his. Preparations are unromantic, she says. So are abortions. She expects her lover to know exactly how to induce "ecstasy"; the responsibility, she feels, is his all the way. Only when she accepts full responsibility for her own pleasure will she get what she really wants and needs.

If any of this is meaningful to you, then you are ready to grow. You *can* make the sensual journey. It has happened to my seminar participants who were ready to follow the map I drew for their private explorations—the heart and substance of this book. All personal examples are based on my work with people who attended the seminars or were referred for counseling in primal sensuality. Their names have been changed. (And while these people have been kind and generous in letting me know that they have benefited, I have been equally pleased to learn a great deal from them.)

It has been documented by innumerable researchers and sexologists that women tend to reach their sexual peaks at least a decade later than men. Most authorities seem to attribute this male-female sexuality gap to basic hormonal differences.

I suspect that just as women have changed considerably in their sexual functioning within the last several generations (and not because one generation differed biologically from another), so will we soon see women reaching their sexual peaks at younger ages.

Just as cultural conditioning has been responsible for other changes in female sexual response, so, I believe, will women realize their full potential at earlier ages—to the extent that they are freed from the trappings of the double standard, the inhibiting "nice girl" image and other Victorian hand-me-downs.

At the same time men will be liberated from the totally unrealistic masculine image imposed upon them.

Unfortunately a great many men have swallowed the stereotype notion of themselves as wordly, infallible lovers. Frequently, when the woman finally overcomes her reluctance to tell a man what she likes, or doesn't like, he won't listen. "Nobody's going to tell *me* how to make love," he says, feeling his masculinity impugned. Obviously, if he's supposed to know it all, then nobody can tell him anything.

I've found that a woman will usually accompany her man if he is interested in my seminars; but many a wife who wants her husband to attend must virtually threaten divorce before he'll go. And a single woman wouldn't dare suggest it to her lover unless he feels *she* needs it.

Learning to pleasure* each other is like cultivating a beautiful garden. You can't say, "I'll only water the seeds when I see them growing."

If a couple doesn't expend the effort without stinting and measuring, they're likely to get weeds and scrubby plants. Blame and recrimination soon follow. It's like trying to grow roses by stomping on them.

Although I may seem at times to address myself mainly to heterosexual lovers, most of what I have to say is applicable to homosexual love, which I do not discount. When I speak in terms of heterosexual relationships, it merely reflects the nature of my own adult sexual experience. Yet my sexual preference for men certainly allows ample emotional space for loving people of both sexes.

To some extent we are all androgynous, a happy (if we accept it) mixture of maleness and femaleness. Recognition of this aspect of our nature by the ancients is evidenced in mythology, in the hermaphroditic qualities of many of their gods.

The focus of this book is on the mutual discovery of ways—*ad-*

---

* I use "pleasure" as a verb to indicate an *active process* of doing rather than a feeling or passive receiving.

ditional ways—to pleasure each other sensually, tenderly, lovingly.

As preparation for your adventures in sensuality, I'm also going to teach you how to intensify your orgasms, and connect up your entire body so that any part of you can be an exquisitely erogenous zone—to the point of orgasm, *if desired.*

When you combine sensuality, sexuality, and love, you enjoy a peak experience, a high High without drugs and artificial assists. Stir those highly volatile ingredients, and—enjoy your trip!

> Every time
>   I think I've
> reached The Top
>   you take me
> through another
>   stained glass door . . .

1

PLEASURE! WHAT KIND
OF A GOAL IS THAT?

IN Greek mythology Pleasure was conceived from the union of beauteous Psyche (soul/mind) with Eros (god of love). The child of this marriage was a girl, aptly named Voluptas (pleasure).

In more recent centuries, however, Pleasure fell into disrepute on earth. She was called wanton. A gratuitous gift of the gods, she was shunned. Those who courted her risked many a raised eyebrow and were punished in all manner of ways.

Though no longer stoned and exiled, Pleasure still languishes beyond the pale. She is embraced freely only in the first few years of our lives.

Paradise Lost

On the first day of school (or sooner) pleasure for its own sake is banished. Its pursuit, for no "better" purpose, is suspect.

Pleasure is tolerated only as part of a socially acceptable goal (*winning* a game, for instance, rather than just having fun).

We empathize more with pain than pleasure.

A child, wanting to share its pleasure at the smell and feel of a favorite something, is told mother doesn't have time for that sort of "nonsense." (Food is to swallow—not smell, feel, lick, taste, crumble or smear all over you. Eat it because it's good for you. And don't dawdle!)

A healthy baby likes his body. He enjoys it and its functions. He does not make a distinction between his bodily excretions and himself. Soon, however, he picks up a negative, critical reaction from parents and others. The genitals then become associated with this repulsion.

The child is receiving conflicting messages. If he chooses to believe his body and continues to show good, pleasurable feelings toward his excretions and genitals, he will probably incur parental disapproval. If he opts for parental approval, he internalizes the message that body excretions, certain good feelings and the places they come from are "nasty." He has taken his first small step toward a mind/body split, away from primal sensuality.

In the mind/body split our intellectual thought process gains a stranglehold over our physical senses: Some of the connections between the brain and the rest of the body are blocked; messages are not properly registered by the brain; they may be garbled, misinterpreted, or very faint and ignored. We begin our internal and external dialogues with "I think," rather than "I feel."

As we grow up we are assaulted from all sides with the message that all bodily excretions are nasty, dirty, offensive enemies, to be fought unceasingly with every deodorizing drug and cosmetic that promises a new "inoffensive" you.

That dictum is a lie. In some cultures people are distressed if they cannot sense each other's body odors.

Normal body excretions are good.

A healthy sweat is good. It may not smell so pleasant after it gets stale and the bacteria have been multiplying for a while. But even then, some women, like Sally, treasure the smell of an absent lover's sweaty shirt (or whatever)—and she's healthier than the compulsive bather, or Bob, who wanted his woman practically boiled in Lysol before they "indulged in intercourse."

Healthy urine is sterile. One of my vivid childhood memories is the time an angry little boy deliberately urinated on me, and how horrified my mother was. She put me in the shower and scrubbed my skin red with antibacterial soap. (The boy ended up a career army officer. In the artillery, I believe.)

Menstruation is not "bad blood" as some people believe. A psychologist at one of my seminars asserted peremptorily that it's toxic. Poppycock. Any medical doctor will confirm that there's nothing toxic about normal menstrual blood. It's the essence of being female. Taste a dab. If you are a woman and the idea disgusts you, examine your feelings about your sex. I get a distasteful grimace from at least one or two women when I make the suggestion during a seminar. They react as though I were asking them to taste excrement. Actually it tastes just like the blood you might suck from your cut and bleeding finger.

Sexual excretions taste marvelous when your feelings about sex and your partner are good. When a man gets excited, a clear excretion that is pure ambrosia may ooze from his penis—the sweetest nectar you could desire. The vaginal odors of a healthy, aroused woman are a tremendous turn-on, but most women don't realize that.* (Vaginal deodorant ads promise "security" against offending, but gynecologists report increasing infections from these sources!)

In a culture that bombards us with deodorant ads and vilifies natural smells, children grow up with the idea that any odor emanating from the body is bad—especially when the area is in proximity to the anus and urinary outlet.

When I first refer to body odors as positive and exciting, I get initial resistance from at least a third of my group. Once they adjust to the idea that body odors and excretions do not equal filth—that I am not referring to habitually unwashed bodies— they begin to entertain the idea that their conditioning is what makes the odors of reasonably clean bodies seem unpleasant. (Dr.

---

* Adelle Davis says that vegetarians who become deficient in Vitamin B 12 develop irregular menstruation and a bad-smelling vaginal discharge, which is eliminated by the needed vitamin B 12.

John M. Knox, chairman of the dermatology department at Baylor College of Medicine, has stated that Americans are harming themselves by too much bathing, cosmetics and deodorants.) The first step, then, is to reevaluate one's attitudes about healthy excretions.

A Sensual Revolution

The Victorian era symbolizes an anti-sensual/sexual society, which culminated in a struggle to enchain the sexual life force.

A genuine sexual revolution, then, must begin with sensual awareness—a sensual revolution! When the sensual and the sexual are revalued and reintegrated, when the pernicious double standard is laid to rest, then it is possible to achieve our sexual freedom and natural potential.

Nudie and porno shows do not represent sexual freedom. *Exploitation* of nude, writhing, human bodies performing for profit is only the other side of the Victorian coin. It's just as much a devaluation of sex—and just as dehumanizing.

More healthy are the free nude beaches and private nudist or therapy groups where the body is not ogled as an object but accepted naturally and unashamedly as part of a total human being. This sort of genuine acceptance of our natural state can be liberating, as I hope you will discover personally. (Explorations B and C.)

Sensual suppression has reduced us to a nation of deodorized spectators, living a vicarious, plastic existence.

In using sex as a spectator sport, people are seeking ways of awakening their ebbing passion. They watch synthetic lovemaking, and they substitute words for the experience. The real thing is too risky. It makes them vulnerable to pain, to loss. Better to be numb.

Good sex requires you to immerse yourself *completely*, focus completely, on the here-and-now experience—on the sensual—on the sensations. You must lose your *self*. A full orgasm is a total *letting go*.

The life force is expressed through sex. Each complete act is a death and rebirth.

Existential psychologist and author Rollo May reports in *Love and Will* that many members of the sexually "permissive" generation are telling him that they're doing it more but enjoying it less. My young seminarians corroborate that. Why? Because the passion is lacking, says May. I would add, of course, that *sensuality* is lacking.

Ben, for instance, complained that while he had no trouble producing an erection and copulating for long periods of time, his orgasms gave him little or no pleasure—the whole experience was dull, lifeless. Sometimes he didn't have an orgasm at all. He thought the trouble was with his partners: One was "too devouring," another "lay there like a dead-ass," a third "didn't know how to suck me off," etc., etc., etc. He even counted the number of contractions when his partner had an orgasm—and let her know that so-and-so had more. His turnover was like a roadside diner's.

Ostensibly he was seeking his "dream girl" lover. What he didn't seek was caring, affection, emotional intensity and genuine sensuality. He was constantly on guard against letting a woman "get her hooks into me" or make emotional demands. What he didn't realize was that his sexual feelings were intimately connected to his emotions—rather, their suppression. Feeling was blocked in the mind/body.

Sensuality and passion are equally important to men and women.

Ben's female counterpart is Janet—twenty-six, hip, pretty, with a lithe, slim body given to staccato movements. Wide-eyed and breathless, she speaks of her sexual adventures in a little girl voice.

Flashing her large, dark eyes, Janet attracts men easily and when she meets someone "sexy" she wastes little time "trying him out." He gets one chance in bed. If he doesn't pass muster—she shrugs her shoulders—"he's out."

She has no time to waste—she's a study in perpetual motion—

bolts her sandwich while driving to shops on her lunch hour. If she could do three things at once, all the better. Only when she slows down and turns off her racing computer mind, does she feel the stirrings of her primal sensuality.

Sensual Training and Self-Love

Small but growing segments of our society are reacting to one of our must dehumanizing taboos—no touching. It begins with the taboo against touching one's self and gradually extends to others.

Nonverbal touching and tactile experiences are always part of primal sensuality seminars. Every so often, however, I get someone who recoils at being touched or massaged. One such person suffered through an Esalen-type massage that is ordinarily deeply relaxing and then confessed that massages made him tense. His inner taboo was too great and the next day, when the loving massage was scheduled, he didn't show up. Perhaps because they have been conditioned to put up with being touched even when they don't like it, I have encountered fewer women with this problem. In general such people have been rare at my seminars because most of them would not attend in the first place.

Adults raised with a dread of touching themselves and others perpetrate pernicious myths about masturbation.

If all those masturbation tales were true, most of us would be in institutions for the insane, blind, debilitated or terminally ill.

Masturbation is normal, healthful and often preferable to certain kinds of sexual release. (As Louise asserted about a stranger who propositioned her in a bar, "Let him go masturbate in someone else's hole!")

Few of us have been lucky enough to escape masturbation guilt. Victorianism dies hard and slow. Yet a guilt-free attitude toward masturbation plays an important role in our ability to enjoy other guilt-free sexual pleasures.

Masturbation is normally our first genital-sexual experience.

When we enjoy it without guilt, we can go on to greater sexual enjoyment with others. It is to sexual training what crawling is to walking. It is self-love, *basic to primal sensuality.*

My work has largely confirmed the studies showing that women who masturbated to climax as girls made the transition to orgasm during coitus more readily than those who had not practiced masturbation.

One young woman who came for help in achieving orgasm had never masturbated or had an orgasm in any way. She was so guilt-ridden that when I encouraged her to learn the pleasure of self-love, she resisted until I labeled it self-stimulation instead of masturbation.

A great deal of pleasure in this activity was erased for me in my late teens by an "authoritative" article that stated categorically that masturbation impeded full orgasmic response for women in marriage. Those were the days when Freud's myth of the vaginal orgasm reigned supreme and clitoral orgasm was dubbed "immature." It was years before the harm of that notion was undone for me.

Even children raised in enlightened households with positive attitudes toward masturbation pick up negative feelings from the majority of their less fortunate peers.

Like guilt about intercourse (to which it's related), masturbation guilt can take most of the pleasure out of what should be a highly enjoyable activity. Instead of doing it strictly for pleasure, enjoying the sensations fully and prolonging them as long as possible, the guilty masturbator has in mind the *goal* of orgasm—i.e., release of tension—and proceeds to get it over with as rapidly as possible. This attitude can be unconsciously carried over into partnered activity, particularly in the case of the "quickie." (Slam-bam, thank-you-ma'am!) It all happens so fast, she's not even sure anyone's been there. It's one of the most common complaints I hear.

Conversely, prolonging masturbation is excellent training for prolonging intercourse. When the experience is wonderful, we do want to extend it to the maximum. The primal sensualist understands how to achieve the maximum experience.

That many men can be content with intercourse that lasts but a few minutes is all the more curious when you consider the orgasm is the *end result* of his pleasure (unless he's rather young or exceptional).

The best approach to lovemaking and masturbation alike is to focus on pleasure alone. The more you enjoy it, the more you want to prolong the pleasure, and therefore the more intense the orgasm when you finally have it.

Children—some as young as four months old—masturbate simply because it feels good. They never heard of orgasm. On the contrary, when they develop skill, they will deliberately postpone the orgasm as long as possible.

Before you can genuinely love someone else, you must first love yourself. The same is true of lovemaking. It is important to start with yourself and *feel good about it.* That is the contribution of such books as *The Sensuous Woman*, *The Sensuous Man*, and other bestsellers that teach and preach masturbation as basic training.

Even if you have been convinced by medical authorities that masturbation is good, clean, healthy fun, there's another possible hangup.

Do you really feel all right about giving/allowing yourself pleasure for no productive purpose—with no other goal? Can you set aside hours for no other purpose than sexual pleasure? Or are your puritanical forebears looking over your shoulder disapprovingly?

I have been asked on occasion, "How long should sex take?" Hard to believe, but true. There are some individuals who do not wish to spend any more "precious time" than is absolutely necessary.

Goal-Free Sex

Can you make sex the main event of your day or evening instead of squeezing it in after a double feature, dinner party, the theater? If not, you might as well close this book and turn on TV.

To get the most out of the succeeding experiments, give up your goals or expectations of what sex will do *for* you. Seek only to *enjoy* each moment as though it were the very first and last portion of your favorite food, which you must savor now because you will never have it again.

Would you gulp gourmet food, stuffing large portions into your mouth, swallowing it hastily, half-chewed? Or would you approach it slowly, lovingly, inhaling deeply its unique fragrance, rolling it sparingly around your tongue, allowing small amounts to sink into your taste buds, focusing on flavor, texture and pleasure rather than how long it will last, whether you'll get more, and whether you might get indigestion or hives?

Put aside everything you ever read or heard about how to arouse your partner—even if it's "correct" and "works" in every detail. If you are doing these things *in order to* arouse your partner, then you're doing the right things for the wrong reason. Arousal, in this case, is a manipulative goal. Arousing your partner can happen more fully and spontaneously when you genuinely find *joy* in touching, caressing, exploring this person's body—not because that's what the books say works but because it *feels,* tastes, smells good to you. When you *enjoy giving* this pleasure, your lover's reactions heighten your own pleasure. (This must be done leisurely, to give your senses time to absorb each stimulus.)

The more tender loving care you invest, the more pleasure you will receive. Most people know this and believe it—*intellectually.* But emotionally they are still wary of investing too much. They are locked onto the win-lose frequency and *feel* that the more they invest, the more they stand to *lose* if they don't reach their goal. They hedge their bets, play it cool, and die a little.

When you forget about outer goals and seek only the pleasure that each moment affords, it is *impossible to lose.*

If you're feeling horny and you decide to seduce someone and fail, you "lose." You didn't reach your goal. But if you desire *only* to express your feelings—and do it!—enjoying however much of the other person you can experience at this moment—nothing more—*you both win.*

Accepting such a situation as anything but a loss is more often difficult for men than for women in our culture. Alan, a single young man, protested, "If I can't go all the way and I'm left horny, what kind of winning is that?"

"The winning is in your attitude—your freedom from *expectations,*" I answered. If being left horny is not something awful; if you don't feel cheated or let down by the other person (after all you don't feel cheated if you enjoy some form of entertainment that leaves you horny); if it is *acceptable* to be left in that state—you have won. You have taken the pressure off both of you and enriched the relationship.

When your major interest is in the person, it is possible to receive emotional gratification without the physical, provided you do not require conquest in order to feel accepted.

It is possible to confuse pleasure with self-indulgence, insisting on having your desires gratified—*now.* That, however, is a compulsive* type of short-range hedonism that places the emphasis on *me* rather than *we.* It does not embody the caring and mutuality that is at the core of the kind of sensuality I am talking about. And it is not tuned in to what is happening in the here and now, and therefore to the feelings of the other as well as oneself.

I advocate a more gentle, noncompulsive and mutually accepting hedonism.

A goal is frequently a "must," a "should": You have to reach it or you're a failure in your own eyes. A no-lose approach acknowledges something you would like, but don't *have to* have: You replace the "must" with a goal of no goals. Your only aim is to enjoy whatever is open to you, physically and emotionally, at each moment—sight, sound, touch, scent. There's a lot to enjoy. And later, if you still need a sexual release, you can *enjoy* masturbating.

---

* I use the term "compulsive" to mean a feeling (as opposed to an idea) that one must/should do, or have, something. Such a *feeling* is irrational and cannot—unlike an idea—be changed by reasoning.

Masturbation can fill a need almost as basic as eating. You may prefer sharing a meal with someone, but if no one is available, and you are hungry, you can enjoy food by yourself.

When your only goal is to experience, you can't lose!

This kind of here-and-now experiencing eludes us, however, when our minds are busy mulling over what has happened, or what might happen five minutes or five months from now.

That's Linda's problem. She was head over heels in love—once. She invested everything in one man and it didn't work out. Did they get along? Famously! Did he love her too? Yes. Did they have marvelous times together? Super! Does she have beautiful memories? Yes, it was the big romance of her life and nothing else has ever come close.

Then how didn't it work out? Because he wasn't ready to get married and live happily ever after, as in the fairytales. Her prince charming deserted her (when she got pushy about marriage), and Linda swears she'll never trust another man or invest that much in a relationship again. She's stuck in the past, and she worries about what her new lover will do in the future.

If her goal were simply to experience a new lover—in the here and now—she'd be able to trust him because she'd have nothing to lose (and she'd have real orgasms instead of having to pretend).

Then there's Rick, who had an impotence problem. His first heterosexual experience had been with an older girl who fancied herself worldly and ridiculed his inexperience. After that encounter he boned up with various marriage manuals, visual aids, and became an accredited sexual gymnast.

He was so anxious to show how much he knew, he'd insist on running through a dozen or two positions the first night, depending on his partner's stamina. He did all the right things the wrong way. No joy, passion, spontaneity, tenderness, sensuality. He was too busy worrying, "If she balled me once, will she do it again?" (And the girl—who wanted more than an athlete—didn't.)

His performance was so important to Rick that he frequently

used liquor to relax. One night he drank a little too much and couldn't achieve an erection. Someone with more confidence in himself might have shrugged his shoulders, recognized he just had one too many and left it at that.

Rick had double trouble. Not only was he his own worst critic, but at the time he had the misfortune to be in bed with a hot-tempered contestant for the Miss Universe title (never mind the name) who made the mistake of taking Rick's alcoholic impotence as a personal affront. Leaping out of bed, she screeched, "How dare you do this to me. Do you know who I am? I am Miss _____!!!" Months later he could still close his eyes and see that indignant beautiful face, hear those screams. And die a little.

Rick had immediately recognized that the culprit *might* be alcohol. But Rick the Performer whispered to himself, "Maybe there's something wrong with me. It never happened before." So he set out to *prove* that he *could* get it up. A natural, involuntary reaction suddenly became a must. Of course it was a disaster. You can't *will* an erection. Rick's downfall was that he was focusing on his erection (the goal) instead of on the stimulus that would *effortlessly* produce and maintain one.

Rick's comeback began when he attended a primal sensuality seminar, and realized that part of him was taking the role of spectator at his sexual performance—watching, judging and trying to direct. (In their research and treatment Masters and Johnson found the realization and elimination of the spectator to be the key to curing impotence.)

Attending the seminar with Rick was Anne, who cared for him but felt rejected sexually. She in turn learned to understand the problem and make no demands on him. With her help Rick soon regained his potency.

How?

By focusing on the here and now—the pleasure of Anne's touch; the beauty of her breasts; by noticing how they swelled when she was aroused.

By seeing how her face flushed with pleasure as she fondled his penis (no closing his eyes and seeing Miss Beauty Queen).

By focusing on the joy of touching and pleasuring a woman instead of manipulating her body as a means to an end.

By learning to enjoy sensuality and making the erection secondary.

By making experiencing his only goal.

By approaching experiments in this book with that point of view.

By getting rid of puritanical hangups.

If you perform the explorations as *adventures in experiencing,* then carry that attitude into your daily life, you will find that pleasure is suddenly a much more organic part of your living.

Be prepared to encounter unexpected resistance to pleasure, from yourself and your lover, and to help each other overcome it. Some forms of resistance will be obvious: procrastination, not finding enough time, etc. Others may be more subtle, such as not following directions, leaving something out, changing things or the order of the preparation experiences, which are important.

Once you've overcome any resistance, be prepared for some of the most erotic hours you've spent in your entire life!

Are you ready for all that pleasure?

Can you accept the gift of the gods and welcome the outcast into your heart?

Then open up. . . .

> Primal sensuality is
> *NOW*
>   Suspended in time and space
> Oasis of *HERE*
>   in the desert of Then and When.

2

PRACTICE MAKES PLEASURE

ONE DOES not hasten to the languorous arms of pleasure without due preparation.

To be able to receive as well as give is integral to pleasure.

This chapter will tell you how to practice receiving, something that is difficult for many. To be a good receiver of pleasure means that you are able to accept it from yourself—to be good to yourself.

Basic Preparations

Begin each exploration in this book with the basic preparations, so that your surroundings will heighten your sensual experience.

1. Allow more time than you think you will need, to insure that there is no time pressure (at least several hours).

2. Arrange the place/room where you will be as though you were having a visit from a Very Important Person. *You* are a VIP. *You* deserve to be fussed over. Gratify all your senses with your favorite

music (no records that have to be changed manually),
relaxant (wine or whatever, but not too much alcohol, it dulls the senses),

scent (incense, if you like it, perfume or cologne on your pillowcase, etc.),
flowers and/or other favorite objects that delight you,
lighting—candlelight at night if you like it (doesn't everyone?).

3. Fix the phone and doorbell so they won't ring or you won't hear them. (If you can't do anything else, put the phone under the couch pillows and pile others on top, or wrap it in blankets. . . .)

4. Be sure children and pets are taken care of (walk the dog, etc.).

5. Make sure children cannot barge in on you (have an inside lock on the bedroom door). Choose a time when they are gone or asleep for the night. (The last three items may seem obvious and unnecessary to mention, but they're also easy to forget and can disrupt your plans.)

6. Begin each experiment by taking time to enjoy your accessories (music, scents, flowers, etc.), become aware of your breathing, then take six to eight very deep, slow breaths.

(These are the basic preparations for each succeeding experiment and exploration. See that the room temperature is comfortable for nudity.)

Experience A—The Primal You

In your primal state you were fully sensuous. Your senses were your consciousness.

I ask you now to return to that state, to the infant that does not yet know the strictures "don't touch, no-no, not nice," that does not yet know its body and what it can or cannot do.

Take off all your clothes and lie down, preferably on the floor. Take six to eight, slow, deep breaths. With each breath feel yourself getting younger and younger until you reach your primal self in infancy.

All your senses are extraordinarily acute. The sensation of air currents moving over your skin is highly pleasurable. You enjoy the odors without knowing what they are. You are fascinated by colors and shapes that have no separate identity or meaning. You can hear your heart beat and feel your blood flowing through the veins under your skin (not knowing what they are called or why they exist).

The air, the floor, everything you sense becomes you—and you, it. When you hear a sound, enter into it and resonate with it. *Become* that sound. You do not *see* a color—you *are* that color. Music is color and you; color is music and you.

Nothing is separate. *All* that you perceive each second is the *totality* of you. There is nothing else. A second is eternal. Time is a concept that does not exist for you. There is no *you* separate from what you perceive. You are *one* with your world.

(This is what is meant by expanded consciousness—perceptions wide open.) *This is your primal sensuality.*

Now you learn to move your body. All of you is *totally* involved in each movement of your limbs, head and torso. Enjoy the sensations and process involved in kicking and stretching. Learn to change positions and roll over. You *are* movement.

Discover your hands and fingers—and what they can do. *Learn* how to grab your feet and toes. Suck and play with your fingers. Smell your body.

There is no right or wrong—only what feels good or not-good.

Discover your genitals *for the first time.* Discover their good feelings. Enjoy them as long as you like, then teach yourself to crawl, stand up (how difficult that is!), and finally to take your first steps and walk.

If in the process you recall any incidents when you were admonished not to touch and play with yourself (or others), relive the incident, especially the feelings that you could not express at the time. Allow yourself to feel the full extent of anger, guilt, shame or other feelings that might have been too overwhelming or dangerous for you to experience fully as a young child dependent on your parents. You can do it safely now, thereby freeing that energy. Should you have trouble getting into your feelings, do some deep breathing (Chapter 16).

When you are finished, draw a nude picture of yourself, emphasizing your favorite parts. Exchange pictures with your lover and discuss your feelings about your bodies and your primal experiences.

Experience B—Your Sensuous Nature

If you were successful in reaching primal sensuality during the first experience, then you experienced your organic unity with your surroundings—the universe.

People in Western cultures are accustomed to speaking and thinking of nature as something one goes out into on Sunday or vacations, something separate and outside themselves. And yet deep inside we know better, and that is why we have the urge to commune with nature and why afterwards we feel refreshed and revitalized.

Nature is not something to be labeled; it can only be experienced nonverbally. Since you are an integral part of nature, that is also true of you and all others.

Primal sensuality is the expanded consciousness of a borderless self, which expands, recedes, and constantly merges in various ways with the rest of the universe (as opposed to the lone, individual consciousness).

That is why it is not possible to love another without loving your *self*.

Your *self* is not any of the many labels with which you can be tagged. Your *self* is the primal you before your ego put a tiny mirror in front of your face, narrowed your perceptions and said, "This is your world, and I will be with you always."

An important part of your *self* is your body, which needs to be fully accepted before you can love your *self*.

But the body has been devalued along with nature, sexuality and woman (all of which are linked in the psyche).

The extent of this devaluation and split with nature deter-
mines the extent of sex without sensuality or love. Since you *are*
nature, if you cannot love/accept nature, you cannot love
yourself or anyone else. You have a mind/body split and can
only love the *idea* of love (and the *idea* of love for humanity, which
so many express so eloquently in rhetoric and so poorly in deed).

Intimate love is a personalization of the generalized love of
nature/life/humanity, brought down to the individual level. (A
well-loved child of four spontaneously informed me recently, "I
love everybody," and kissed me—a so-called stranger sharing our
beach).

In the Western world the most common methods for tran-
scending the isolation of one's individual self-consciousness—for
letting go of that ego-mirror and experiencing our identity with
the world/universe/cosmos—have been sex, drugs, or communion with other parts of nature. This is what drug addiction is
about—the magic cure for fragmentation, dissociation, aliena-
tion. But that is typical of the tendency to see everything,
including the answer to one's inner quest, as *outside* ourselves—
something to grasp at and ingest. Those who do not realize that
the real drug, the cure or key, is *within us,* seek outside with an
unquenched thirst.

The most frequent means of losing one's separate*ness* is
through sex. A full orgasm is a gratuitous gift. It involves a
temporary death of the ego, which usually blocks our sense of
organic unity with nature. Through this ego death we transcend
our separate*ness.* Alan Watts* points out that if this is the only
means we have of escaping our isolation, then sex is pursued as
the means to an end, set apart from the natural rhythm of life,
and *used* to compensate for lack of joy elsewhere.

The third most common opportunity for unity is through
communion with other aspects of nature, something we can do
every day if we are so inclined. Even if you live in a cement

* *Nature, Man and Woman,* Pantheon Books, 1958, to be read for a deeper understanding of
our unity with nature.

jungle, you can bring small treasures of nature into your home to contemplate.

However, for me, the most powerful direct experience with nature is outdoors, where you can immerse yourself totally in your surroundings. This is what I propose for this experience with *your sensuous nature.*

Once you are in touch with the primal you through Experience A (or some other path of your own finding), you can reach that open state of sensuality without consciously going back to infancy. Yet you experience similarly because you approach what you perceive from the standpoint of an infant who is experiencing this for *the very first time ever.*

If you are sitting beneath a tree—it is something you have *never* done or seen before. You do not know or care what it is named; you know what it is—part of you.

To help yourself slip into the receptive state, where your senses are accepting rather than straining or grasping for the experience, do your deep breathing.

Eventually, when you find something that particularly intrigues you, keep your focus on it *without concentrating,* just being open and *identifying with it. Allow* the artificial (mental) separation between you to dissipate. (*Whatever happens must be spontaneous;* you cannot *will* the identification, the sense of inseparability, or oneness.)

The key is quiet, nonverbal contemplation—*undistracted, without any expectations or goals.* The merging, the fusion, the sense of timelessness will happen when you don't expect it, *never* when you do.

If it happens, it will only be on one of the occasions when you are enjoying nature for its own sake, having made a practice of doing so whenever possible. And if you *try* to repeat a particular experience, you will fail.

We all have this ability to experience unity. It is part of our animal nature. How else do our pets (and infants) know exactly what we are feeling?

Begin by choosing some part of nature to discover, as

something completely unknown, to experience with as many senses as possible—how it feels, smells, etc. How long since you really experienced/discovered a blade of grass?

To convey a nonverbal experience in words is impossible. I can only talk around it, give you clues and share with you in retrospect fragments of my own experiences of unity with nature.

My first such recollection as an adult (I had many in my first decade) happened spontaneously as I lay beneath a pine tree, alone, gazing up at the patterns of the branches and the pine needles piercing the sky. Nestled among one cluster of needles was a luminous, sparkling dewdrop, which caught my attention. I do not know how long I spent contemplating these treasures, but when I finally became aware of myself lying on the ground, I felt as though I had grown roots into the earth. I was anchored, fused—at one with it. It was only with the greatest effort that I finally made the physical separation and left to join my companions. My body left, but part of me stayed rooted.

A most memorable experience took place as I lay on a large rock in the middle of a small, rushing river. I was lying on my stomach, head over the edge, directly above the flowing water. My companion dozed off and I was alone with my river. First I identified with the constant movement of the river. Then my eye was caught by the way the water cascaded over a particular small, jutting rock, taking on a viscous fluidity in the sun's reflection. I felt myself merging with the water, moving, flowing over obstacles . . . I was entranced. (Meanwhile my friend awoke, had the sense not to disturb me, and made his way to shore while I remained lost in contemplation—or whatever inadequate word you care to use.) Nothing else existed.

When I finally returned to my ordinary consciousness, I was astonished. I had not been sleeping, yet what had seemed like minutes had obviously been quite some time because the sun was low in the sky.

In order to reach shore, I had to make my way by stepping or jumping from rock to rock. On approaching my rock I had been shaky, teetering as I went. After this experience I was surefooted, confident, balanced and relaxed. The rocks, the river, all were my friends, my family. They would not harm me. Later I wrote the poem you will find at the end of this chapter.

There have been other times when I have sat and leaned against sharp irregular rocks as I rose and fell with the ocean—eventually to discover myself wedded, as it were, to the rock in which I nestled, as though it had been custom-carved for my body and my body for it.

There are labels—oceanic experience, cosmic experience, peak experience, religious experience. It all comes down to a rediscovery of our universal inseparability. The expressions "lost in nature" or "lost in contemplation" refer to a loss of the ego-mirror, of its illusion of separateness.

When you experience nature with the eyes of a child, you experience it *for the first time.* It is an exciting discovery. You see, feel things that never before entered your consciousness.

(Much of my poetry has written itself following sensual/sexual/unitary experiences with various aspects of nature.)

For this exploration, choose some aspect of nature and experience it as a baby would, for the very first time, accepting its essence into your center.

In later explorations you will experience your lover in this way.

When you are free in your sensory response to nature (the world, yourself), you are sexually free as well.

Experiencing yourself and your lover as constantly changing parts of nature, you will discover that when you perceive him or her in this way, you will never make love with the same lover twice.

EXPERIENCE C—SELF-EXPLORATION

Begin with the basic preparations. If you're using candles, light several, so that you can see yourself well.

Additional accessories: full-length mirror, hand mirror, petroleum jelly, flashlight (optional).

Do not bathe within the three or four hours before the experiment.

Most of us, when we look at our bodies in the mirror, have a critical eye and think, "If only I could take a little off the middle . . . add a little to the chest," etc.

This experiment is done with mirrors, but the critical attitude should be locked outside the door.

Look at your body from the standpoint of a baby who does not know standards of beauty—labels like fat, skinny, ugly. He only knows his body feels good and he *likes it.* If he has four fingers instead of five, he enjoys them just the same. He knows nothing of how things *should* be.

Enjoy yourself as though you were a baby exploring yourself for the very first time. A baby has no expectations.

Let yourself see how much there is to like about your body. As you examine each part of you say (preferably aloud), "I like the feel of my hair. . . ." (Never mind that it's fine and won't do what you want it to.) Do the same all over.

The hand mirror is for places you can't see directly unless you're a contortionist. Use it. See how much you can like.

Focus your flashlight wherever it pleases you. I especially recommend the genital area.

Seeing is only part of this experiment. This is a sensuality inventory of your body, its attributes and its *responses.* Your skin has different odors and tastes in different spots.

Smell, taste, touch, see, feel. . . .

You may think you know your body, but I guarantee you will make some exciting discoveries. Narcissism is not the dynamic here. Later, with your lover, you will use the pleasure knowledge and practice you gain, particularly during the Minimoon (Chapter 7), one of the most exciting sensuality adventures.

Beginning with your scalp, *slowly* work your way down to your toes. (What an erogenous zone that is!—babies know.) *Experiment* with every kind of touch, rubbing and pressure you can think of *plus* various directions and rhythms of movement, different degrees of contact.

Note your preferences. Experiment with light pinching and

run your nails lightly over your skin. Find the fine line between pleasure and pain.

Determine in each area what kind of contact and rhythm feels best.

Focus on one small area at a time. Notice the various colors and shapes of that area and any changes in appearance as you play and experiment.

On spots that feel especially good to rub, apply some petroleum jelly, oil or lotion to spread the sensation. (Warm it in your fingers.) Notice the difference in sensation.

Don't skip a centimeter of your body.

Men, if you haven't already discovered how erotic your nipples can be, you're in for a treat. (Women, take note if you haven't discovered *his* nipples.) Try the jelly there. When you get to the genital area try running your nails very lightly across the scrotum in addition to other types of touch.

Don't forget the anus. The area right around it is highly erogenous.

It might be best to leave the genitals till last—otherwise you could get hung up there and not complete your sensual safari. When you get there, rub a finger on and around your genitals. Take a deep sniff of that finger. Then taste it. Whenever you get to the point of exuding a little musky genital excretion, get some of that directly on a finger. Again, smell and taste. Note any differences.

The more you can enjoy your own smells and tastes (especially the smells), the better it augurs for your sensuality and sexual sensitivity.

If you don't like your smells, if the idea of tasting your genital excretion disgusts you, then to some degree you don't accept your sexual self. Now is the time to rediscover that body excretions/odors can be good, not evil!

Remember, genital odors are the major turn-on for some animals—and we are all members of the animal kingdom.

It is surprising how many women do not recall ever having thoroughly explored and examined the treasure within the lips of their vulvas, and have never looked at their clitoris. The clitoral head is usually hidden by a hood of soft flesh that must be firmly drawn back to reveal the highly sensitive little head of ecstasy— the only human organ whose *sole* purpose is pleasure.

The clitoris is so sensitive that even the lightest possible direct touch can be too hard. Which is why so many women grit their teeth and silently endure pain instead of pleasure as their heavy-handed, well-meaning lovers dutifully follow some remembered exhortation to rub the clitoris. For many women the lightest possible touch is too hard and the most effective stimulation is indirect, around the clitoral shaft or hood or along the line between the hood and the vagina.

Gently draw the clitoral hood back and scrutinize it carefully. Then experiment to see what's best for you. Don't skip the labia. The inner lips, the labia minora, are especially erogenous, and usually one side is a little more sensitive than the other. Find out which is your best side.

Use petroleum jelly, a slippery lotion, cream or vaginal jelly on male or female genitals and surrounding areas. Notice changes in color, size and shape of the areas as they are stimulated.

Everyone who has masturbated instinctively finds the best rhythm and spot(s) without thinking about it intellectually. This time, as you explore the area, make mental notes about these factors, because later you're going to show your lover *exactly* what's best for you, rather than expecting him or her to divine it somehow. Everyone's different, and your lover's no mind reader.

When you have completed the experiment, compile your sensuality profile, listing your favorite turn-on spots in order of preference. Make a copy for yourself and one for your lover.

On the same list add your favorite music for sensualizing— your favorite scents, flowers, pornography and other props including feathers (peacock feathers are great) and mirrors. (If you've never tried feathers and other fuzzy, sensuous objects on your skin, by all means *do*. And don't forget *hair*. It's even better than peacock feathers. That's the real reason sensuous men flip over long locks. But short-hairs, don't despair; you can still manipulate your head to drive your lover up the wall. (And there's nothing wrong with using her wig or fall.)

List things you like to touch you and what you like to touch.

You can also list your turn-offs, so your partner knows if you don't like being bitten, pinched, having your breasts kneaded like dough, your nipples tweaked, twiddled or rolled. One person's turn-on is another's turn-off.

(I don't think there is any heterosexual woman who hasn't at some time, in order to build a male ego, murmured, "Mmmmm," when she really felt, "Ouch, you clod!" That's where sexual deception starts—fearing that if you don't make him feel like the greatest lover, he may not call again.)

Although the experiment to follow is preparation for new sexual adventures with your lover, its greatest benefit lies in your ability to do it with the idea of giving *yourself* pleasure. You deserve it. Allow yourself to enjoy it.

Become a small child, *exploring for the first time,* with no hangups about enjoying your own body.

EXPERIENCE D—SELF-STIMULATION

This is an experiment in prolonging self-stimulation, which will eventually enhance your experience with others. It's important to *keep from having an orgasm* as long as possible. *You have no goal other than to give yourself pleasure.* It will be beneficial to anyone, but particularly men with potency problems (including premature ejaculation) and women who do not experience full orgasmic response.

If, however, you happen to have an orgasm at the end of the experiment, you will find that it is more intense than usual.

A prerequisite is that you have performed Experience C. Let at least eight hours elapse between C and D. Then do it whenever you're in the mood—horny, that is.

If you are seldom consciously aware of feeling horny, practice letting yourself feel sexual desire—through reading, films, pictures, and *especially* when you see someone who looks attractive to you. It can be a stranger passing on the beach. That's fine and normal. Feeling lust doesn't mean you have to follow through. Just let yourself feel, then you can go home and release those good, lusty feelings when you see your lover or when you masturbate. Women in particular are brought up to repress those feelings, especially with someone we like, so it may take more practice to release them.

Begin with the basic preparations. In addition to your favorite perceptual stimuli, add the conceptual—written or visual erotica that turn you on, plus your best sexual fantasies. (If you've never had that sort of fantasy, it's not too late to start.)

Most important, have petroleum jelly handy. This may be a lengthy session and other lubricants might necessitate an interruption for another application.

(If you discovered during your inventory that seeing yourself and your genitals in the mirror was exciting, you may want to try it again, especially if you are new at self-stimulation.)

Start rubbing various turned-on spots you encountered during Experience C, adding Vaseline as desired. Eventually get to the genital area, apply Vaseline and stimulate in the way you discovered feels best. (If you were going to be sensitive about making love to someone, you wouldn't just dive for the crotch and forget the rest of the body—so don't do it to yourself.)

When you are on the verge of orgasm (just before the point of no return), *back off* by stopping momentarily, breaking the rhythm. Then continue until you are close again and back off once more. Continue this pattern as long as possible. If you have an orgasm, maintain genital contact and start rubbing again until you feel no response to pressure. A completed orgasm leaves the genitals in temporary anaesthesia.

EXPERIENCE E—WATER STIMULATION

This experiment is optional, unless you've never had an orgasm. Then it can be a magic key or an important first step. If, in addition to a subconscious fear of letting go, you have an aversion to touching/rubbing your genitals, this experiment bypasses that taboo.

It is imperative that you *not* expect or desire an orgasm when you perform this experiment. It can also be satisfying to achieve a high peak of excitement and pleasure, then gently simmer down.

Nobody can *will* an orgasm (or erection). Trying and straining for it will only insure "failure." Again, if your *only genuine* desire is to experience whatever pleasure there is, *you can't lose.* (I stressed "genuine" because it is possible to play games with yourself, pretending you don't want an orgasm so that you will have one. It won't work.)

Eliminate all other goals, musts, shoulds, expectations, self-evaluations and judgments of your performance. Don't perform. Experience.

(If you are unable to drop the performer role, then assume it consciously. *Deliberately* perform and watch yourself till you're tired of it, then let go.)

Again, begin the experiment with the basic preparations. Just because this will be done in the bathroom is no reason not to arrange it to pleasure your senses. Today you're entertaining (*you* alone) in the bathroom. (If you've never made love there, add to your *future* list doing it with one of you seated or on the sink counter or together in the tub or shower. But not yet.)

The ideal accessory for this experience is a spray head that comes off the shower, or a spray extension. Otherwise you can use a faucet spray attachment for washing your hair. They're inexpensive and well worth the investment. Even a garden hose will do. If you get your legs up at right angles you can even manage without an extension.

Get your spray set up and partially fill the tub with water slightly above body temperature. Add bubbly bath oil. Enjoy the scent, the rainbows in the bubbles. Lie back, breathe deeply. Luxuriate. Soap your hands and let them slip and slide over your skin. Enjoy the silky sensuality. Slide the bar of soap over your body; play with the spray. Then raise your hips slightly so that your most turned-on genital spot receives a comfortable, even stream of lukewarm water. When you reach the place that feels best, just keep the stream of water there—and *enjoy*. If you're willing to try only for pleasure and *forget* about having an orgasm (or erection), you'll probably have one because it's something the body knows how to do *by itself.*

If you find your mind wandering, to routine matters, problems, what you have to do tomorrow, recognize that part of you is resisting. One way of keeping your attention on the erotic is to fantasize. Come prepared with several exciting sex fantasies, so that when you tire of one, you can go on to another. If desired you can include erotic literary or visual material.

Should this experiment lead to your very first orgasm, try it again another time, *still not expecting an orgasm.* Much as you tell yourself not to, you may end up expecting an orgasm, and not having one for that reason. No matter. Keep practicing. When a concert pianist masters a piano concerto, he doesn't say, "Well, that's done. I don't have to play that any more." When you are having orgasms three times out of four, go back and try Experience D.

For women a good time to try these is just before your menses, when changes in hormonal balance bring most women to their peak of sexual tension. Most women are aware of premenstrual tension, but few realize that it can be relieved by more frequent sexual release at that time. Since I told Carol about this, she has discovered that she can avoid headaches at the onset of her period if she masturbates when she gets the first warning.

Couples may also try this exploration together, soaping and spraying each other in the tub or shower. A stream of water hitting the right spots as you near climax can supplement the attitudinal difficulties of shower or tub. Or, you may choose to get out and continue your sensualizing elsewhere.

Life is a Dance . . .
We can rush through it
   carelessly
bumping, jerking,
   not noticing . . .
We can stiffen our limbs
   and resist
Until we are taut and brittle
Or we can bend our knees and move
   softly,
   gently and surely,
Feet caressing the earth
Body embracing the inexorable
   ebb and flow
   of the life force
   that makes us one.

3

HOW TO TURN ANY PART
OF YOU
INTO AN ORGASMIC
EROGENOUS ZONE

EXPERIENCE F—RECONNECTING YOUR BODY

This could be the most important experiment in the book for you. It is a means of reconnecting your sensual/sexual responses so that the whole of you can become an erogenous zone. You will learn how to intensify your sensations by reestablishing a direct line of communication with your genitals. Then, when desired, you can have an orgasm from the stimulation of any spot you choose—even a fingernail.

Make your basic preparations. Have the Sensuality Profile of your most turned-on spots as well as erotic material, fantasies—and petroleum jelly. Prerequisites are Experiences C and D.

Begin with the same kind of self-stimulation as in Experience D but before you get to the back-off point, take your other hand and start rubbing your second most turned-on spot, synchronizing the rhythm to that of the hand that continues rubbing your genital area. When it's feeling good in both places, take your hand away from spot number two *but feel as though it's still there.* If you can't feel that, imagine you feel it. Stay with it. Then put your hand back and rub both places again. Without breaking the rhythm on spot two, take your hand off your genital spot and feel as though *it's* still there. Now put it back, and after a while take your hand off spot two, again feeling that it's still there. Put it back, then take the genital hand off, feeling even more keenly that it's still there.

Keep alternating hands that way until you have an orgasm with your hand on spot number two alone. If you accidentally come while rubbing your genital area, try again later.

Once you connect up spot two, you can do the same with spots three, four, etc.

Once you start connecting up, more and more places will continue to connect spontaneously during lovemaking.

Soon you'll find that your entire body is connected up.

Because women are naturally multiorgasmic, the uninhibited woman will find that she can have one or more orgasms during foreplay alone, sometimes without even being touched—just from the excitement of making love. Then when he enters, it is easy for her to enjoy several more.

A man will now be able to get more intense pleasure from being stimulated in areas other than his genitals. He does not have to reach orgasm during love play when he prefers to wait, but there are many situations in which he can use an orgasmic nongenital erogenous zone to advantage. Most men have had the frustrating experience of being stopped short while making love—left out on a limb, you might say. It would take a stony heart to refuse to rub the palm of your hand—or whatever—when you're left all stirred up with nowhere to go.

I might also point out that in the case of public situations, nobody was ever arrested for merely rubbing his wrist.

Experience G—Intensifying Your Orgasms

Done correctly, this experiment will result in a greater letting-go at the time of orgasm, thus intensifying the experience.

It involves fully relaxing the muscles around the anal, urinary and vaginal openings.

Most people unconsciously clench these muscles during sex to avoid the embarrassment (to them) of an anal or vaginal fart in the midst of everything.

There is also the unconscious fear of defecating or urinating. Some women who completely let go can leak or flood if they didn't empty their bladder beforehand. It's not really as dreadful as it sounds. A physician at one seminar had a girlfriend who always, as he put it, "flooded me," and he loved it! Of course, as a doctor he knew that urine is sterile. Some leakage is more likely to happen to a woman whose deep pelvic pubococcygeus muscles are sagging.

Clenching cuts off some of your sexual sensation, as will any nonsexual tension. This experiment reconditions your body to let go. If you do it correctly, you'll only have to perform the experiment once. From then on, your muscles will involuntarily relax as you reach orgasm.

Before doing this experiment, you may want to check with your lover to satisfy yourself that a fart now and then during sexing is not really objectionable. I know it was a tremendous relief to me when my husband gave me that assurance. If it's objectionable, consider changing lovers.

After making your basic preparations, insert the finger of one hand just inside your anal opening and start masturbating with your other hand. When you get to the point of orgasm, simultaneously push *gently* on your finger as though you were pushing it out. The objective is to have the pushing out activity coincide with the orgasm. Once you synchronize it, your body will take over happily ever after. The ability to relax those sphincters is also helpful for anal sex.

For women to increase their pleasure it is necessary to relax the muscles around the introitus of the vagina as well as the anus. For this you use a narrow, rounded, soft plastic bottle, a cosmetic container, for instance. Lubricate it with petroleum jelly and insert, bottom first, into the vagina. Masturbate, and when you reach your peak, gently try to push out the bottle. That will

locate the muscles involved. At first the conscious pushing out
will probably back you off from the orgasm, but keep masturbating and try to connect the pushout with the orgasm. Once
you've located these pushout muscles, you can use them to keep
from being "nailed" (hurt) if someone thrusts too hard in a deep
position. Just push out as he pushes in. It doesn't detract from
anyone's pleasure; in fact it can add to it.

The basic experiments in Chapters 2 and 3 will greatly
enhance your sensual adventures together. I will refer to some of
them as an essential prelude to certain joint explorations, such as
the Minimoon. Most of the others in succeeding chapters do not
require that you complete these basic experiences before you try
them. The only prerequisites for those are a nongoal openness to
experiencing in the here and now . . . together.

Bon voyage.

How well can I
love you
my love?
As well as I
can love
my Self.

4

EYE SEE YOU

IN OUR culture the eyes have it. Our visual sense overshadows others to the extent that if we wish to focus exclusively on a feeling, thought, or piece of music, we often close our eyes or focus on the floor, ceiling or other "unseeing" spot. This dominance is reflected in our language. For example, "I see" means "I understand."

But because we see with the brain, not the eye, most of what the retina picks up is filtered out, censored by the time the brain's translation reaches our awareness.

Therefore, the proverbial husband can look at his wife without *seeing* a significant change she has made in her appearance.

Have you ever had trouble remembering who was waiting on you in a restaurant?

We can look at a person and see a stereotype instead of a human being.

Dr. Frederick Perls, the pioneering Gestalt therapist, was fond of pointing out that people have various perceptual holes. Some look but cannot see. Some don't really hear. Some can't feel.

In our culture the senses are dulled and ignored.

How do *you* see?

Close your eyes and visualize someone you know casually, but see fairly often. Someone you work with, perhaps, or a neighbor.

See the person's face. What color are his or her eyes? How is the nose shaped? Are there any scars, freckles, etc.? How thoroughly can you describe this person?

Check your oversights the next time you see that person. Note any holes in your perception and work on those areas with others.

EXPLORATIONS FOR LOVERS

EXPLORATION A. Begin with the basic preparations (Chapter 2).

Stand face to face. Close your eyes and take four or five very deep breaths. Continue to breathe deeply and slowly as you become aware of the muscles around your eyes, those behind your eyes and those holding them shut. Relax them. Feel the warmth of your blood circulating in, around, behind your eyes.

Make your eyelids very light, as though they were gossamer. Let them cover your eyes very lightly. . . .

Rub your palms together till they are quite warm and cup them around your eyes.

Silently say to each eye, three times:

"Relax, relax, relax. A little more, a little more, a little more."

Very *slowly* take your hands away, a fraction of an inch at a time, keeping them parallel to your eyes.

At the same time let your eyelids part gently and open your eyes ever so slowly, keeping them soft, relaxed and effortless.

See whatever portions of your palms are visible, but *make no effort to focus* and see clearly.

By the time your hands are far enough away to see all of them, your eyes should be open but not staring. Keep them relaxed, make no effort to focus sharply, and *allow* yourself to experience your hands, to be aware of their colors, their lines, the shape of your fingers, without strain.

Slowly lower your hands and in the same relaxed manner *allow* yourself to see your partner's face. Enjoy it.

Finally, spend at least one minute (or as long as is comfortable) looking and *allowing* each into the other's eyes.

When either one of you is ready to look away, you can break the silence and tell each other how you feel.

EXPLORATION B. Be sure you are not interrupted. (Basic preparations.) Your lighting should be bright enough to see well, but not harsh. At night four or more candles are soft and warm.

Each of you will take turns being active while the other is passive. Agree beforehand who will start.

Stand face to face in the nude and begin with Exploration A.

After looking into each other's eyes, stay silent and keep your eyes soft, relaxed, loving—the opposite of staring.

Allow yourself (the active person) to see and enjoy your partner's face, body, hair, from head to toe. Touch only with your brain, not your hands.

When you have seen your fill from one side of your partner, move around to another side as you would to enjoy a sculptural work of art. Admire all angles, enjoying the various curves, spatial composition, textures, colors.

See how many aspects you never noticed before.

Then verbally share your experience and tell your lover all the things that please you about his/her body. Your partner accepts your honest comments without answering verbally.

The more personal and detailed your comments, the better. Instead of saying, "I like the hair on your chest," it would be preferable to say what it is about the hair that you like, such as, "I like the way your hair curls on your chest; I love to play with it and brush my cheek against it."

Although your point of departure is visual, include the other senses when appropriate. If you like the smell of your lover's skin and genital odors, tell him/her so.

This sort of communication can add exciting dimensions to your relationship.

In admiring a woman's hair, for example, a man might also let her know that it excites him when her hair brushes against his skin, and the particular places of contact that excite him most. She can put that information to very good use later. (And now that some men have longer hair, they too can use it in lovemaking.)

The passive person, eyes open (unless that's too difficult the first time) simply *allows* and accepts.

The better you like your body, the more comfortable you will be with this exploration.

Take note of anything that makes you uncomfortable. See what feelings about yourself, your body or sex you can associate with your uneasiness. You may even be reminded of an incident from the past. If so, relive it, now or later. (See Primal Ice Cubes.)

Do you feel uncomfortable when you are told complimentary things about yourself? Can you believe them?

Feelings about your body are tied up with feelings about yourself as a person. The better you feel about one, the better you'll feel about the other.

EXPLORATION C. This exploration can be done right after B, or some other time when you are making love. Take turns being active and passive, as you did in B. Allow at least an hour or two to pass between the time you've bathed and when you begin.

This time the focus of your mutual explorations is the genital area, and you include the sense of touch and smell.

In addition to soft lighting, you will need a flashlight.

Explore every fraction of an inch, very slowly, deliberately, searchingly. Get to know intimately every wrinkle of skin, every ridge and hollow of your beloved's most erogenous zones. See how many things you can find to please you. Start with the flashlight, unless it's too embarrassing for you.

Gently pull back her clitoral hood to reveal its treasure. Part the lips of her vulva and look within.

Breathe deeply of each other's natural fragrances.

Take his penis into your hands, examine it from all sides and delight in its swelling reactions to your touch. Put your nose right on it and sniff up and down its exciting scents. Gently examine his testicles all over and enjoy the subtle changes within those soft, sexual sacs.

Then tell each other all that you have discovered to pleasure you.

If you were unable to use the flashlight, try it some other time.

The more difficult you find this experiment, the more embarrassing it seems, the more you will gain if you bring yourself to *allow* this.

Too many of us grow up feeling that genitals (including ours) are ugly, forgetting that such a judgment is in the brain of the beholder.

Genitals are beautiful. The better we feel about ourselves, others and sex, the more we will like the equipment nature has chosen for her purpose.

If you are uncomfortable with B or C, I suggest you repeat them some other time until you feel acceptable and comfortable. Under the latter conditions Exploration C can be fantastically exciting, something you may wish to include in your lovemaking from time to time.

De-light

Unaccepting feelings about the body usually spill over to sex. Persons who relegate sex to the unlit dark of night are ashamed of both their bodies and their sexual desires.

They should, as soon as possible, gradually increase the amount of light during lovemaking.

If accustomed to total darkness, the first step could be to leave the light on in an adjoining room or hall, and leave the door open a slit, gradually opening it more and more until it is wide open. Then introduce a candle or soft night light in the bedroom, and eventually try making love in daylight or soft morning light.

Instead of leaving your door open, you may prefer to introduce a dim light by leaving a candle at the opposite end of the room.

There's an old joke that goes:

"Why does a wife keep her eyes closed during intercourse?"

"Because she can't stand to see her husband enjoying himself!"

Actually people close their eyes for a great variety of reasons. Many people think that's the normal and natural way to make love. Their eyes close involuntarily, perhaps the better to concentrate on their sensations. For others, however, it is an escape from their sensations. It becomes much easier to let the mind wander from the here and now, back to the day's happenings, or some nagging problem. It will effectively cut down on enjoyment. I have known some women who actually plan their market shopping during intercourse. Orgasm was an unknown, frightening phenomenon to them.

Premature ejaculators try distracting themselves, but it usually doesn't work. Their problem is not enjoying too much, but not having learned to really enjoy.

Another reason people close their eyes is to fantasize, a very common aphrodisiac that I occasionally recommend, with a caution against undue dependency.

For most women in our culture, orgasm during intercourse is achieved through a learning process rather than an immediate, automatic, natural function. To learn how may take several weeks, months, or years. (More on that in Chapter 15.) It is sometimes helpful for a woman seeking to make the transition to orgasm during intercourse to utilize fantasies as a familiar means of achieving a climax. However, once she is able to reach orgasm most of the time (which won't take long after the initial breakthrough, all other factors remaining equal), I then encourage her to drop the fantasies to avoid feeling dependent upon them.

How? That's our next exploration.

Exploration D—here and now sex. When you are with someone you truly enjoy and care for, seeing that person can be more exciting than any fantasy. (If not, why are you in bed together?)

If you are in the habit of keeping your eyes closed during intercourse, try it with eyes open—both of you. That way, in addition to watching the movement of your lover's body and enjoying the view each particular position affords, you can get the tremendous emotional kick that comes from seeing the expression of pleasure on the face of your loved one (depending on the position) and fully consummate the union by opening up and entering into each other's eyes.

As you approach climax you may involuntarily close your eyes, but keep them open as long as possible.

If you want to enlarge the visual experience, you may enjoy the different views you can get in front of a mirror—or two, or three. . . .

Exploration E—body braille. With your eyes shut, could you pick out your lover's hands or face from among many about the same size? I've put people through this in my seminars, and what a shock not to recognize your spouse's face with your eyes closed!

Pretend you're going to have to pick out your lover's body from among others, with your eyes closed, and you're practicing for the challenge. Begin with the basic preparations.

Take turns exploring each other's bodies. Begin with your eyes closed. Then try to maintain the same kind of gentle touch and do it with your eyes open. Before starting, rub your hands together or run hot water over them till they are good and warm.

Begin with the hands, then move slowly up along the arm to the shoulders, exploring neck and face, back down the neck to the chest and the rest of the body.

Explore slowly, using the tips, front and back of your fingers and hands as though they were the only eyes you had.

When you are being touched, let yourself surrender completely to your lover's touch. Keep your eyes closed throughout, and try to detect when your lover has opened his eyes. At the same time your lover should try to keep you from perceiving the transition.

When you are moving from one part of the body to another,

keep one hand on the old spot and do not remove it until your other hand is on the new spot, so that at least one hand is on your partner's body at all times.

Remove your hands slowly, reluctantly, lovingly.

When you have each taken a turn, give yourselves time to absorb the experience quietly. Then, if it feels right, discuss your reactions and how you feel about each other.

> I surrender to
> the touch of You
> I bare my
> tenderness
> discard the armor.
> Into your Loving
> I release my Self

5

THE LOVING MASSAGE:

An Exploration with Eros

IN THE loving massage, the *loving* takes precedence over any techniques involved.

The massage is the message.

It is an incredibly beautiful way of communicating to someone, from deep within, "I care—I love."

You are making love in the truest sense, whether or not this leads to intercourse.

The loving massage is the expression of eros within the context of a peak sensual/sexual experience. It relaxes as it arouses, and when properly approached, what emerges is a profound emotional encounter.

This should of course be performed with both partners nude, although it is not necessary that both receive the loving massage on the same occasion.

(In case of potency or orgasmic problems, I highly recommend this massage, *without intromission* at least the first few times. It is also good training for the woman who is shy about actively making love to a man.)

Some men think they *should* have an erection when giving or receiving a massage with their lover. This is not so. When you are giving, you're not likely to have an erection because all your attention is on her. When you're receiving, the massage, although sensuous, is very relaxing and that includes the penis. You may get an erection at some point, but don't *expect* it. If you are experiencing in the here and now, you won't even think about whether you have an erection.

Ideally, at some point when you're together, one of you suddenly feels like giving the other a loving massage and you get it together.

Unfortunately that sort of spontaneity does not always fit in with other planned activities, so especially if your lives are heavily scheduled, it is wise to plan ahead and set time (lots of it) aside in advance for this experience. If you're not in the mood when the time arrives, don't push it. See a movie and try again some other day.

It is my observation that people who need these explorations the most have the greatest difficulty finding time. A couple who could find the time an average of once a month for each to give the other this massage would do much toward keeping the relationship healthy and loving.

At no time should the person who has just received a loving massage feel that it is now his or her turn to massage. Nor should this be expected by the initiator. Your entire reward is in the mutual pleasure of the massage—in giving a gratuitous gift. Roles can be reversed another time.

Understanding that you do not *plan* to reverse roles at the end of a massage leaves you freer to take all the time you want and follow your instincts later on.

If you have the time and the desire to take turns, by all means do; but it is better not to count on it.

Allow at least ninety minutes for each person plus an hour (minimum) for additional intimacy and coming back to earth.

As accessories I recommend you have a peacock (or other) feather and/or long hair, and body lotion or oil (my preference is oil).

Make your basic preparations (Chapter 2) and warm up the oil.

Keep in mind these basic massage principles:

1. Remove rings, watch, etc.

2. Before starting, rub your hands together, making them as warm as possible.

3. Most important, pause for a moment before you begin, and *put your heart into your hands*.

4. Begin at the extremities (head, hands or feet) and work toward the heart.

5. Keep at least one hand in contact with the body when moving from one place to another.

6. Never remove a hand abruptly. Withdraw very slowly, reluctantly.

7. Keep a flowing rhythm with your hand movements, as in a dance.

8. This is a nonverbal experience, so do not speak if possible. Pleasure noises by the receiver are recommended.

9. When you get into your hands, you are ready.

Each movement that I describe should be done over the entire body, paying special attention to the head and feet. Complete the entire sequence of movements on the back side of your lover, then start over on the front.

Begin with the receiver lying on his/her stomach.

1. This is coordinated with slow deep-breathing through your nose. As you inhale, your stomach should expand (instead of your chest). As you exhale, press your hands firmly down on your partner's body (begin with the head in this instance). Exert a loving pressure during your slow exhalation, which should last a slow count of five at the minimum. As you begin your inhalation, gradually lesson the pressure of your hands until you raise them off the body (at the end of your inhalation). Place them in an adjoining spot as you begin your next exhalation. As you press, hands and fingers take on the contour of the body.

2. Run your hands lightly over the body, enjoying the various textures and conformation of the skin.

3. Tap lightly with your fingertips.

4. Run the tips of your fingers over the body in varying rhythms and directions with both hands. The spirit here is playful, one of surprises for the receiver, who should not know what to expect next.

5. The same sort of playful approach, running the tips of your nails *lightly* over the skin.

6. Blow your breath over your love's entire body. When you purse your lips the breath will be cooler than it is when you blow with your mouth open. Try it both ways on your arm, so that you know the effect of each. You can make your choice according to the room temperature, or alternate the two. (At no time blow directly into the vaginal opening. That could be dangerous!)

7. Run a feather and/or long hair over the skin, again playfully altering rhythm and direction. In addition to using long hair to titillate, try drawing it *slowly* across the body (head to toe) as though it were a blanket. Short-haired persons can use a wig or fall, holding or wearing it.

8. *Loving* kisses. This is the single most powerful part of the entire massage. If you have ever been kissed on every square inch of your body, you will know why. If not, you will find out, I hope. For added pleasure, breathe deeply of your beloved's skin with each kiss. Take your time.

9. Anoint your lover's body with warm oil or lotion (only the side you have been working on).

10. Turn and start over on the other side.

11. If you wish to continue making love after completing the loving kisses, anointing the second side of the body is optional. You may prefer using your tongue or other forms of improvisation.

Do improvise, sensualize, enjoy.

6

SENSUALITY MEALS

TWO universally favorite pastimes are eating and lovemaking. When all the right elements are combined (including ambience), a supremely voluptuous experience is inevitable.

Unfortunately there are many people who get only a fraction of the pleasure possible from both activities.

In our busy, tension-filled lives most of us don't consciously taste our food after the first mouthful or two. The first bite usually serves to reassure us that the food is edible and acceptable to our palates. We then make a value judgment as to its quality. We may compare it with a similar dish eaten in the past. Occasionally we may try to identify the various ingredients. Usually after a few bites we are off talking or thinking about something else and all those delicious sensations go unnoticed.

Many of us eat too fast and bolt our food practically unchewed. The amount of antacids and digestive aids consumed by the public is testimony to poor eating habits.

Thoroughly chewing and mixing food with the saliva can help turn an acid food into an alkaline-forming one, through the action of mouth enzymes. The digestion of starchy foods is initiated by the salivary enzyme, ptyalin. Starches commonly go unchewed, which can contribute to subsequent indigestion.

Not fully tasting, chewing and enjoying our foods frequently causes us to eat more than is healthful, as we seek more enjoyment through quantity. When we take smaller bites or portions, chew leisurely, concentrate on the tastes and delicious odors, we can be more satisfied with less.

Much of the taste that tickles our palates comes from our sense of smell rather than our taste buds. The major function of those buds on our tongues is to differentiate among sweet, bitter, sour and salty. That's why the taste of food seems flat when we get a head cold.

The really sensuous eaters are small children. When allowed, they will smell, fondle, mush, smear, bang and lick their food before eating it. All their senses are involved in the experience. They smack their lips and make pleasure sounds. They either enjoy the food thoroughly or spit it out. Their concentration is total, and only when very cleverly distracted can they be fed more when they've had enough.

Sensuality meals involve enjoying a figurative second childhood; forgoing our textbook table manners; forgetting our conditioned distaste for dirtying our hands; eating lustily and noisily. (At an ordinary meal, note the tension involved in keeping food off your hands, face and body.)

Let's Eat

I am going to describe two sensuous meals. The first concentrates on the food. The second combines the sensuality of food with sex play in gastronomical lovemaking. You'll get the most out of the second if you begin with the first.

The same basic guidelines apply to both meals (in addition to your basic preparations).

No utensils are used to transport food to mouth or to cut portions once you begin your meal.

No talking. Sounds, noises, grunts, growls, or nonsense syllables can substitute for words.

Plan your meal in advance, including foods each of you chooses as your favorites. Browsing together through markets and food shops to select your gastronomical delights can be fun in itself (especially if expense is no object). Some delicatessens, bakeries, Italian or Jewish markets in particular, offer a free feast of delicious smells.

Dress (or undress) in such a way that you don't have to worry about getting food on yourselves.

Be playful! Give your imagination free rein.

Approach each food as though it were the first time you had ever seen, smelled, felt, tasted anything like it.

Sensuous Dinner, Brunch, Whatever

When you sit down for the meal (on the floor, perhaps?), pretend you are a baby, discovering one new delight after another, thoroughly exploring the mysteries of each. Relish it as something that you will never experience again.

Enjoy the arrangement and appearance of the food. Admire the colors and textures. Enjoy the feel of them. Hold each up to your nose and breathe deeply of its fragrance. Lick it.

Foods that are somewhat spherical, such as fruit, can be rolled around on your skin. Feel the coolness and texture on your face. Move it around in both palms and listen to the sound.

Very slowly stripping an orange or grapefruit is a highly sensual experience when done properly. First examine it. Feel, smell, roll it around on each other's skin.

As you gently start peeling the fruit, notice the juice and pungent odor that oozes out. Notice the peeling sound. Examine the underbelly of the peel and absorb its aroma. When it is all peeled, focus all your senses on the treasure you have exposed. Then part it ever so slowly. Open gently into its center. Share tenderly.

Feed each other.

Sniff deeply before you bite.

Focus on the texture of the food in your mouth.

Try to liquefy each bite of food before swallowing it. Notice any changes in flavors as it is liquefied. Starches will taste sweet as they become sugar.

Take mini-portions.

Make love with your eyes.

Take turns closing your eyes and being given foods to feel, smell, touch and taste. Do not try to identify them, just enjoy the sensations.

Tear or bite off chunks of beef or chicken, caveman (or Henry VIII) style. Make appropriate growls and noises. Do that with other foods as well.

Have some gushy foods that you can gush your hands around in and eat off your (and each other's) fingers. Have you ever felt cottage cheese? It's more fun to gush than to eat. Mashed potatoes are gushy good, too.

Feel free to slurp and make noises that would horrify Emily Post and your Aunt Gertrude. Things like uninhibited belching should be checked out with each other beforehand. However, if you take small portions and chew them thoroughly as described earlier, there is less likelihood that belching will be necessary.

Plan your dessert ahead of time. There are an endless number of possibilities. I'll just mention a few.

A pudding that's on the loose side and usually eaten with a spoon can be put in a shallow bowl, to be lapped up with the tongue. If you're uninhibited enough, it can be fun to add animal sounds to the pleasure sounds I hope you're making throughout the feast.

After dinner (while waiting for that full feeling to subside) is a good time for getting into the rhythmic basics of music—using drums, pots, pans and table utensils. Explore various combinations of "drums," and/or glasses with varying amounts of water for different tones when struck by a fork. Your combo might be so good you'll want to preserve it on tape, listen later and perhaps dance to your own music.

GASTRONOMICAL LOVEMAKING

For this, most intimate sensual dinner, you do all the things I described above, with these additions:

Take any round fruit and roll it over your lover's skin with your palm. An apple feels particularly good on the back, arms and legs. For more intimate, sensitive parts of the body try grapes, cherries, nuts, olives, whatever will roll. Don't neglect the face, either. Try grapes, unpeeled and peeled. Do roll them around genital areas.

Peel an orange or grapefruit as described earlier; then take a piece of its peel and play it over your lover's body, especially around the face and under the nose so that the sensation merges with the tart oils. Experiment with both sides of the peel. Surprisingly, the grainy inside might pleasure you even more than the smoother exterior. Play with different degrees of pressure, from lightest to firm. Banana peel is interesting as well.

The Sensuous Vegetable

We usually think of vegetables as "nutritious and low-calorie" rather than sensuous. Much of the sensuality is ignored or thrown out, such as the leafy tops found on carrots and celery. What fun to slowly draw the soft bushy tops over your lover's body, like a handful of feathers. We eat but don't play with parsley, bean sprouts, alfalfa sprouts, spinach, endive. . . .

Choose one or two bean sprouts to draw and dance over the skin.

Have a raw spinach salad, but first play with the leaves.

Then there's cornsilk.

When playing with vegetables, let the receiver close his/her eyes and experience the sensations as surprises, not knowing what it is or what to expect.

Mouth to Mouth Recreation

Are you one of the lucky people who has already discovered how delicious it is to pass and receive a sip of wine (or whatever) to or from the mouth of your lover? To try it is to love it! You simply pass the liquid from one mouth to the other while you're kissing. Mmmmm. Nectar of the gods!

In your gastronomical lovemaking you carry this practice even further by swapping food the same way.

Take a bite of any fruit you enjoy and pass it on. Ambrosia!

Try it with anything and everything.

There are so many delightful things you can do with so many different foods, you are bound only by the limits of your imagination and inhibitions.

Be daring, playful, inventive—*but do not continue anything that is not pleasurable to both of you.*

While the ideal foods will greatly please all your senses, you may choose some primarily for their pungent odors, some because they are fun to play with, and others for their tactile and visual effects as well as oral pleasures.

Select a combination of foods that roll on the body, squish in the hands, slip, slide and spread on the skin.

Everything you eat is either fed you by your lover (sometimes with your eyes closed) or licked off his/her skin. Spread some foods on places where *you* want to be licked.

Enjoyed this way, every food on your menu becomes an aphrodisiac. Although the stories about aphrodisiacs have not been substantiated, it is what goes on in connection with their ingestion that gives them an aphrodisiacal quality. Therefore, on the basis of my own experience and that of many others, I can say with certainty that a sensuous meal as described is an aphrodisiac.

Obviously you will be taking turns giving and receiving sensations and food. When you are receiving, surrender totally to the sensations. Let go and soak them in, like the sensory sponge that you are.

A sponge is not meant to be dry.

Sop up the wet rainbow feelings.

7

THE MINIMOON

THE minimoon is a special kind of one- or two-day honeymoon—and the only license you need is issued by your heart and mind.

It is an intimacy marathon, a peak experience in intimate sensuality.

It is a voyage of discovery (no matter how long you've been together). You are going to explore each other even more thoroughly (and more pleasurably) than you explored yourself (Experience C). It involves spending a leisurely day or night—or two—in the pursuit of carnal knowledge.

By the end of the minimoon there will not be a spot on your lover's body that you have not caressingly traversed.

Together you will smell, taste, touch, see, feel, love.

Preparations

Your basic preparations are more important than ever for this prolonged exploration.

For couples with children, it will mean sending them off to relatives, friends, overnight camp, or a sitter.

Stock up on favorite foods and beverages so that you do not have to go out to eat or market. Plan the dishes you would like and prepare them ahead when possible (precooked casserole for dinner, perhaps). Don't forget to ice the white wine!

Leaf through the entire book (I assume you'll both have finished it by the time you reach this planning stage) and pick out all the things you'd like to include in your minimoon. You probably won't get to them all this time, but then you'll have something to anticipate for the next.

Instead of preparing just one room of your home to please all your senses, prepare all—do it together so that the senses of both are pleasured. Be prepared to use all your rooms for a variety of settings—perhaps even a closet! If you have a secluded outdoor area (and the weather to enjoy it), all the better. An area that might not be visually private enough in the day might be suitable at night.

Decide together what accessories you would like, such as feathers, pure silk, and other sensuous substances. Choose lotions and scents that please both of you. Have blossoms, leaves and ferns around the house for admiring, smelling, and drifting playfully over each other's bodies.

Make your music selection together.

Decide on whether you would like to have champagne, caviar, or any other festive treats for the occasion.

If possible, discuss any sex fantasies that might be suitable for inclusion in this minimoon. (*You* may think your fantasies wild or shocking, but anything *you* can envision has occurred to many others as well. A fantasy that you choose for this occasion should be enjoyable to both, not just something your partner will go along with. That's all right for some other occasion but not for your minimoon, which is a peak experience, a time for those things that pleasure you the most. Your lover need not partake of your favorite food if he does not enjoy it, but a fantasy game that involves two people requires the genuine commitment and enjoyment of both at this special time.)

Getting Started

There is no specific order, routine or ritual of things to do, but if you find yourselves uncertain about how to get into it, here are a few suggestions. They are all optional and not meant to be followed in any particular order. The first few would be particularly helpful if either of you tends to feel anxious or tense.

Give each other a relaxing massage or backrub. (I don't suggest my entire loving massage for inclusion in the minimoon, unless you're spending more than one full day and night; it is a separate event in its own right and extremely time-consuming. However, you can certainly use some or all aspects of the loving massage in spontaneous ways during the minimoon.)

Enjoy some wine and music, whatever relaxes you—preferably something that enhances the senses rather than hard liquor, which dulls them.

Take turns lovingly undressing each other in *very slow motion*.

Explorations for Lovers A or B are excellent ways to begin.

Or, you might try some back play (it's fun for this or any occasion.)

Back Play

Stand back-to-back, completely nude. Once you begin, do not speak.

Using no hands, only your bodies, simultaneously explore each other's backs and buttocks.

Be playful and have a "back conversation."

Get into an argument.

Make up. Be tender and loving.

Do a back dance, exploring various motions and rhythms in unison.

Gradually slow down and be still, just experiencing each other.

Say good-bye with your backs, then very slowly separate. Experience how you feel, starting with your back. Then turn, and say hello with your eyes.

Explorations

During your self-exploration you experimented with many different kinds of touch, rhythms and pressures, to find those that are optimum for you. Now is the time to explore all these variations to discover what is optimum for each other, not in a deliberate, methodical way—but with the joy, tenderness and passion of making love.

The primary emphasis, however, is on pleasuring, knowing, exploring, enjoying the various textures, smells and tastes of your lover's body, rather than on sexing (though it certainly can be included).

Approach him or her as though it were your very first opportunity to see and experience a person of the opposite sex in the nude, totally without shame, actively using all your senses at their maximum—and it really will be a *first* in many ways.

Frequently both parties in a sexual relationship are eager to demonstrate what good lovers they are, how much they know about pleasing the other.

During the minimoon I ask you to do exactly the opposite. The basic attitude is, "I know very little about what is actually best for you, but I sure am going to find out everything I possibly can during this minimoon."

How can you do that when you've been together for years and know each other intimately? If you do it properly, you'll discover how much more there is to know about each other. And people change constantly. What made you climb the wall at one time may do little for you now, and vice versa.

Still, if you think you know her/him like a book, all I can say is, *pretend* it's a new book. If it helps, you could even change the cover—with both of you wearing wigs (different from your usual color) and pretend you're new lovers living only for the moment. Devise a Walter Mitty scenario if you like. Be a movie star, a bullfighter—or you!

For those who enter into the spirit of the minimoon, new and exciting discoveries are inevitable.

Although each of you sets out to find as many ways as possible of pleasuring the other, this is not a competitive Easter-egg hunt to see who finds the most goodies. On the contrary, the idea is to *help each other* find them. There are many ways of doing that.

You can show what feels good to you *by example*. You can also give verbal hints—"That feels pretty good—and if you lightened up just a shade it would be fantastic." Be careful to limit yourself to suggestions and avoid anything resembling an order. Many desires can be indicated by body language.

Sounds are perhaps the very best way of keeping your lover tuned into what feels how, where and when. The most subtle variation in enjoyment and intensity can be beautifully communicated through moans, groans and other nonverbal noises. Spontaneous growling while you are actively and passionately making love can also prove to be a big turn-on to your partner.

If you are not accustomed to reacting with sounds, you will find that letting yourself go this way adds immensely to your pleasure. To practice, start groaning and moaning during an ordinary body massage, when it's a good "hurt" or feeling. Then consciously, if necessary, do it during the loving massage.

If you're not sure exactly how your lover is responding, ask, "How does that feel?" If the answer is enthusiastic, you might volunteer, "Good, that's one of my favorite places, too." But *never*, "Oh, I thought you'd like it; that always made Harry climb the wall."

(Frequently, when they're getting over a recent breakup, people have a need to talk about their ex. Even when the current lover is being compared favorably to an ex, it's a real turn-off. It doesn't belong. It's past. This is *now*.)

Try to begin your explorations at one of the extremities (scalp and face, hands, feet). Leave the genitals for last.

Let not one centimeter of your lover's skin go unexplored noting any changes in texture, colors, shapes.

Sniff and taste; be a sensuous epicure.

Experiment with different kinds of touch, rhythms, degrees of contact; with various oils, lotions, petroleum jelly; with sensuous

objects. Put a piece of very fine pure silk on your lover's skin and
caress the skin through the fabric.

Use your hands, fingertips, nails (ever so lightly), lips, tongue,
breath, hair.

Pay special attention to fingers and toes, especially the space
between and behind them.

All hollows, the insides of joints such as armpits, crooks of
elbows and knees, arc especially sensitive. The inside of the wrist
can also be particularly responsive to light touch.

The eyelids usually respond happily to the lighest possible flick
of the tongue.

Try butterfly kisses on the face or other delicate areas. This is
done by flickering your eyelashes up and down over your lover's
skin. This is not just for women to do to men. Men frequently
have thicker natural lashes than women.

Alternate giving and receiving; exploring, being active and
then being passive.

Men, try caressing various parts of her body with your penis
(you might want to put some oil or lotion on it) and especially
her breasts and nipples.

Women, use your nipples to caress parts of his body, especially
his nipples and genitals. Lubricate one of your nipples when you
do this and compare the sensations with the unlubricated one.

Run your nails lightly over his testicles. Take as much as you
can *gently* into your mouth and simultaneously run your tongue
over the skin.

Be sure none of his skin comes in contact with your teeth.

Another especially erogenous area is the perineum (between
the testicles and the anus for the man; between anus and vagina
for the woman).

Don't forget the voluptuous area right around the anus. (Each
of you should make sure that area is well cleansed.) Some people
also enjoy the stimulation of a well-lubricated finger in the anus.
Consult your lover before deciding whether to try that. The
finger should be cleansed before it contacts the vagina, to guard
against infection.

No form of pleasuring is improper or perverted as long as it is mutually enjoyable, and not compulsively practiced to the exclusion of other lovemaking.

(Some places still have antiquated laws against oral-genital stimulation, holdovers from the sex-is-for-procreation mentality. Lawyers' associations have gone on record favoring repeal of such medieval nonsense. If it were ever truly enforced, there would certainly be more people in jail than outside.)

Genital Love

When exploring your lover's genitals, speak endearingly to them. Play with them. *Make up pet names for them.* Yes! Your very own pet names are a tender, fun, turn-on! Speak nonsense syllables to them—as you would when playing with a baby.

Once you've enjoyed the sights, tastes and smells, ask your lover to *show* you his or her favorite masturbation technique. To learn what sort of motion, rhythm and pressure is best, each of you in turn puts your hand over his or hers, guiding its movement and using pressure to indicate a lighter or firmer touch.

When the woman is guiding the man in this way, a good position might be for her to sit in his lap, leaning back on his chest, while he rests his back against a headboard or wall.

For reversing roles and exploring the man's genitals, the woman can sit against the headboard while the man lies on his back facing her.

Learn each other's methods thoroughly. This is essential to a successful love-in and a sensuous love life.

Let primal sensuality pervade everything you do: When you wash hands, wash each other's, gently, lovingly, then apply lotion (men with rough hands who do not use softening lotions are losing much of their potential sensuality. A sensuous woman is very sensitive to rough or dry skin); bathe each other; feed each other; have sensuality meals with gastronomical love play

(Chapter 6). Allow everything you hear, touch, smell, see, taste, feel, to be a total sensory experience.

Sometime during the minimoon try coupling without planning to go any further. Just cuddle, caress, talk, joke, enjoy each other without moving toward orgasm.

You might also enjoy spending some time dancing in the nude and/or listening to music you both enjoy.

In addition to all the pleasure, which is its main purpose, the minimoon offers an opportunity to synthesize and integrate many of the ideas put forth in this book.

It is an opportunity to find out each other's secret desires.

Do you enjoy being "spanked" with a towel? That's not as unusual as you may think. It doesn't make you a pervert. If it gives you an extra thrill and your lover doesn't mind (and may like it as well), why not? Nobody is being harmed.

So you get turned on high when she wears high heeled backless shoes with black lacy stockings, a lace garter belt—and nothing else. You're not alone.

You go wild when he licks between your toes? If he doesn't discover it himself—tell him!

You love to have your perineum stroked or pressed just before you come? Say so, and show her.

If it's easier for you, put it on your written sensuality profile. At the end of this minimoon, add all your new discoveries and make any necessary changes in your list of favorite turn-ons. Try to guess each other's order of preference. Then exchange profiles.

If you haven't already done so, this is an opportunity to exchange fantasies that you might perform together some other time. That can be added to your profile, if you like.

When you know each other well enough, this might be the time to try some new exotica (see Chapter 11). If your relationship is fairly new, you might save those for another minimoon.

Trust Game

This game combines trust and sensuality, two key factors in a good sexual relationship. It's a fun activity you can try during your minimoon or at any other time, and it's a variation of a trust game played by some fortunate people exposed to the human-potential movement. I have included it in my seminars and it has never failed to be one of the highlights remembered by participants long afterwards.

Partners take turns being blindfolded and gently led around (indoors and outdoors) by the other, being given things to touch, taste, feel, smell and hear.

When you are in private, I suggest you do it in the nude and in addition to objects, give each other parts of yourselves to feel. The object is *not* to guess what it is you are feeling, smelling, tasting, hearing, or being touched or stroked with. The object is *not to know, not to care* what it is, but rather simply to enjoy absorbing the sensations while turning off your mind, which analyzes, labels and judges things.

You will find that those things you enjoy the most are the ones you cannot identify.

It also helps to disorient your partner somewhat, by gradually turning her/him this way and that, until she/he no longer knows exactly where she/he is. Another way is to ask your lover to lie down and give her/him things to feel that she/he wouldn't ordinarily experience in that position, such as touching a painting or the back of a chair.

If you peek, that is simply cheating yourself; it indicates a lack of trust. Try it over again another time until you can let go of the visual security and control.

Special Situations

Although the major focus of the minimoon is not on sexing, there is no sanction against it—except in the case of primary and secondary impotence or orgasmic dysfunction.*

When the man is not always able to achieve an erection, there should be no *expectation* of erection and no intromission even if he does achieve some erection. Should he maintain an erection for any length of time (perhaps while his penis is massaged with oil or petroleum jelly in the way he has indicated is best for him), he can then be manipulated to orgasm (*but again, that should not be expected*). During this time his eyes should be open, enjoying the sight of his lover and the pleasure she is experiencing. She should expect only to be manipulated to orgasm, this time.

The main focus for both is to enjoy all the sensual pleasures, with no goal in mind.

The man who wishes to increase the amount of time he can maintain an erection before he ejaculates should explore and play as long as possible while erect (from a twenty-minute minimoon to hours) before he finally enters his lover and continues their leisurely lovemaking trip.

At least once during the minimoon, enter with the idea of simply lying together quietly and enjoying the intimacy.

The woman with orgasmic difficulty can, during the minimoon, build a tender, playful relationship with her lover's penis before it ever enters her (and then only at her initiative, when she *really* wants it). This should be done with her sitting astride her lover, leaning slightly toward him, with her hands on the bed or his shoulders for added support. He should do no moving, thrusting or demanding, but simply lie back and enjoy the sensory pleasures at hand, possibly caressing her breasts and communicating his love.

At first she can merely sit still, experiencing completely the warm, loving fullness within her. Her eyes should be open to the here and now, to look into his eyes in a spiritual as well as

---

* Primary impotence defines a total inability to achieve erection. Secondary impotence defines an inability to achieve erection on at least 25 percent of all opportunities. Orgasmic dysfunction (in women) defines a consistent inability to achieve orgasm after effective arousal, intromission, and continued thrusting at a desirable rhythm for her for at least five minutes or longer.

physical union. When she is ready, she can experiment with various angles, movements and rhythms. On the first minimoon both should expect orgasm solely through manipulation.

To this woman I would say:

Take this penis to be your very own, to have, to hold, to play with, to enjoy, to experiment with, to love . . . and then let go.

I come to this experience
  Open
All of me . . . Giving
  Receiving
    Receptive
Expecting
    Nothing
Accepting
    Everything
    It
Chooses to Grant
    Whether different from
Expectations
    dream/hopes.
Embracing All
  So do
I come to you

8

PRIMAL LOVE-IN

IDEALLY you will have had your minimoon before you embark upon the love-in. This exploration does not require quite as much time as the minimoon—one entire evening will suffice, in addition to preparation time.

If you have not been able to set aside the time and privacy needed for the minimoon and are eager to take this intimacy trip, it is possible if you have each done the following:

1. Your self-exploration
2. Written down and exchanged your sensuality profiles
3. Followed the instructions in Chapter 7 for showing each other your optimum method of genital stimulation to the point of orgasm. (This requires that you already know your optimum method, as achieved through self-stimulation and Experience D, Chapter 2.)

The above factors are essential to this particular exploration and if any are missing, you may follow the rest of my instructions and have an experience, but it will be another kind.

The primary purpose of this, as in all the explorations, is to give and receive pleasure; but in this one particularly, the giving and receiving of *eros* is paramount.

Various fringe benefits accrue from this exploration.

Stereotypes

It can help release persons from their inhibiting stereotyped masculine-feminine roles in sexing. Each love-in has only one giver and one receiver. The giver must actively initiate and carry through the entire event. The receiver remains receptive, participating by accepting and enjoying all the pleasure possible, while the giver is dedicated *solely* to pleasuring his/her beloved in every way possible. Any reciprocation must be *postponed* for another occasion.

Obviously this would be fairly easy for the passive-female and aggressive-male stereotype couple when the man initiates the love-in as giver. However, when it is his time to take the receiving role (and the woman the assertive one), that can involve the uncomfortable—but exciting—stretching of personal growth.

Surrendering Control

This exploration involves giving over complete control of your body to your lover. A woman does this when she has an orgasm while sexing. (And the fear of doing this can keep her from having one.)

The man, however, is not accustomed to lying back (his privates all hanging out and vulnerable) and simply allowing a woman to do with (and to) him as she wishes. Being a human being first and male second, he also has a passive side, which is often suppressed but *which needs expression.* The more he feels the need to *prove* his masculinity, the more he will resist being the receiver.

The receiver gives up every form of control up to and including the moment of orgasm. Toward the end of the love-in the giver, during extended genital manipulation, will literally decide exactly *when* the receiver shall have his or her orgasm.

When you are no longer able to choose *when* to have an orgasm, you can no longer choose *not* to have it, either. (Therein lies the significance of this love-in for orgasmic dysfunction or impotence problems.)

The greater the need to control situations, the more a person will resist following through with the surrendering role. And what we resist tends to persist. The fear of losing control is one of the most common anxieties of twentieth-century Western humans.

A benefit for those with sexual anxieties and dysfunctions is that the love-in does not necessarily involve copulation. It calls for assertion but not insertion. Many factors that are experienced (often unconsciously) as pressures by such persons are relieved or eliminated.

The man with anxiety about his potency can feel assured that he is giving his lover a peak experience in lovemaking (much more than orgasm is involved) plus one or more orgasms that may well be the most intense she's ever had. (And he won't have to worry about getting an erection, keeping it, satisfying her with proper movements, rhythm, positions—or *holding out.*) She won't have to worry about any of those things either, or having to rush to get hers before he comes.

The woman with orgasmic difficulties doesn't have to worry about taking too long, tiring him out, proving anything, faking an orgasm, or getting pregnant.

When free of their anxieties, these persons are then able to reopen their pathways to arousal.

STARTING POINT

The basic agreement between you is that the receiver will allow him/herself to receive pleasure and will do everything to make sure he/she gets it, while the giver does everything possible to provide it.

The receiver must not view this as altruism or a favor from the giver. It is important to reach an understanding that the *giver* will not initiate the love-in unless he or she genuinely wants to and feels like doing it; that never will it be done "because he did me, so I guess I should really reciprocate pretty soon." The feeling that you *should* do anything has no place here!

You must be in the right mood for this. Even if you have put quite a bit of time and effort into preparing for the love-in, should something happen to change your feelings, scrap it and try again another time. Unless all signals are Go, your receiver will pick up any inappropriate feelings. (On the other hand, should you pick up some resistance from your receiver, you must decide before actually getting into the lovemaking, whether the resistance is strong enough to keep you from carrying through and whether or not to postpone.)

A degree of resistance is to be expected and is surmountable. But if something quite unsettling has happened and the person can't put it aside or relate to anything else, give it up for now. Assess the mood in the early stages, and once you get started, *don't chicken out!*

PREPARATIONS

The basic preparations are made ahead of time by the giver alone. However, this time instead of pleasing *your* senses, use your lover's sensuality profile regarding favorite music, wine, scent, etc., everything and anything else that you know is a turn-on for him/her. Use fantasy material when appropriate. You might want to put a surprise love message in the room where you'll be making love. Or even write "I love you" on the ceiling over the bed. One seminar member made a special dinner for his lover and the pièce de résistance turned out to be love notes scattered all over the entrée.

Allow at least six hours for the actual love-in, but begin building up to it long before that. Let's say you have picked an evening for your love-in. What you're trying to show, from beginning to end, is how much you love this person. Start in the morning, by indicating how much he/she pleasures you. (That's sex appeal—the ability to communicate to others that you are pleasured by them.) Look for all the ways your lover pleasures you and then let him/her know about it.

So often people do not allow themselves to express fully the love they have within, because others might then expect a commitment beyond the present. Here are ways of expressing love without verbal commitment when that is not possible.

DOING HER

If you wake up together in the morning, let her know how wonderful it is to see her there beside you, how much you enjoy looking into her eyes, smelling and touching her hair. Hold her in a warm embrace.

As you go about your early morning activities, take every opportunity to touch her, be it ever so brief, like running a finger lightly across her wrist or neck as you pass.

The more little things you can think of to let her know you love her, the more turned on she will get. To her, the *little things are the important things.* That includes spontaneously helping her with a chore or stopping somewhere to pick up something she needs.

If you're going out to work or wherever, you might hide a love note someplace where she'll find it while you're gone. You can make up your own "Happiness is . . ." card.

If you do not see her in the morning but have a date for the evening, phone her if possible during the day just to hear her voice, to be pleasured, and to ask how she is. (Lovers who don't live together are more likely to do that as a matter of course, but it's really a big event for a wife whose husband's call usually means he forgot something, or the car broke down.) If she ordinarily cooks dinner for you, tell her not to bother tonight.

Pick up some dinner she likes on your way home, take her out for her favorite food or cook it yourself. If you eat in, make it romantic with candlelight, perhaps in a different room (like in the living room, sitting on pillows at a coffee table opposite a flickering fire). Arrange your setting as though you were preparing to seduce her—and do it.

When you get home on this special evening, it is essential that you leave all your worries behind you. Think only about seeing the most important, exciting person in the world—your woman.

Look at her, really see and appreciate her. Look into her eyes and see her beauty. Enjoy the sound of her voice, the smell of her skin, the feel of *her* wrapped in your arms.

If you're fixing dinner at home for her, send her out of the kitchen, insist she do something to pamper *herself* while you decorate and cook. (I have never forgotten the few times in my life a lover has baked me a cake.)

She might want to take a luxurious, leisurely bath (without worrying about keeping you waiting), a sauna, a sunbath or do other personal things for herself that usually get put off. While she's relaxing, bring her a glass of champagne or anything else she likes. Scrub her back, or wash her from head to toe.

Have your accessories planned out beforehand. Bring or send her favorite flowers. Know what music you will play, or set the radio to her favorite station. Prepare the bedroom (or wherever the lovemaking will be) with luxurious things like fur, satin or velvet to lie on and feel. Have her favorite treat on hand, to feed her later.

Leave a jar of petroleum jelly at the place you have chosen for lovemaking. Use jelly because it is not water soluble and it's less likely to require interruption for a refill during genital manipulation (which should last as long as possible—a half-hour minimum). If you're really ambitious, you can scent the jelly, heating it in a double boiler.

Assuming that by now you have let each other in on some of your sexual fantasy material, use that information in planning your accessories. Have available visual or reading material you suspect will arouse her. This may range anywhere from love poetry to a nude male pinup.

Before you sit down to dinner, encourage her to unload her day's headaches, so that she can relax and more fully enjoy her love-in. If the day has been so bad that she can't get those things off her mind, if she is so irritable that *you* no longer are in the mood—at this point you can still cancel the lift-off.

If all systems are Go, then light the candles and proceed. Should she be compulsive about doing dishes after dinner, do them yourself, while she bathes or otherwise relaxes. Give your food a little time to settle before you get into the heavy part of the love-in. Meanwhile you can take a walk, listen to music, dance, make love with your eyes, enjoy your turn-on props, read to her.

Back at the love-in, everything is going well and you are ready to get it on. If you feel she could use further relaxation, offer to give her a massage. That device is centuries old for a very good reason. It works. You may wish to undress her, slowly, lovingly (and get your clothes off, too). Be sure the music won't require any attention.

You can begin with a regular massage if you like, and work onto the loving massage, or start right off with the latter. Just so you don't dive for the crotch!

Begin with her head, hands or toes, and cover every part of her body before you get around to the genital stimulation.

Before, during or after kissing her mouth, flick your tongue *very lightly* across the center ridge of her upper lip. Another highly sensitive area well worth exploring with the tongue is the armpit and its surrounding erogenous zone. Be sure any deodorant has been washed off, otherwise you're likely to find it distasteful.

(Many of these suggestions for her can be applied to him, and vice versa, so read both sections with that in mind.)

Keep your motions irregular, unpredictable, so that she has a pleasant sense of suspense and surprise at what you do next.

When you get to her breasts, don't grab for a nipple. Start running your fingers or tongue lightly around the outer circle of the breasts and ever so suspensefully spiral your way toward the peak. Then work from the center to the outer edges of each breast. The nipple, like the clitoris, can be so sensitive that only a delicate touch is a turn-on. (This varies with the person, of course.) The areola, the dark area surrounding the nipple, is more receptive to direct stimulation and transmits the sensations to the nipple.

Stay one step ahead of her, moving elsewhere before she starts wishing you would. But don't rush either. This is a very slow buildup.

If you are really tuned into her, you will be experiencing this together with her. By putting your full attention on her you'll know what she feels and when it's time to move on. You can be certain that when something gets less pleasurable for you, it will be less for her as well.

Much of the time she'll probably lie rather still. The less she moves, the better. If she starts flopping around like crazy, don't assume she's in ecstasy. If your touch is too heavy, she may be trying to escape.

Should she ask you to stop at any time, *don't* (unless you're doing something new and exotic in which case just go on to something you know she likes). If it's not something objectionable or downright painful, and she asks you to stop, she probably wants some control. Say, "Just a minute," *lighten up* and slow down, but *keep control* of her body. *She really wants that.*

When you get around to the genital area, tease a little. Get close, then back off. Drift a finger across the mons or vulva, then carry the movement out to other parts of the body (another connecting technique). When you finally do zero in, warm some petroleum jelly in your fingers (no cold globs, please), and start with large circles moving from the perineum up around the outer lips, then down the more sensitive inner lips. Although they meet at the clitoral hood, bypass the clitoris other than letting a finger (or your tongue) drift over it *ever so lightly.* (Any oral-genital lovemaking should take place before you start the manipulation. If she gets too close to orgasm when you go down on her, back off and use your fingers in the way she has previously indicated is best for her.)

If you like, make up a story that fits one of her sex fantasies and tell it to her while you caress her genitally.

Speak lovingly to her vulva as you play with it, using the pet name you chose during your minimoon. If you are uninhibited, speak nonsense syllables to it or make animal noises.

Once you start the prolonged genital manipulation which culminates the love-in, all spontaneity and inventiveness cease. You are guided by what *she* has previously demonstrated is the optimum stimulation for her. Get in a position that will be comfortable for thirty minutes to an hour, or she will pick up your discomfort. Don't move in time to the music or anything other than *her* rhythm, and maintain the steady, even motion that she likes. For most women, any change in rhythm or movement will cause them to back down. That's exactly what you do for this exploration—but *only* when she gets extremely close to orgasm. If you feel she's just a step away, then she is. (Just before the orgasm she'll probably be rigidly still, though there may be some leg twitching, and her breathing will change.) Back her off by stopping a fraction of a second. Miss one or two strokes, then take her back up again.

She may moan and groan, but women have a greater tolerance than most men, for going up and down like that. So keep taking her to the edge and backing off until *you* decide to let her have the orgasm. If she begs you to let it happen, say, "All right," but keep taking her up and down. Don't let *her* manipulate *you*. Each time you take her back up she'll be just a little higher.

When she's peaking as high as *you* want her to be, then let her go over by maintaining the rhythm, and easing up. Do *not* move harder and faster unless she's *previously* shown you that it's best for her that way. For most women, it's not.

Some involuntary muscular twitching of limbs, face, or body frequently accompanies the orgasm (that's a release of tension), plus a series of irregular vaginal contractions which you can feel when your finger is on the vulva above the vaginal opening.

When she finally has her orgasm after going up and down a

number of times, it will be more intense than usual. Meanwhile, keep your hand on the spot you were stimulating, but without pressure. When the orgasm is over, she may say, "Wow, that was good," which might really mean, "don't touch me" because the area is ultrasensitive at that point. Just lighten your touch but don't completely remove your hand. Wait several minutes (women's orgasms last longer than men's) and when you can't feel any more vaginal contractions start stimulating her again. Use fresh lubricant, a lighter touch, and continue *if she is responsive.* When she is satiated, the area will be temporarily anesthetized.

An alternative to resuming manual stimulation is to enter her. Although you will *not* have had an erection previously because your full attention was on *her,* the peak of her excitement and orgasm may stimulate an erection. When you enter just after her orgasm, she'll be as turned on as she was *before* her climax, so she may get back up and have another.

However, at this point she'll be ecstatic and satiated, whatever you do, or don't.

The woman with the greatest anxiety over whether she can reach orgasm is likely to protest the most at the idea of being brought to the brink and being taken up and down at the whim of her lover. Yet she is the one who needs it the most! If she can give up control, and discover that she *can* go up and down many times and still experience orgasm, even more intensely—that confidence will keep her from panic or mounting anxiety when she inadvertently backs off and "loses it" during intercourse.

Primally for Him

The same benefit accrues to the man who is not sure how long he can keep his erection. Such a man fears that if he got close to orgasm and were backed off, he would lose the erection entirely, so he resists that aspect of the love-in. His fear is unfounded. With effective stimulation (in the way *he* prefers), the only thing that can cause him to lose the erection is thinking about whether he will keep it. Discovering that he can postpone ejaculation without completely losing his erection will give him confidence.

A major difference in doing the man is that—for the first time at least—you should back him off no more than twice—three times if you *know* he has more tolerance. Most men don't have the tolerance for being taken up and down as often as women.

If you have trouble getting him to lie still for the love-in, convince him that it's fun for *you*, which it will be as long as you genuinely feel like doing it. With the man who has bought the masculine-aggressive stereotype (to whom "passive-receptive" means feminine) your hardest job will be to get him on his back. Here the age-old massage comes in handy again. But that's later.

The love-in begins much earlier. Should you get up together that morning, let him know how much he pleasures you, how you enjoy feeling him next to you, the touch of his skin, the warmth of his body. Snuggle, cuddle up, tell him things about himself that you enjoy.

After you get up, let a hand seek his body whenever you come close. If you pass behind him while he's sitting, kiss him softly on the back of his neck, or drift your fingers across it. Don't be afraid of touching his genital area or buttocks.

If he's going to work, leave a love note someplace where he'll find it later—in the car, his briefcase, his lunch or pocket. If you're at *his* place, leave one where he'll find it after you're gone.

If his/your work allows it, phone him during the day just to say, "I love you," in your own way. Let him know you miss him and look forward to seeing him later.

Try to have the place and yourself all spruced up by the time he gets there. Wear something you know *he* especially likes. Decorate the room you pick for lovemaking with *him* in mind. Be guided by *his* taste, bring in things *he* likes. You might change the pictures on the wall for the occasion, catering to his taste and what turns him on. If you know he enjoys skin flicks, you could be terribly daring and rent some for the evening.

Utilize your knowledge of his sex fantasies in planning your outfit and accessories. Prepare any erotic reading material that turns him on. Write him a big love-note—perhaps in lipstick on the mirror! If there are certain erotic words that turn him on, include them.

If your love-in includes dinner, plan to take him to a favorite place or cook something special. This is your night to seduce *him*. If you don't live together, you might discuss the idea of reversing roles entirely: You pick *him* up at his place and *take him out* to dinner. If either of you is really uncomfortable about that, save it for another experiment.

About flowers. Who ever said men can't receive them? And why? Both married and single men at my seminars have loved the idea of being sent or brought flowers, be it a single perfect blossom or a bouquet. There again, you must know your man and what pleasures *him*.

Be guided by his sensuality profile.

Doublecheck your basic preparations (Chapter 2).

As part of your preparations, shake off any problems that have been nagging at you. If you can't put them aside for the evening, cancel your plans.

When you greet him, let it be as though the sun just burst out and the world started spinning; nobody, nothing else exists, for now.

Encourage him to talk about any problems he had that day, so he can get them off his chest and unwind. Don't let him make any decision, like whether he wants a drink. Just fix him what you know he likes.

For real luxury, run a bath for him with bubble bath and oil. (Who says men can't enjoy and have soft skin?) Then give him a drink in the tub. Scrub his back (or anything else) if you like.

Meanwhile make your final preparations. Have the petroleum jelly ready for use later, and *take off your rings*.

If he says he's tired, had a hard day, offer to give him a massage. *Once you get started, you've got to see it through to the end.* If he offers resistance and talks about "some other time," say yes and keep right on. If he gets too tense, just put your hand on his genitals. (If he has potency difficulties do not attempt the love-in when he is tired or after a big meal; and read Chapters 16 and 17 before making plans.)

You might start by massaging his feet firmly (warm oil is recommended), and then as you work up to the thighs, lighten up on your touch. If he needs and wants it, give him a good relaxing massage and backrub before easing into the sexual stimulation.

Keep in mind the discoveries made during your minimoon as to what pleasures him most.

When you're ready, approach him as though he's a gourmet banquet and you're a gourmand. You have two hands and a mouth. Try to use them simultaneously. Work your way up and down his body, but don't wait too long before getting to his genitals.

The testicles are very sensitive. If they are squeezed, it must be very gently. With one gentle fingertip make tiny little circles over every last centimeter of his genitals.

The Primal Lick

For an exquisitely arousing treat, try the following: Gently raise his knees toward his chest and run your tongue tip from his glans penis down the corpus spongiosum, which resembles a vein running down the underside of the penis, over the balls, down the perineum to the anus which can be licked and flicked lightly. Then travel the same route back up to the penis, flicking rapidly at the frenum (a membrane on the penis rim where the foreskin is or was attached) and the penis tip and then down and up again as many times as pleases you. If he doesn't react strongly, take his pulse. He may be dead!

(The anus should be washed carefully with soap and water before this sort of lovemaking.)

If he enjoys fellatio, fine, but use your hand to bring him to orgasm. The hand is best for taking him up and down because it has the best stamina, agility, and can duplicate his optimum self-stimulation. Warm some petroleum jelly in your fingers and apply it when you begin manual stimulation. (You should have tried this sort of stimulation on at least one other occasion so you know that you're doing it the way he likes it.)

By now you should know the kinds of genital stimulation he likes best. Your goal is not to get him hard, necessarily, but rather for him *simply to enjoy* everything. An erection is for insertion, which is not going to happen—at least the first time around.

Be sure you get into a comfortable position when you get to his penis. (You might like to sit cross-legged between his legs.) Adjust your position to the natural angle of the penis and do not force it from its natural angle or you can hurt him.

His noises and other responses should reassure you that you have the right pressure and rhythm for him. When he gets close to orgasm the glans will be shinier, tighter. It may swell slightly and look as though the skin is going to burst. At that point back him off by cupping your hand around the head, *briefly*. Then resume stimulation and back him off just once more. Plan to spend only five or ten minutes taking him up and down when you don't know his tolerance level.

To bring on the orgasm, just continue instead of backing off when he reaches his peak—or slow down imperceptibly and lighten the pressure.

Keep a light contact while he comes. A nice way to bring him down is to suck him dry. He might also appreciate having his pelvic area gently washed with a *warm* washcloth. (Let him know what you're going for before you up and leave him.)

Afterwards, he'll probably want to hold you close, kiss you and express his pleasure in various loving ways including stimulating you to orgasm—but no reciprocal love-in at this time.

FRINGE BENEFIT

Bringing the man almost to orgasm and then backing him off is also good training for satisfying a woman who likes to have one or more orgasms before he has his. He can then thrust at the rhythm *she* likes (or let her do the thrusting), pause when she climaxes, then resume thrusting in the same or another position and repeat . . . until he is ready to come.

VARIATIONS

Once you have tried the love-in as described, you can then do it again, but this time switch to intercourse after taking the person up and down a few times. In the case of ongoing impotence, however, insertion should *not* be expected.

INSURANCE

The best insurance for making this a memorable experience is to read and *discuss* the chapter together, thoroughly, especially those suggestions that are new to you. You might want to try some of them when you're sexing sometime, to see whether they would add to your love-ins. Talking a fantasy, for example, is something that can be a big turn-on for some people and a turn-off for others.

Should you plan to have a love-in before you have had your minimoon, review the aspects you can incorporate into your love-in.

9

SEEING I TO I:

Explorations in Sexcommunication

DON'T talk about sex.

That unspoken taboo against such *intimate* discussion is one with which most of us have grown up. When the taboo is broken, embarrassment is the norm. The sexual revolution in its fullest sense has as yet reached only the growing edge of our neatly bordered institutions.

Many of us who do feel free enough to break the taboo frequently refrain for fear of embarrassing or intruding upon another's privacy.

Lovers also fear they may embarrass or anger each other, and thereby suffer some sort of reprisal.

"Not us," you may say. "We have no trouble talking about sex." Talking *about* sex is relatively easy. But communicating about aspects of your lovemaking that leave room for improvement is more difficult.

Lovers not only hold back on things they don't like about their sexing, they spend a great deal of energy pretending to like what they don't. And pretending to feel more than they do.

I have spoken to many a woman who was afraid to tell her husband that she was interested in a seminar about sensuality because then he would know that she felt their sex life was less than perfect.

The charade begins early. It starts with learning to hide feelings from Mom and Dad in order to get love. The same pattern continues with others.

Sharon is parked with Ted, captain of the basketball team. As they kiss, she thinks, "Please, please ask me to the prom." Suddenly he grabs her breast as though he were reaching for a rebound. Then he tweaks her nipple. "Ooooh," she murmurs—when she really feels, "that hurts, you oaf!"

Ted the Tweaker is following the instructions of a "more experienced" friend who assured him that this gets a girl really hot. Another girl, maybe. Sharon, no. After the prom, she gets tired of getting tweaked and tells him to dribble on another court, rather than let him know that her oohs and aahs were fake.

So poor Ted goes on thinking that there are certain things that arouse *all* girls. If someone doesn't respond, he'll assume there's something wrong with *her* instead of trying to find out what things arouse her as an individual, distinct from anyone else.

There are few women who have not sometimes feigned or exaggerated their enthusiasm out of tact, a desire to please and gain or keep a lover's favor. Some of it is rather minor, but some fakery is important enough to merit tactful revelation. The earlier in the relationship it is revealed, the easier it is to accept. It is also easier for a man to accept something displeasing when his lover has been quite openly appreciative of the things he does that *are* pleasing.

You may start faking because you think you don't want to hurt someone, but if it becomes a long-term relationship, chances are the truth will eventually come out. Keeping your finger in the dam can siphon off so much energy and generate such tension that you tire and let it out (possibly in a moment of anger). What you rationalized as a desire not to hurt another can end up hurting more. Where phony orgasm or other major faking has gone on for years, the aid of a therapist may be needed to guide a couple through the transition toward authenticity and genuine intimacy.

Some pretense is more difficult for a man. If he is too tired, tense, or just not in the mood for sex, the message is conveyed graphically—without words.

If you are thinking, "Well, I never pretend," rerun the reel on your sex life and look carefully. Have you leveled with your lover about *everything* you like and don't like?

COMMUNICATION AIDS

Should things get difficult between you during any of the verbal explorations to follow, the Revolving Discussion Sequence (RDS) has proven to be an effective communication technique for couples. Developed by general semanticist Ted Crawford, its aim is to help each of you understand and grow toward each other.

RDS consists basically of three segments:

STATEMENT
Party A makes a statement to you.
UNDERSTANDING
1. You don't answer that statement yet. Instead you concentrate *completely* on understanding A's message, his or her way, as fully as possible. To assure that you understood it correctly, you restate the same message *in different words*, concentrating on the significant aspects and *feelings*. Then you ask, "Is that what you mean?"

2. If you have restated his ideas or feelings correctly, Party A says, "Yes."

3. If the restatement does not *completely* satisfy him, Party A *first* tells you what part was *right* and then makes the correction.

4. You go through the same process of understanding and rewording the correction until A is satisfied. To be fair, A should keep to *one* point and not add any *new* ones as he corrects B's understanding of the original point.
AGREEMENT
This can be quite challenging when your feelings are in total

disagreement even though you think you understand how A feels.

1. Search for at least one aspect of what A said that you can agree with even if it's only conditional, such as, "If I were in your position, I might feel the same way"; or confirming agreement such as, "I can see by the look in your eyes that you are feeling hurt. . . ." A partial agreement might be: "You call me a liar, implying that I'm *always* a liar. I agree that I've lied on *some* occasions."

2. If you can, find and relate something in your past experience that was similar in terms of feeling or incident, to reinforce the understanding and empathy.

3. It is a copout merely to say, "I agree with everything," and not specify *what* you agree with or support it with brief, specific examples.

New Round

After you have stated your agreements, the cycle starts again. It is now your turn to state your own view, be understood and experience some agreement.

This process is useful because the same words and phrases can have different meanings to different people, causing incredible labyrinths of misunderstanding. This is one way of preventing and resolving such problems. It takes the emphasis off your disagreement by switching the focus from *your* protests and desire to *make* A understand or agree with you, to the effort of understanding A, knowing she/he will do the same for you. It works, *provided* both parties sincerely stay with the format as described.

For example:

Statement

A: "I've helped show you all kinds of different things that turn me on during love play but you hardly ever do them, unless I hint or ask. When you don't do things on your own that you know I enjoy, I feel as though you don't care about pleasuring me."

UNDERSTANDING

B: "Are you saying that you wish I would be more active during lovemaking and do more things that you like—and when I don't do these things without prompting, you feel like I don't care about you? Is that what you mean?"

A: "Yes, mostly, in terms of wanting you to be more active and spontaneous. But my emphasis is not that you don't care about me. It's that I feel like you don't *enjoy* giving me pleasure, the way that I enjoy pleasuring you."

B: "Oh, I see, you feel as though your pleasure isn't gratifying or important to me in the way that mine is to you. It sounds like you're disappointed because that's really important to you. Does that fit for you?"

A: "Yes."

AGREEMENT

B: "I can see that you are disappointed that I don't do a lot of the things you like on my own and I agree that I'm not as active as I could be. I also don't keep a mental list of your turn-on preferences in my mind during lovemaking and tend to forget until you remind me. I may depend on your hints because then I don't have to remember. I also agree that it's much more meaningful when I do something to pleasure you without being asked verbally or nonverbally. I know that when you do something nice for me without being asked, it also means a lot more to me that way, and I dislike having to ask you to do something that you could have thought to do on your own. I hadn't considered my role in lovemaking in that context before."

B has now done a substantial amount of agreeing and is ready to make an independent statement, with A doing the understanding and agreeing. It is nice, but not always necessary to agree to the extent of the example given.

I *Messages Versus* You *Messages*

The above discussion sequence might not have elicited the amount of agreement it did in the example if B had been someone who was sensitive to criticism, because the complaint was made with *you* messages. Telling someone that "You do or don't do thus-and-such" has the structure of a reproach or accusation. It encourages the accused to summon up arguments in his defense instead of using his energy in trying to see the other person's point of view as well as his own.

In using the more effective *I* messages, the speaker tries to express the situation in terms of his *own feelings* about it. If A had used *I* messages in stating the problem above, it would have sounded something like this:

A: "When we make love, I frequently find myself wishing you would take me by surprise and do some of those things I've shown you that I like, without my having to ask in one way or another. It would mean a lot to me to feel that you really enjoy pleasuring me the way I enjoy pleasuring you."

When people send *you* messages, they are frequently taking on the role of judge and jury. They are notifying the defendant that his actions have been judged wrong. Telling someone he is not doing the right thing is taking a much greater liberty than exercising your right to express how *you* feel about something.

To say, "*You* upset me when *you* don't want sex," is quite different from, "*I* feel upset when *I* get turned down for sex." The sender of the *you* message is *blaming* the other person for his own upsetness. The *I* message puts the responsibility for the upsetness where it belongs—on the person who is upset. He has a right to get upset and express his feelings—but not to blame them on another.

If your first impulse is to say, "You always . . ." change that to something like, "I feel annoyed when you . . .". You may notice that you no longer have an "antagonist."

If your lover tends to be touchy and defensive, especially about sexual matters, you can start off clearly stating your *I* orientation with, "*I* have a problem."

Diane, for instance, wanted to let Bob know that he was moving too fast and changing rhythm too often for her maximum pleasure. She and I discussed attitude and approach. This is how she broached it:

"I have a problem," she began. "I don't seem to be able to get very excited unless the thrusting is rather slow and constant, without changes in rhythm. But I don't know whether that will be enjoyable for you."

Her approach was not critical of what he *had* been doing, and she expressed concern for his enjoyment as well as hers. He responded positively and they worked it out so that he did it the way that was best for her to reach a climax at least once, and then he did it his way.

SEXCOMMUNICATION

It would be ideal if you could set aside a certain night or two each week for the explorations to follow. As you get into discussion try to keep sending *I*'s and minimize the *you*'s.

Hold hands as you talk. If one of you pulls his or her hand away, you are probably on a blaming/defensive track and need to work harder on *I* messages or try the RDS technique.

Within the sensual/sexual context, take turns telling each other:

1. Something your lover has done that you like but you never mentioned before.

2. Something your lover does (or omits) that bothers you but you don't recall having mentioned it. (If it turns out to have been mentioned previously, discuss it anyway, using *I* messages this time.)

3. Something you could never tell before.

4. Something you would like but could never ask for.

5. Your sexual fantasies, particularly those that are feasible to enjoy together. There are many things people fantasize but would not like to experience in reality (such as rape). However, parts or all of some fantasies *can* be carried out *or modified*. A woman who fantasizes being a stripteaser might never wish to

actually become one, but with encouragement would enjoy stripping for her lover or watching *him* strip.

If you have previously shared some fantasies, I commend you on your degree of intimacy and candor, because this is one of the more difficult things for couples to do.

6. Kinds of movies and other visual/aural material that turns you on the most.

7. Kinds of activities that help get you in a sexual mood (for instance, dancing, wrestling, horseback riding).

8. Personal hygiene preferences (bathing, mouthwash) vis-a-vis what turns you on and off for lovemaking.

9. Discuss your early feelings about masturbation; how you feel about doing it now, in the presence of your lover.

(Many seminar participants express feelings about masturbation as an act of "desperation and loneliness." But masturbation often fills a need that cannot otherwise be met, even by a spouse. Marriage should not make masturbation taboo or indicate that one has "failed" the other if one resorts to self-love instead of mutual love on occasion.)

10. Feelings about fellatio and cunnilingus.

11. In writing, separately, list aspects of your lovemaking that are predictable or have become habitual; what could decrease predictability and what else you might *add* that would be exciting. Then discuss possible changes in your patterns.

12. Any other aspect of your relationship that needs to be discussed more openly, using *I* messages and possibly the RDS technique.

13. AGGRESSION-GENTLENESS PROFILES

Rate each item according to its turn-on potential for you, on a scale of zero to ten. Zero would indicate indifference; ten the greatest degree of turn-on. If it definitely turns you off, write OFF. Fill in details, where appropriate.

I like it when you:

Rating

_____a. are assertive

_____b. are firm and moderately aggressive

____c. make animal/caveman noises

____d. are forceful and dominating, but not hurtful

____e. say things like (fill in)_____

_____

____f. make verbal threats of physical violence if I don't do as you wish. (It should be *clearly understood* if you desire threats to be *verbal only, not* physical.) State any specific kinds of threats you prefer.

____g. use *mild* or reciprocal violence (such as wrestling)____ or squeezing____; biting____; pinching____; scratching____; slapping____; pushing me around____; pinning me down____; tieing me down (loosely)____; anything else_____

____h. are assertive at the outset (as rated above) followed by tender gentleness.

____i. are gentle and seductive at first, gradually becoming more assertive as checked above.

____j. are gentle but lovingly passionate

____k. are very gentle

____l. are receptive and responsive

____m. are passive

____n. are resistant

____   (other)_____

Should you end up checking both aggressive and gentle items, this is not surprising. Uninhibited people can enjoy aspects of both, changing their preferences with their mood and their particular lover.

Now fill out the second half of the profile covering the sort of roles *you* enjoy playing. Use the same rating scale.

Part Two

I like to:

____a. be assertive

____b. be firm and moderately aggressive

____c. make animal/caveman noises

_____d. be forceful and dominating, but not hurtful

_____e. say things like (fill in)_____

_____f. make *threats* of physical violence if you don't do as I wish. (It should be *clearly understood* that these threats would be *verbal only not* physical.) State any specific kinds of threats you prefer.

_____g. Use *mild* or reciprocal violence (such as wrestling)_____ or squeezing_____; biting_____; pinching_____; scratching_____; slapping_____; pushing you around_____; pinning you down_____; tieing you down (loosely_____; anything else_____

_____h. be assertive, at the outset as rated above, followed by tender gentleness.

_____i. be gentle and seductive at first, gradually becoming more assertive as checked above.

_____j. be gentle but lovingly passionate

_____k. be very gentle

_____l. be receptive and responsive

_____m. be passive

_____n. be resistant

_____ (other)_____

Fill these out before you see your lover's profiles. You might try guessing each other's answers before exchanging and *discussing* them.

GAMES

Exploration Fourteen: CENTER TO CENTER

Take several deep breaths, then look into your lover's eyes for a minute or so. When you are ready, close them and picture what your lover would be if he or she were:

a. an object

b. an animal

c. part of nature

Don't think about it before or during the exploration. Just stay in the nonverbal here and now, simply *allowing* any images that come.

Do not force, question, or analyze. Just be open and accept, without effort.

Now take the nature image that feels best and allow it into your center. Stay with the experience as long as you like. Time does not exist.

When you have both opened your eyes, share your experience.

Some of the ways your lover saw you will feel right and some may not. Those that don't feel on target may actually relate to him or her rather than to you since we often see ourselves reflected in others.

Exploration Fifteen: TOUCH-A-THON

Take turns spending a half-hour sensualizing—giving your lover a wide variety of sensations ranging from highly erotic to *mildly* unpleasant, from delicious warmth to cool, from the lightest of touch to firm pressure to light pinching/nipping/biting.

With each new sensation, stop and wait for your lover to indicate *by sound* (not words) the degree of pleasure or displeasure. *Anything communicated as unpleasant should be discontinued immediately.*

As a receiver, if something is neither pleasant nor unpleasant to you, then make no noise at all.

Those sensations that are communicated as pleasurable should be continued for a while. As long as you really enjoy the sensation, *keep making pleasure sounds. Stop them* the moment it gets boring or you find your mind wandering. If what was pleasant at first suddenly becomes irritating (as it will if kept up too long), *change your sounds* accordingly.

If you are not in the habit of letting your lover know what you are feeling through noises (and silence when nothing's happening), repeat this exploration until you can integrate sounds into your sexing.

Exploration Sixteen: ANIMAL PLAY
Each of you takes the identity of an animal of your choice.
Close your eyes and take five or six slow, deep breaths. Let the
image of your animal appear. Continue breathing slowly and
start *feeling* like this animal. Feel your skin taking on its
characteristics. Feel fuzzy, hairy, thick-skinned or shelled. If
you're an elephant, feel yourself growing a trunk. Start moving
like the animal, and *make its noises.* Take on its sense of smell.

When you are ready, open your eyes and relate to the other
animal you sniff/see. Smell it from a distance, then closer, to
ascertain its intentions. Communicate one way or another.

Be playful. Fight or have a tussle. Chase one another. Be
friendly or make up. Feel free to do anything short of actual
violence. *Play* violence is fine. Do not be afraid of baring your
fangs and claws; showing anger. It can expand your love and
sensual channels.

Growl or make other guttural sounds. (Don't worry about
whether the sounds match the animal when you find yourself
spontaneously making noises.) You can even change animals
whenever you like. Gobbling up the other animal is proper, as
are horseplay and wrestling. Whatever happens, make friends at
the end.

If you find yourselves too inhibited when getting started, try
taking a drink or something that relaxes and releases you. See if
you can recapture your primitive and uninhibited *self,* for a little
while.

Should you find any part of the exploration sexually arousing,
you can incorporate those aspects (like growls, perhaps) into your
lovemaking—or use them to signal that you're in the mood.

Try this more than once, as various animals. It can be a fun
kind of love play, providing a change of pace to your sexing
pattern.

Structured language is far removed from actual experience,
from gut-level feeling, from sensuality. Other forms of communication, such as these, can help us get further into primal
sensuality.

Exploration Seventeen: SIGNALS

Think back to times when you have felt shy about letting your desires be known, and discuss them. Then explore various possible means of letting each other know while you're sexing what you want (and don't want). Think *primal*.

Look for specific ways of signaling that feel right to both of you. It is best to do this after experimenting and completing the explorations in this chapter.

Desires can be communicated by words, sounds or gestures. A direct gesture would be to gently guide your lover's hand or head toward the desired part of your body; opening or closing your legs; raising your hips or feet if you wish attention there. A rhythm you want can be indicated by tapping it out with fingers or hand.

Signals can be as subtle as inclining your head or your eyes or placing your own hand where you crave attention. If you are in the mood for a particular accessory (a feather or whatever), you can indicate this verbally or by putting it out beforehand or using it first on your lover.

If you do not ordinarily speak during sexing, make an effort to do so. After a while, it should become comfortable.

Although you probably have some informal communication system going, see if you can expand it and fill in any gaps.

EROTIC TALK

Luck, coincidence and conditioning in our sexually formative and impressionable years largely determine what sort of things arouse us later in life. For most people, various words and expressions are very powerful. These run the gamut from the romantic whisper of "I love you" to the lusty or whispered exhortation, "suck my cock" or "eat my pussy"—or "fuck me."

It's good to know and to be able to accept each other's verbal turn-ons. They're just words. They're not "sick," as Edith had thought when she was asked to say, "I'm gonna suck your giant red cock." She also objected to hearing "hot juicy pussy," something Laura mentioned as very enjoyable for her.

There's no need to analyze why something excites a person; just be glad you discovered it so you can use it to advantage. Erotic and colloquial expressions are also a turn-on for the speaker, so it can work both ways.

Viv and Frank said they enjoy "Sock it to me, baby!" while Bill felt it was too demanding or crude. "Fuck me" is a common turn-on, or turn-off when "fuck" is experienced as hostile or vulgar.

On the whole, I think "fuck" is more of a turn-*on*, being what Eric Berne called a wet word as opposed to a dry word such as "intercourse." Balling is another wet word that may be preferable to "fuck" because it does not carry the same cultural hostility. Neither does it have the potential for arousal, however.

Words that have objectionable associations to one person but arouse the other can be discussed in terms of defining their meaning *to each other*. A word can mean (between you) what *you want* it to mean.

Getting hung up on semantics is antisensual. If the *feelings* are warm and lusty, the sounds are right, no matter what dictionary definition or historical derivation is quoted.

Sometimes an "objectionable" word may be involuntarily spoken in the heat of passion.

Passion is more important than semantics!

Defuse negative reactions to your lover's turn-on expressions by talking about them and saying the word(s) over and over. You may find that when the revulsion leaves, it was masking an arousal potential.

> Energy
>   is giving and receiving
>   passed
>   lovingly back and forth.

10

PRIMAL SENSUALITY SEMINARS

THE CONCEPT of a group of people getting together for a seminar in primal sensuality has aroused considerable curiosity and a flurry of fantasies.

There are those who have instant visions of orgies, even though seminars have been held at reputable growth centers, and my literature has stated "no nudity."

The no-nudity restraint is not because I am opposed to nudity; I think relaxed social nudity can be fun (especially around a pool) with people who are not trying to prove anything.

However, only a small percentage of our population is relaxed enough about the body to participate in nude seminars, therapy or bathing. Women, in particular, did not flock to the first nude marathons pioneered by Paul Bindrin.

(I remember vividly my first experience with "public" nudity eleven years ago. It was my initial visit to the Esalen Institute, and I had heard about the *coeducational* hot-springs bathing. I felt it would be one of the most difficult things I had ever done, but determined to do it because, like spinach, it would be "good for me." When the moment finally arrived, it was so easy that after all my nervous anticipation, I was actually disappointed. But I was not disappointed in another discovery I made at those baths. Relaxing in the rhythm of timeless waves crashing below us, I looked about and found that all bodies are beautiful—young, old, fat, thin—all part of nature's beauty.)

Yet for the sake of those people—even if it's just one in the group—who would be uncomfortable with nudity, I ask people to wear bathing suits for group lessons in Esalen-type massage and an abbreviated version of my own loving massage.

In one group a woman refused to allow her husband to give her the massage; she later confessed she was afraid it would become an orgy. Yet at no seminar, even among very sexually liberated groups, has anyone ever gotten out of line.

As I expected, most participants turned out to be thoroughly likable people—aware, intelligent, with a sense of humor. Many have been exposed to some aspect of the human-potential movement; they have seen life as a process of developing their potential in many areas and are there for their additional discoveries.

Quite a number of them seem to have had better-than-average sex lives (not perfect—whose is?) and are interested in expanding their sensual horizons, adding to their knowledge and variety. Many of them are curious and interested in my techniques for experiencing "new" body sensations, for turning any part of the body into an erogenous zone, in the loving massage and a general heightening of sensual awareness.

Most of the people in my seminars are in their twenties, thirties and forties, with a few fifties. Now and then we get a juicy old man who refuses to accept the retirement mystique. The oldest woman was sixty and looked younger.

Sex Life Data

During my last dozen seminars, in order to best fill the participants' needs, I distributed questionnaires inquiring why they were there, how they functioned sexually, their specific interests and problems.

I have compiled statistics based on 180 questionnaires (100 women, 80 men), not as part of a scientific research project but simply as a matter of general interest. Although there are some parallels, I doubt whether this data could be taken as representative of the average American. The human-potential movement as yet attracts only a small percentage of our population, usually from among the more sophisticated and economically advantaged groups.

This sample is also more adventurous than average, I feel, because when I first introduced primal sensuality seminars, there were no others dealing with sensuality and sexuality readily available in Los Angeles, and to my knowledge, only one other program in all of California. I have been glad to note, that others have sprung up since then to fill the wide sensuality/sexuality education gap.

Potency

One of the questions for males was: "Do you have difficulty with your erection or orgasm? Occasionally; never; often." Only 9.7 percent checked "often"; 38.9 percent "never"; and 51.4 percent "occasionally." This included men who felt they ejaculated "prematurely," as well as those with erective difficulties.

Orgasmic Function

Six percent of the women had never experienced orgasm by any means. All, however, said they enjoyed sex.

Orgasm during coitus with a man was reported by 72 percent of the women, with 48 percent experiencing it more than 50 percent of the time. "Most or all of the time" was reported by 32 percent; "more than half the time," 16 percent; "less than half," 9 percent; "seldom" 15 percent. Another 22 percent, plus many of those who did not have consistent orgasms during coitus, had orgasms with their lovers through other means of stimulation. Multiple orgasms during coitus were reported by 31 percent, and during masturbation by 27 percent.

Masturbation leading to orgasm was reported by 76 percent of the women. In addition to other methods, 26 percent used vibrators on occasion. There was a high degree of correlation between masturbation experience and amount of sexual experience (such as marriage affords) and the ability to reach orgasm during coitus.

Duration of Coitus

My figures on rapidity of ejaculation are almost a reversal of the estimate by Dr. Alfred C. Kinsey in the *Sexual Behavior in the Human Male*. He estimated that for three-quarters of all males ejaculation is effected in less than two minutes after intromission. (Perhaps he had no information on such groups as the Panopeans, Trobrianders and Marquesan men who develop good control and make it a practice to prolong coitus.)

Only 23.2 percent of the men from my seminar samples reported ejaculating in less than five minutes after intromission. Between five and fifteen minutes was estimated by 30.2 percent, while the majority—46.5 percent gave figures ranging from fifteen minutes up to an hour or more.

The picture given by twenty-seven women talking *about* their husbands or boyfriends at women-only seminars is quite different. They reported 40.7 percent less than five minutes; 33.3 percent five to fifteen minutes; and 26 percent fifteen minutes and up. For such a small sample, the percentages are remarkably close to those based on interviews with 362 American married couples by Dr. Robert L. Dickinson, published back in 1931. His figures were 40 percent under five minutes; 34 percent five to ten minutes; 17 percent fifteen to twenty minutes; 9 percent thirty plus. He reported 3 percent able to copulate any length of time and climax at will. That too parallels my reports.

There is a distinct possibility that men who are interested in primal sensuality are more concerned than the average male with postponing their ejaculations. They make considerable effort to do so, and a greater than average number succeed. This would support my theory that for most men the ability to prolong sexing is a learning process (like the ability to reach orgasm for a woman). They learn to tolerate and sustain more excitement. Those men who feel that quick ejaculation is gratifying and proper, and who are able to satisfy their partners or don't care, make no effort to prolong it. In this respect my male data is somewhat supportive of the Kinsey report that showed men on higher educational levels being more concerned with foreplay, satisfying a woman, and prolonging their sexing—a description that would fit a majority of the men in primal sensuality seminars. (I have also found them more liberated from stereotypes and double-standards, inhibitions and other hangups.)

Among the men who ejaculated in less than five minutes, only 10 percent said their lovers climaxed during coitus, whereas the percentage rose dramatically to 76.5 percent for men who reported five to fifteen minutes and 87 percent for the lovers of men who continued fifteen minutes and longer.

The Larger Picture

Statistics, however, cannot give a good picture of the amount of pleasure and joy experienced by these couples. A man who ejaculates in two minutes may give his lover so much sensuous pleasure and love before, during and after, that she is completely satisfied and doesn't care whether she has her orgasm(s) before, during or after.

Then again, many a woman who easily has more than one orgasm during sex, has made comments like, "Our sex is not right."

Janine told about one night when in the midst of sexing she heard an odd noise. She opened her eyes and couldn't believe what she saw. "What are you doing?" she shrieked. "Winding my watch," said her boyfriend matter of factly.

Yet the woman who is trying to achieve orgasm during sexing, and fails, thinks that everything would be perfect if she could only achieve that goal; she can't understand at all why her neighbor, to whom orgasms come as easily as turning on the light, watches the late late show to avoid sex.

Goal vs. Pleasure

During my seminars when we discuss difficulties in achieving erection, orgasm, or ejaculatory control, I use an analogy that has proved helpful to many people:

If you were hiking up to a waterfall, would you run, huffing, puffing and scrambling to get there as fast as possible? Or would you enjoy the hike *for itself, moment to moment* (making no comparisons with your last hike). If you spend the entire hike agonizing over whether you'll reach your goal, pleasure and appetite are lost; you might as well give up and go home.

When you approach lovemaking like a leisurely hike, what happens on the way (sensual pleasure) is more important than the goal (erection and/or orgasm).

People who are struggling toward the waterfall frequently relate this analogy to a recent "failure" (that's what it is to the goal-oriented person).

Sally, for instance, clasped her head and gasped, "Oh, my God. There we were making love next to a beautiful stream, under the sun, surrounded by trees and absolute privacy—but I didn't enjoy any of that—all I could think of was, 'Will I make it?' "

The next time she and her lover visited his vacation home, she focused on the *experience* with all her senses. Not long after, *when she wasn't expecting it*, what was no longer a goal, happened.

The Sensuous Parents

I found less than a handful of people in all of my seminars who said their parents had communicated positive attitudes toward sex. (Nonverbal messages—body-language—can be most important, because a parent can say the "right" words but the child reacts to the underlying anxiety and tension.)

Whereas most participants said their parents avoided the subject and/or tensed up when confronted with it, and many were verbally negative as well, the picture given of sensuous parents was quite different.

Lisa, a highly sensuous and sensitive woman in her early thirties (herself a mother) recalled that her parents were naturally affectionate in her presence; and her mother, in relaxed conversation about sex, made it clear that it was a very enjoyable and beautiful experience *for her*. Moreover, she assured young Lisa that when she grew up it would be the same for her. And it was. Her mother's *joyous* verbal assertions were also reinforced for Lisa when she identified the sounds of her parents' lovemaking. "I could tell they were really having a ball," she said.

Lisa attended the seminar for a number of reasons not uncommon to singles (she was divorced). Her good friend Gloria had signed up; she was interested in new sensual pleasures; she was presently uninvolved and didn't like going to phony cocktail parties or dances in order to meet men.

The young couple next door to Lisa were keenly interested in the seminar but couldn't afford even the student rate, so Lisa took careful notes for them. Following the basic primal sensuality exploration techniques, the wife was able, within a very few months, to achieve orgasm for the first time in their three-year marriage—and multiple orgasms soon after. But first they learned how to enjoy the "hike" and forget the waterfall.

Imagery

One of the explorations we do together in a seminar involves the use of inner imagery to find and remove something that interferes with one's *full* expression of primal sensuality, of wholeness and oneness with nature.

Gloria, an orgasmic single woman whose only "problem" was that she was sickened by the idea of a man ejaculating in her mouth, conjured up a bright electric sign that said "should."

Then she deliberately unscrewed and removed each light bulb and tossed it out. She was responding to a discussion we had had about various sexual activities becoming *shoulds* and *musts*—which are highly antisensual. As a nurse she knew that semen was clean and harmless and felt she *should* go down on a man to the point of ejaculation. I told her that I overcame my fear by first tasting semen on my finger and her face lit up.

Jack, in his mid-twenties, recently divorced and bitter about "critical women," relived an incident when his mother caught him masturbating with a sex comic book. Later, when he was giving his seminar partner a massage, he got a muscle twitch, which promptly disappeared when I suggested that he *allow* himself to feel any sexual arousal he might experience. This sort of twitch had frequently plagued him when he had felt such "improper" feelings. He subsequently phoned me to say that he was experiencing new joy in his life from everyday sensory pleasures that he had not felt since childhood (in addition to a new set of sensual/sexual feelings he was now allowing himself to experience).

Masturbation Guilt

I have found a very strong correlation between guilt feelings after getting caught and chastised for masturbating and later impairment of adult sexual response. Such traumas have been recalled regularly, either during the seminar, as with Jack, or on a questionnaire, as with Kim. In response to one of the questions, Kim wrote:

"I was criticized for masturbating and have since felt guilty about sex. I now compensate by thinking I'm being subjected to pain whenever I masturbate and usually when I have sex with a man (which in turn makes me feel like I'm some kind of a pervert for being turned on by thinking about being tortured or punished)."

Although she said she loves her husband, Kim had stopped enjoying him sensually as soon as they were married and stopped sexing with him six months later, "even though he was the first man I ever achieved organism (sic) with (manually)."

Kim resented criticism of her masturbation pleasure, but as a youngster she *believed* her parents were right and felt guilty. Since she believed it was wrong, she simultaneously punished herself with torture fantasies. This only made matters worse because now she labeled herself a *pervert*, a complete washout as a human being. And to have such fantasies with her husband, stimulated more self-hatred. She felt he couldn't *really* love such a despicable person—and she didn't deserve his love! From a rational-emotive viewpoint, she was using these irrational hidden beliefs to put herself down. Such beliefs can be challenged as false, then changed and disconnected from one's *intrinsic value* as a human being.

As we discuss self-stimulation and its use to heighten one's own sensuality, frequently some person who is guilt-ridden about masturbation asks anxiously whether one might not come to *prefer* it to intercourse. To this I answer that it is *remotely* possible *if* the person is psychologically unwilling to relate to any partner.

Sexcommunication

For couples attending the seminar together I emphasize sexcommunication. Sex is an excellent barometer of an overall relationship.

In the case of Paul and Doris, her lesser sexual interest had resulted in discomfort for both. During sexcommunication explorations she revealed for the first time that she was hurt by his subtle criticism of her paintings, whereas Paul had not even been aware of his negativism. We also discussed her "irrational" feelings—that she *should* want sex as often as her husband and that if she didn't, she was therefore a lesser woman. When I saw them a few months later, there had been a positive change in their sensual/sexual/marital relationship.

Barbara and John had been married more than ten years, with Barbara averaging about one orgasm per year, until the ninth year when she had an affair that afforded her orgasms with great ease. The problem with her husband had been that when she became very excited and started accelerating her movements, he would lose his erection. During sexcommunication he said that he experienced pain at the point when that happened. "Oh! I didn't know that it *hurt*," Barbara exclaimed, her entire demeanor softening. I suggested checking out and experimenting with the position, and several weeks later they said the problem was solved.

Menopause and Sensuality

While some women go through menopause without noticing much more than the fact that they aren't menstruating any more, many other women have symptoms ranging from "a dragged out feeling" to extreme physical debilitation. The only symptom most people know about is hot flashes and not everyone gets those.

A rather distraught husband phoned to inquire about a seminar, asking if I thought it might help his wife. "We used to have a good marriage and a good sex life," he said, "but the past six months things have gone from bad to worse. First she started having pain when we used the deep positions so those had to be cut out. Then she said my snoring bothered her and started sleeping in another room. She used to like sex as much as I did, but now she's tired . . . or her back hurts. She's only forty-two but she acts like an old lady!"

There are innumerable causes for most of those symptoms, but the pain in deep thrusting reminded me of the shrinkage (shortening and inelasticity) of the vaginal barrel that results from menopausal hormone deficiency.

"Did she ask her gynecologist about the pain during sex?" I asked.

"Yes, but he just sloughed it off. I guess he thought it was psychological."

I suggested she go back to him or another doctor and insist on a simple Maturation Index test that would measure her hormone level. It turned out that she needed estrogen replacement although she was still menstruating. Menopausal symptoms, like irritability, headaches, dizziness, insomnia, vaginal dryness and itchiness, skin dryness, loss of muscle tone and strength, heart palpitations *and more*, can turn a sensuous woman into an invalid. And they can appear as early as age thirty-five. Yet according to Dr. Robert Wilson who pioneered in menopausal hormone treatment, a doctor's training may include no more than a thirty-minute lecture on menopause and innumerable women do not get the hormone replacement they need.* All the symptoms except "dowager's hump," he says, are reversible. Fortunately, hormone replacement is now so simple that a woman need not lose her sensuality together with her reproductive function. For some women it opens them up to much greater sensuality by removing their anxiety about unwanted pregnancy.

Sex and Beauty

Although hormone replacement may eliminate or retard various unpleasant aspects of aging, it cannot prevent eventual aging. If your enjoyment of sex is dependent upon your own and your partner's physical beauty, this can become a problem in the sunset years. Therefore in my seminars I urge couples to remember that it is the human being, not the physical facade that is loved. When couples can free their sensuality from vanity and false equations with youth, they may then appreciate each other sensually, sexually and humanly all their active lives.

* *Feminine Forever* by Robert A. Wilson, M.D.; M. Evans and Co.

11

VARIETY:

Sensual Exotica

VARIETY is fun. It also relieves a sameness that can turn live lovemaking into a taped rerun.

Variety may be an extra fillip in a scene that already has the windows steamed up. Or it can be a restorative—stirring up renewed interest through the surprise or anticipation of something pleasantly different.

A certain category of sexual sybarite feels called upon to earn sensuality badges, count orgasms and regale intimates with stories of how it was all accomplished standing up on a surfboard while being buzzed by a student pilot.

Exposed to the comparative, competitive, status-seeking mentality, a couple could get the *idea* that if they are to qualify as a sensuous couple, they *should* engage in more experimentation and variety. This *idea* is quite different from the genuine or spontaneous desire natural to primal sensualists.

There do exist couples who are satisfied with a few basic positions they select as optimum for both of them and who seek no further experimentation. They may experience more sensuality from their simple, relaxed lovemaking than do others who surround themselves with mirrors, Jacuzzi sprays and reels of pornography. (Because sensuality comes from within not from without.) On the other hand, the dry rot of sameness may eventually eat away at their pleasure—and then they may seek the stimulant of sensual variety.

Couples who are secure in their sensuality have no need to count orgasms or prove *anything*. That does not mean, however, that they have no need or desire for variety and exotica.

I consider variety most important during foreplay (which starts before you even touch each other.) This requires more imagination, more sensitivity, and more spontaneity than the adoption of a new position or partner. My focus is on *emotional-sensory relating* rather than with whose-leg-goes-where.

THE MANY FACES OF YOU

For those of you who might enjoy a change of face but do not want another lover, here are several choices:

One of the common pitfalls of marriage or living together is that after a while couples cease to think of each other as lovers. With a set of his-and-her wigs, each of you can have an affair with a "new" lover.

A wig in another color and style can change your appearance remarkably—and make you *feel* different as well. If you are a cool blonde, you can put on a dark wig and feel mysterious, fiery, exotic. And dress accordingly—different from your usual style. You can wear different colors, assume another personality (some aspect of yourself that is there but hidden in the wings, off-stage . . .). Even your manner of speaking can change according to your role. Naturally your style of lovemaking would differ as well. Some psychologists say everyone has several personalities waiting to be discovered.

With the wig on (or without it if you prefer sheer imagination) he can be another lover making hay. Another time she wears a wig and he gets a new lover.

If you wear the wigs now and then just for fun (not necessarily for sexing) you'll find scripts developing spontaneously, even when neither of you is wigged:

(*He comes "home," kisses her amorously.*)

SHE: (*turned on and wriggling up against him*) We'll have to hurry. My old man will be home any minute!

There are innumerable scenarios that can be played. I offer just a few, to serve as a springboard. (Neil Simon please skip!)

HE: (*rings bell*) Did you call for a repairman, lady?

SHE: Yes, I need some work on my chassy.

Doctor-Patient

DOCTOR: My, that's quite a swelling you've got there.

PATIENT: Yes. Is there something you could do for it?

DOCTOR: Ah, yes (*examines*) Hmmm. Very interesting. (*rubs*) Yes, I think I can take care of that. But I'm afraid it will require extended treatment. Like this. . . .

PATIENT: Mmmm. Yes, well whatever you say, doctor.

DOCTOR: I think I'd better take your temperature.

PATIENT: My, that's quite a thermometer you've got there.

This scene can be played with role reversal (the "thermometer" being optional) according to which of you feels like being patient or doctor at the time. Of course it's best when spontaneous, with one person opening the dialogue in the role he or she has chosen and the other falling into the opposite role.

You Don't Have to Be Young to Be Young Lovers

This first scenario involves seduction. Both of you can wear wigs and create new identities if you like.

The initiator telephones the other: "Hello, I'm Dick Lovitt from Chicago and Harry Telall suggested I call and give you regards."

Either one of you can suggest meeting somewhere for lunch, dinner or drinks. You work out ways of recognizing each other and spend time getting acquainted (with your new personalities). If you're turned on, you end up making love in a motel or some secluded spot. In the case of married couples, you part as clandestine lovers, take off your wigs and change clothes if possible before you meet as husband and wife. If it feels right, you can kid each other about some "other" woman or man. (Be sure the new lover wears a scent that is also new and different.)

Joan told the seminar group that she was really excited when her husband phoned and introduced himself with another name, saying he'd heard she was a very interesting person and he would like to meet her. Recognizing his voice, Joan promptly changed her plans for the day, dressed up and met him for lunch at an elegant restaurant. He seduced her with stories of his adventures in foreign lands, then drove to a motel. . . .

Joan's face lit up as she told the story. "He was so fascinating and charming, I fell in love with him all over again!"

A variation of that scenario is for you to "accidentally" meet as strangers at a bar, discotheque—even a drug store or park.

The following variation was the brainchild of Art Buchwald. The lovers (man and wife) have their "affair" on an ordinary work day. He leaves the office and she the house, meeting near a motel for lunch. After exchanging accounts of how they kept their affair from being discovered, they check into the motel. A couple of hours later they reluctantly part, until next week. When he arrives for dinner, the conversation goes something like this:

> SHE: Hello dear. How was your day?
> HE: Dull, one of those long conferences. How about you?
> SHE: Oh, just the usual routine.

Persons who enjoy the wig game might wish to invest in several different styles and colors to express various facets of their personality.

The Art of Seduction

The practice of seduction is a ritual game that singles play, soon forgotten by those who really need it—the couples, married or not, who have come to take sex (and other things) for granted.

Because of her upbringing, it is usually more important to the woman that she be seduced. With the man she cares for she enjoys giving in, being overpowered (not necessarily physically) and overwhelmed by the man's desire for her. She was brought up with the image of being "taken" by an aggressive, forceful man—a fearless knight who would sweep her onto his horse, off her feet (and onto her back).

Women usually prefer a tender, loving seduction, but one which overcomes all objections and is powered by a passion that will not take "no" for an answer. *Many a woman would forget her headache when properly seduced.* By this I do not mean, "Hey, baby, let's fuck" or "How about a little action?"

A seducer does not ask, he acts—and overcomes resistance with hands, mouth and ardor. He is strongly demonstrative and nonverbal in action, although spontaneous expressions of love and passion are always welcomed as long as they're not just words.

Seduction can range from the subtle, "You're tired? Poor baby, let me give you a relaxing massage" to "But you're so exciting I just can't keep my hands off you" or a forceful, "Yes, now!" coupled with physically chasing her around the house if necessary (or desired, as many women do). You can tell if she's "running away" but loving every minute of it—unless you're blind and deaf (in which case maybe you'd better change tactics).

Another thing a woman adores and remembers forever is being unexpectedly picked up, even tossed over your shoulder (if you can swing it) and bodily carried off to bed, with your lips and tongue busy all the way. (The old sweep-her-off-her-feet gambit.)

I am not advocating anything akin to rape! Seduction involves *arousing* someone to the point of *agreeing* and *desiring* sex *before* intromission takes place. Otherwise it's a rape, even if she's your wife.

The verbal proposition is much easier than the nonverbal,

demonstrative effort at seduction. In the former, the person who is turned down can tell himself, "Well, I wasn't all that interested, anyway" or "I can take it or leave it." He can stay cool and casual about it.

But in the seduction by action he has put himself on the line, he has gone all out, committed himself, unfettered his primal sensuality. It is this very act of courage, desire and *total* commitment that is the major ingredient of success and excitement.

Men: know your woman and allow your intuition to guide each seduction. With sensitivity, persistence and *confidence* you can without much difficulty transform "Don't! Stop!" into *"Don't Stop!"*

The willingness to *risk* failure and the ability to sustain and overcome rejection are essential to the seducer. Many a man does not try, for fear of failure. And women, especially, can be paralyzed by this fear when they would like to seduce a man. Even when a woman is no longer trapped in the passive web and is fully aware of her sexual desires, she may still not make overtures for fear of rejection.

This fear can be a realistic one, as in the case of Bill, who could not step beyond the masculine stereotype and was turned off (frightened) by his wife's advances. Not wanting to leave the marriage, she revised her technique, learned how to use subtle means to arouse him, letting him think sexing was his idea. A woman learns very early how to turn a man on while dancing, by wearing something sexy, by accidentally revealing parts of her body, by the way she sits, walks, talks, smells, strokes his neck, cuddles up and teases. But body language can be used to better purpose than snagging a marriage ring or a fur coat.

Two people who live together over a period of time are not always likely to be in the mood for sexing at the same time. If the woman must always wait for the man to be the aggressor, she is missing out. On the other hand, if the woman ends up initiating things most of the time—or the man merely waits for her to get undressed and in bed, always taking for granted that she is willing and available—she is being deprived of the *joy of surrender*.

The greatest fun and variety is available to the couple who can each, in turn, feel free to seduce the other without restraints, in all manner of ways—subtle and overt.

I do not mean to say that seduction should be a constant component of monogamous sexing. That would lose its spontaneity and veracity. I simply feel that when used spontaneously, appropriately, judiciously, it can add a great deal of excitement to lovemaking and engender many a peak experience.

One of the peripheral but important emotional benefits of seduction is that it reassures a person that he or she is attractive, highly desirable and exciting to you. Everyone needs that sort of message, and *the ability to send it in a way that is received ungarbled is what gives a person sex appeal.* You become attractive to someone who gets that message from you. (I do not refer to empty cliché flattery, which can be spotted by any perceptive person, but to a genuine expression of your feelings.)

Seduction is only one of many methods (verbal and nonverbal) of getting the idea across. Harry, one of my seminar participants, reported to me that when he was finally able to tell a woman how attractive he found her (he was previously afraid of being too forward), the response was *consistently* gratifying.

"I used to think," said Harry, "that a beautiful woman would know she was beautiful and it would be silly telling her the obvious—but I sure found out different."

Men, too, appreciate messages about how attractive they are to a woman. Too few women tell a man that they enjoy his body, his lovemaking, his personality, style. That is part of the power behind Exploration B (Chapter 4) and the love-in.

Overt seduction by the woman might include initiating lovemaking and rubbing her hand, body or mouth against his genitals, kissing and licking, undressing him, actively wooing him. . . . Less direct, but quite overt, is a striptease or a belly dance performed just for him. That has the advantage of being exotic—and the fact that you will knock yourself out for him in this way will make him realize he is quite special—a VIP to you.

When I mentioned this at a Women's Center seminar (knowing it would be controversial there), Joyce objected.

"That's the sort of thing that makes us sex objects," she protested.

"Yes," I said, "done before strangers for monetary exchange it does make a woman a sex *object*, but not so when neither you nor your lover relate to each other as sex objects. Then it simply becomes another way of expressing your love and sensuality."

If a woman is hypersensitive about being a sex object (Betty said she wouldn't wear sexy nightgowns on that account) I would suspect that she herself *feels* like one and the lady doth protest too much. She can be *treated* like a sex object at times but cannot be made to *feel* like one unless she already does, within *herself*. This is entirely understandable because our culture has certainly brainwashed us in that direction.

Although there are women who feel they don't want to do anything that promotes the sex-object stereotype, to me that's akin to blacks refusing to dance or eat watermelon.

Striptease

You have an opportunity to do a striptease every time you undress in the presence of your lover. (A woman who gets turned on by looking at her lover's body will enjoy watching him strip as much as he enjoys her.) It doesn't have to be anything fancy or freaky—*just very slow!* It's the *suspense* that makes a striptease effective, so that's what you build. Of course soft lighting helps—or the opposite, a strobe or spotlight (a flashlight can be manipulated for special effects). Again, the more senses you please, simultaneously, the better: music, incense, perfume. However, in the case of an impromptu strip, the spontaneity will more than compensate for any lack of atmosphere.

A variation on the striptease is letting your lover undress you, ever . . . so . . . very . . . *slowly*.

It's great fun, however, to do a grand production (complete with rehearsal if necessary). Here you start out fully clothed, wearing the maximum layers of pretty lingerie. The record player is offering up sensuous music. Strut, dance, use your body, hips, bump and grind any way that pleases you. From time to time remove a bit of clothing and waft it toward him. When you're nude, a scarf can be used to tease in the way that strippers have used fans. Indulge your imagination and inclinations.

Belly Dancing

Arabic dancing enjoyed low prestige in the West for many years because it was likened to burlesque. Belly dancing, as it is popularly called here, is a bona fide Arabic folk art and tradition, with ancient ethnic origins.

As we have become more sexually liberated, Arabic dancing has regained status along with other things sensual. It is not only a tremendous turn-on for men (more than stripping, for many) but also a turn-on for the dancer herself. Most Middle Eastern nightclubs feature belly dancers; the better the club, the better the dancers, usually. If you've never seen a show, it's well worth experiencing. Many of the performers give belly dance lessons or can tell a woman where to find them, should she be interested. Not only is it sensually stimulating, but it is very exhilarating, increasing flexibility and freedom of pelvic and hip movements. It is also creative and expressive, because once you learn the basic movements, you are then free to improvise, using your vocabulary of movements to express spontaneously whatever you feel from moment to moment.

Get a few records that move you, and put on a private show for your lover. But don't expect to finish your dance uninterrupted. . . .

Body Light Show

Try dancing in the nude while your lover focuses a slide projector on your body. Any slides will do, as they become psychedelically distorted by the contours of your body.

When you have each had your fill of watching the other as a dancing kaleidoscope, you can turn off the projector and dance together, getting closer and closer until you are moving in unison, body to body. *Don't stop.* . . .

The Dance

The dance has always been one of the most sensual of art forms—for the spectator and participant alike.

Instead of going to a dance or discotheque, plan to stay home and dance, just the two of you. Dance together, dance for each other, dance dressed, partially dressed, nude. Dance any way you feel. (A woman might enjoy wearing a sheer negligee or gown.)

Center to Center

Close your eyes and feel the music. Do not will your body to move. Be still and feel your breath move, your heart beat, your blood pulsating throughout your body. Let the music seep in, merge with your inner rhythm until your body starts moving of itself, *from your center—independent of your mind.* You are not concerned with how you look, the sort of movement you're making, or what you'll do next.

Let the music take over and become one with you. Flow as a meandering stream or a turbulent river, changing with the music and your mood.

You may find yourself repeating one movement many, many times before your body is finished with it and ready to go on to something else. Or it may stay with the one movement (as in trance dancing).

This sort of spontaneous, primal dancing can lead to various peak experiences (but not if you *expect* it). If you have never tried moving in this manner before, you may wish to experiment at first by yourself—or if together, with both of you closing your eyes to eliminate any self-consciousness. If you have trouble relaxing into it, a drink might help.

Hand Dancing

Stand face to face, a little less than arm's length from each other. Place your hands palm to palm, about shoulder height, elbows bent out to the side. Close your eyes and feel the music. Let the music, your partner, or both, move your hands and arms. Flow with whatever's happening, even if it seems like nothing is.

Let the music, your emotions and your lover's touch fuse, filling your body with rhythm. Let your movements respond: Expand, contract, large and small, fast, slow, rise to a peak, subside, peaceful, joyous, sad, turbulent, loving. . . .

Allow your hands to curl and slide around each other; caress each other's hands and arms in tune with the music. Make love with your hands. . . .

Bath Play

Shampooing each other's hair can be a beautiful, sensuous experience. The scalp gets touched much less than other parts of our bodies. It is delightfully sensitive. (Sensuous people usually love having their hair played with and washed by someone else.) Do it very slowly, massaging the scalp, playing with the hair, feeling with your eyes closed now and then, enjoying the sudsiness, smells, wetness.

Get into a shower or bubble bath together. If you have any sort of detachable spray or jet spray, use it on each other. Take turns washing every part of each other's bodies with your hands, slowly, enjoying the sudsy slipperiness. (The person being washed should close his/her eyes.) When you get to the buttocks, gently bend your lover over so that you can thoroughly cleanse the anus with soap and a soft, sensuous touch. Rinse, and if it pleases you, run your tongue around and into the anus, teasing and flicking forth and back with tongue-tip. This is a highly erotic experience. Another part of the body that is especially pleasurable to lick while it's still wet is the armpit. Licking a wet body can induce extremely voluptuous feelings. Notice the difference between licking wet and dry skin when you do this.

You may enjoy licking the water off so much that you end up using your tongues like towels.

Should you find the shower or tub uncomfortable for completing the lovemaking, try it with the man sitting on the closed toilet seat (or a chair you prepare earlier) and the woman seated on his lap, either facing toward or away from him, bending slightly. Or, she can sit on a pullman countertop, leaning back, hips thrust forward while he stands between her legs. Another possibility is for the woman to stand, bending forward from the waist, either slightly or at right angles, hands leaning on the counter while the man enters the vagina from the rear.

It may not be as comfortable as a bed, but the variety and spontaneity can more than compensate. (The last position described is particularly enjoyable in front of one or more mirrors.)

We See Us

Seeing yourselves and each other simultaneously in the midst of sexing can be highly exciting. For this reason there are people who have an entire room mirrored, including ceilings. However, one or more ordinary mirrors are quite adequate. An alternative to mirrors are sheets of aluminized plastic that reflect like a mirror. Hand mirrors can also be used to observe the genital movements in various positions. It's pretty hard for your mind to wander when you have such erotic sights to enjoy.

Another turn-on for many couples is picture-taking, preferably with an instant camera so you can see the results immediately. You can also use a timer to get both of you in the picture.

Photos, movies, or drawings of the sex act are commonly used methods of heightening arousal, and are beginning to gain in favor among less inhibited women.

ADULT MOVIES

Perhaps the most important potential revolution in "erotic" filmmaking is its changing audience. In the old days you had to break the law in order to view a stag film, and the whole affair had a rather sordid connotation, to women in particular. The label was indicative: stag films were made for men. Until recently few women would venture into a skin flick theater.

The controversy and ensuing popularity of *Deep Throat* developed a new audience for porno films. The lines of couples waiting to see that film were very much like those queuing up for any GP first-run movie. However, like most of its genre, the acting and plotting in *Deep Throat* were quite poor, although the film had its moments of campy humor. Certainly the idea of a woman having a clitoris in her throat does seem to tickle the male fancy.

The potentials of a new market of middle/upper class couples (as opposed to the old stereotype of the porno moviegoer as a dirty old man with a vibrating overcoat on his lap) would hopefully inspire better and more truly erotic adult movies, someday.

Movies built around the full-color, larger-than-life explicit closeups of sexual activities, which multiplied in number and popularity between 1969 and the 1973 Supreme Court obscenity decision, will be affected by that judgment. How much and for how long is another question. Four of the nine justices opposed the ruling and with one more vote their minority opinion favoring repeal of all laws interfering with what the presidentially appointed Commission on Obscenity and Pornography said is favored by the majority of Americans—"that adults should be legally able to read or see explicitly sexual materials if they wish to do so"—would have prevailed. I believe that the courts will eventually be more responsive to the average person's laissez-faire attitude reflected in the Commission's report, particularly in light of what has happened in countries such as Denmark. A marked reduction of sex crimes (especially child molestation) was seen after its pornography laws were liberalized in 1969.

In their efforts to circumvent the previous "obscenity" tests and appeal to their new and substantial audience of wives, girlfriends and students, the porno films (advertised as "adult movies") began, in the early 1970's, to beef up the flimsy plots, which they attempted to represent as having "serious" social value. From what I have seen they succeeded only in reflecting some of the worst aspects of our obsolete moral codes, including the exploitation of sex.

Movies like *The Devil in Miss Jones* are more likely to be praised by basically moralistic and prudish persons who find it easier to watch something that pretends to be more than hard-core pornography, and in which the woman is punished for her sins.

I see nothing of social or serious value in their plots. Unless a film is well-written and acted, I'd just as soon its creators did not inflict their psychic idiosyncrasies upon me and would stick to honest pornography, which *in itself* may be said to have a serious social value. Let me explain.

In cultures where families sleep together without privacy, children naturally gain familiarity with the adult sex act. It is not a mystery, viewed with ignorance, anxiety and fear. Books, pictures and the right sort of films can provide a modern-day substitute for such direct, experiential learning—providing they are fairly genuine and realistic. There is much that a sexual neophyte can learn from a *good* explicit film and it might stimulate new ideas for the most experienced of couples, in variety of techniques and positions. Pornography can also help to open up sexual discussion, experimentation and to free inhibitions, as attested by many psychiatrists and psychologists.

Unfortunately most of the films are as yet exploitative, unsensual, without affection or lovemaking. They may also be sexually misleading. For example, the erroneous impression has been given that anal sex is easy and always enjoyable for the woman, requiring no special care or preparation.

If *Deep Throat* were used by a neophyte as a model for giving head, she might feel inadequate if she could not get down as far as the movie's oral athlete.

It is healthy to see fellatio unashamedly and avidly relished. Women are depicted voraciously worshiping the phallus and its secretions, getting all choked up about its beauty, raving how delicious it is. That's fine (though sometimes overacted) but what about some reciprocation? While the men regularly go down on a woman, they do not express similar appreciation or extol the delights of women's juices.

I also notice that their threesomes consistently involve one man with two women but rarely the reverse.

If there were more women behind the cameras instead of in front, the end product might be something more appealing to both sexes.

Another common lapse of realism is the absence of sexual sounds and changes in breathing on the part of women *and men* (the men stick to the "strong," silent stereotype).

With the exception of two half-hour features labeled "hard-core" (in a converted store-front theater containing four other spectators—men) the movies I have seen treated both men and women as nothing more than sex objects. However, they have improved tremendously upon stag films in terms of quality photography, providing good shots of (among other things) explicit genital, oral-genital and anal sex in a number of positions and ingenious camera angles. At the time of the 1973 revised pornography definition, the movies were becoming less male-oriented and attempted to tell more of a story.

As Tom said during a seminar (and many agree), "You can enjoy watching cunts, cocks and balls for just so long. After a half-hour, if nothing else is happening I'd rather go home and do it myself."

Nevertheless if you haven't seen an "adult movie" since last decade, and there are any such theaters left in your city, it's worth one visit to judge for yourself.

We frequently discuss films in our seminars and most women, in particular, seem to need more of a feasible plot—some emotional progression or content with which to identify in order to get aroused. (I believe that greater freedom from sexual guilt and repression will enable them also to respond—on another level—to unembellished sexual stimulus. That plus the ability to identify with *all* women would enable them to identify at will with the woman in a film, even without a story line.)

Only one movie (not an "adult film" but rather an artistic masterpiece) elicited unanimous and enthusiastic agreement among women who had seen it that this had indeed turned them on. It was *Women in Love,* based on the novel by D. H. Lawrence. They responded sensually not only to the spectacular male nude wrestling scene, but perhaps even more to the emotional dynamics and photographic artistry employed for some of the most beautiful lovemaking scenes I have ever seen. One woman (I'm sure she wasn't unique) said she actually had an orgasm while watching one seduction scene. Sensuality is, of course, only one aspect of the film's many levels and attributes.

During seminar discussions of movies some couples have mentioned that they have the most fun shooting erotic pictures of each other. And of course home movies go one step further. As closed circuit erasable video-tape becomes more accessible it presents the perfect solution for people who don't want their private films to be accidentally viewed by anyone else.

Some couples have taken photos during various primal sensuality explorations, and have keepsakes of their artistic endeavors at body painting both with the special paints for that purpose or with foods during a Sensuous Meal. Viewing their pictures or movies later on is yet another erotic experience.

X-RATED MOTELS

At this writing the latest wrinkle in skin flicks is "adult movies" on closed circuit television in motels. We decided to check into a motel that advertised water beds; color TV or black and white; and mirrors. The mirror is simply a large one hung on the wall in front of the bed. We chose the color TV, which was very poor. There were two films, each an hour long with about a half-hour pause between, presumably for the viewers to take their turn. "Something like a teaching machine," commented my husband, dryly. There is, of course, the opportunity to watch the films while sexing, and for many people a porno film may heighten their sexual excitement. At any rate it can be a new experience.

In comparison to the genitally explicit color films in the theaters the past few years, the motel movies were rather dull (to me). The sex was obviously simulated and in one film the sound was very fuzzy. Visual stimulation depended almost entirely on nude bodies and the *idea* of what they were doing. The camera focused mainly on the female bodies and genitals, practically ignoring the male physique. There was hardly a phallus in sight (and never erect). My husband enjoyed these films, in the motel setting, more than the highly explicit theater flicks. My preference was the reverse.

Motel cost for the night was $25. I think it's worth it as an experience (especially with the water bed if you don't own one).

FANTASY LAND

Many of my suggested explorations can be combined with fantasy material that you have shared with each other. That is the main purpose of sharing that information. If you fantasize making love with a movie star, you can help choose a wig that makes your lover resemble that person, plus clothes to go with the wig. If you're going to change identities for your "affair," you can consult together on the sort of identities you choose. You might consider getting two wigs each, one to please your lover and another to express yourself (and perhaps spring it as a surprise together with a new identity).

Sex with more than one other person—simultaneously or in rotation—is a fairly common *fantasy* among men and women. If that includes you, I hope you don't feel guilty about it; remember, monogamy is more culturally imposed than biologically ordained. Nevertheless, only a very small percentage of people in our society can actually allow themselves to do it and enjoy it. Do not ask this of a lover unless he or she would *truly* like multiple sex. Going along with something like that for a lover's sake alone is not a good idea.

When your fantasies mesh, that is truly fortuitous. Should both of you independently happen to cherish a sultan/harem-girl scenario, you've got a certain hit on your hands.

While most women have no desire to experience an actual rape and would not enjoy it in the least, one of the most common of women's fantasies involves being ravished. A rape play (*without any physical harm*) is quite simple to enact if she specifies her *limits* and scenario. If she wants the experience of her clothes being ripped off, paper dresses and bikinis are quite practical. Or she may prefer that you *make* her do a slow strip. Do not tie her down unless she has indicated beforehand that she would like it. Also check out whether she wants you to take her with or without some physical stimulation in addition to that of the simulated rape. She may have a plot or setting she fancies, for example: a pirate raid or a more contemporary plot.

For any fantasy you plan to stage, discuss as much detail as possible beforehand, including the kind of dialogue, if any. Improvisation is best of course.

(One of the factors that sends a man to prostitutes is an intense desire to act out some fantasy he thinks is unacceptable to his wife or lover. If he could talk about it, have it understood and accepted, it would alter their psychosexual life.)

Happy Hour

You meet at a bar (or wherever), have a few drinks and go to a motel. When you get inside, she throws off her coat—and is wearing nothing underneath. What a lark, to go out wearing nothing under your coat!

Fire and Flowers

Fire and flowers are ancient and universal sexual symbols. Fireworks were a traditional part of wedding ceremonies in the Orient, while flowers still play a role in ours. These powerful forces of nature are yours to enjoy and integrate directly into your loving.

I was greatly moved by a Spanish gypsy wedding in the incredibly beautiful Spanish movie, *Los Tarantos*. Although it was many years ago I remember the scene vividly.

> Outside the guitars
>   sing and weep
> a flowing river
>   endless deep
>
> Inside the bride
>   her body bare, is
>   lovingly with
>   oil anointed
>
> One by one the
>   women come with
>   flowers, reverently
>   her to cover
>
> Skin ablaze
> with blossoms strewn
> gypsy bride
> awaits her groom

How exciting to await your lover bedecked with flowers for him to pluck off, one by one, kissing and loving each trembling spot as it is uncovered!

Cover your naked body with blossoms and free the gypsy within you—earthy, sensuous, deeply passionate and loving.

Listen to the Flamenco guitar and let your loving fuse with its primal life force.

Since this is *your* festival, who is to say that a *man* cannot also bedeck himself with flowers and await his lover?

You have only a few flowers this night? Why not entwine some in your *pubic* hair? Start the music . . . and light the fire.

Make yourself a bower. Bed down upon aromatic rose petals, strewn lovingly upon the place where you would lie together.

Fiction

You can be inspired by a scene from a book, a poem, a movie or play that excites you. You can also create your original scene by discussing and combining elements from various scenes that have aroused one or another of you in the past.

Fantasy situations that are easy to act out include: seduction scenes; prostitute (or gigolo) and customer; cowboy and dance hall girl; mobster and gun moll or kidnap victim; rape; teacher and student; doctor/nurse/patient. The possibilities are endless.

Whatever you do, let it be without pressure, coercion or guilt. *If the idea is distasteful to one of you, drop it.* If you're not sure you will be able to go through with something but would like to try, have that clearly understood beforehand so your lover will not be too disappointed if you decide not to go on with it.

If you feel something is too far out and freaky, if you would feel guilty about doing it—*don't.* In some cases it is possible for extreme guilt to turn a one-time experience into an obsessive compulsion (an irresistible impulse to do something against the conscious will).

Should you find yourself hooked on some fantasy or fetish and be unable to function sexually without it, psychotherapy could be indicated. The sorts of scenes that frequently become obsessive compulsions include bondage, slave-master and other sadomasochistic activities that are extreme or *without which* the person cannot get sexual gratification.

Is That Perverted?

There was a time when almost everything but the missionary position (man on top) was called perverted.

It is now recognized by most modern sexologists that very little is "perverted" unless it involves *real* physical or psychological *coercion*—a *mutually* staged *play* rape, or whatever, does not come under that heading—or if it is practiced *compulsively* to the *exclusion* of all other *available* forms of sexual behavior. According to Albert Ellis,* a man or woman is not necessarily a homosexual if he/she had homosexual experiences in his/her teens, became heterosexual by adulthood but occasionally (especially when isolated from the opposite sex, as in prison) engages in homosexual acts. Ellis states that an exclusive homosexual "is a deviant not because he engages in inverted acts but because out of an *irrational fear* of heterosexuality, he does not desire heterosexual activities."

Sadistic impulses can be said to reach the deviant stage, according to Ellis, when "one *always* requires intense sadistic behavior for arousal or satisfaction or one is *intensively* and *extremely* sadistic (particularly with unwilling partners). . . ." As for masochism, "the desire to have some degree of physical pain inflicted upon oneself in order to aid sex gratification is another aspect of sexual *normality* when it is kept within reasonable limits. As soon, however, as one is unable to achieve arousal or orgasm without having fairly intense physical pain or mental humiliation inflicted upon oneself, one begins to lap over into sexual deviation."

Even bestiality (when a person is sexually aroused or satisfied through animal contact) is not necessarily abnormal or perverted, says Ellis, if it is practiced to a mild degree or when no other sex outlets are available. In summing up, he says, "it is often not the *kind* of sex act that makes an individual a deviate but the *manner* in which and the attitude with which he performs it."

* Albert Ellis, Ph.D., *Art and Science of Love.*

On the other hand, even those who are labeled deviates should have a right to be so as consenting adults.

ANAL SEX

As I hope you have discovered during your minimoon explorations, the nerves surrounding your anus respond voluptuously to the erotic stimulation of your lover's tongue and lubricated finger. Why not, then, to a penis?

Anal sex could be considered perverted only if it were practiced compulsively, to the exclusion of other forms of sexing, or if one partner insisted when the other disliked it. When approached gradually and sensitively, it can offer new sensuous enjoyment for both.

For the anal virgin who is somewhat reluctant about this, an association of pleasure with stimulation of the area can be built up with tongue and finger, gradually extending deeper into the opening. Such manipulation can also coincide with coitus, especially in the rear-entry position.

(Anytime a finger or penis is withdrawn from the anus it should be thoroughly washed before contacting the vagina, to avoid infection.)

Stimulation of the anus by the penis can begin with placement of the *lubricated* penis head on the anal opening. By tightening your pubococcygeus muscle so that your head quivers and by moving it back and forth with your hand, you can induce some voluptuous sensations.

I suggest that the woman get on her hands and knees and rest her head on one or two pillows.

For the next stage both the phallus and the anus should be generously lubricated with surgical jelly. The penis should be very slowly and gently inserted—no further than the head the first time—with sensitivity to any discomfort. In case of pain, withdraw at once. If her anal sphincter and pubococcygeus muscle are relaxed it will probably be all right to continue and thrust the *penis head only* in and out. You can either climax in this position or withdraw. Let her wash your penis with soap and water and then continue sexing within her vagina.

Even greater care and gentleness must be taken for penetration deeper than the penis head in order to avoid the possibility of injury.

For the woman, an alternative position is to lie on your stomach, with a couple of pillows under your hips. If you're sore the next day, it probably means you were not completely relaxing your muscles. Push out gently as he enters. Do not be shy about expressing any discomfort. This isn't supposed to hurt (unless you enjoy pain). It's supposed to feel good. And it can if you relax.

To increase the pleasure for the woman, bring her to a high state of arousal before entering, and stimulate her clitoral area with one hand while you thrust.

A relatively small percentage of women at my seminars have talked about experiences with anal sex, and those mainly in women's groups. Norma's experience was likened by her to a rape, because it was done suddenly, without warning and without her consent. As her legs were on her new lover's shoulders, he quickly withdrew from her vagina and plunged into her rectum. When she screamed he hastily withdrew and said, "I thought you were sophisticated!" She said she now takes the precaution of telling a new lover, first off, that she doesn't want anal sex.

Fortunately, Norma's experience was the exception. Several other women had much better experiences and enjoyed it. Julie said it was "all right" until her boyfriend got carried away in his thrusting and hurt her. She did not sound as though it were highly enjoyable for her, so perhaps she wasn't fully relaxed.

POTPOURRI

Always keep an ear open for new turn-on music and an eye for new sexing locations, especially isolated places out in nature.

Have you ever tried making love in the summer rain?

The Sensuous Breeze

Among all the accessories for voluptuous sensations is one that you can feel but not see—air. If you enjoy your lover's breath on your body—or a sensuous breeze—try an air hose. (But use cautiously.) That can be more erotic than the water spray. It even feels good through your clothes.

Good Eating

On occasions when you'd like a variation in your diet, but nothing lavish like a sensuous meal, just have a can of prepared whipped cream handy and/or some warm fudge, butterscotch, whatever. (You can warm it in the container. Leave the whip out of the refrigerator a while to unchill.) Spray or smear your dessert over various parts of your lover's body, and lap it up!

Synthetic flavored preparations are continually appearing on the market such as scented "joy jell" or pineapple-flavored spray cans. They are meant mainly for applying, smelling and licking or sucking off, although at least one "joy jell" that I sampled made the skin feel quite hot when rubbed a few times. Some people enjoy these tremendously, and others don't at all. As one outspoken husband declared during a seminar:

"I like pussy to smell and taste like pussy, not like some phony pineapple!" Others may occasionally enjoy the synthetic as a change of taste.

Surprise!

A happy surprise a man can give his lover is to secretly place a little sauce (such as chocolate mint) under his foreskin. And a woman's genital lips can hold many a dainty.

An unexpected erotic sensation can be arranged by placing a

cup of coffee or tea beside you, taking a sip when your lover is too involved to notice, then take his penis into your heated mouth, or use your hot tongue where it counts.

Another special treat is licking up and down your lover's spine. There's usually one spot somewhere around the middle that's especially responsive.

Head Trip

As already stated, the scalp and head are highly sensitive to pressure and massage. If you fondle and massage your lover's head with both hands and fingers during coitus it can intensify the feelings and possibly bring on an orgasm. You can have fun experimenting to see what sort of touch and pressure is best.

Sensory Grab Bag

Fill a pillowcase with as many new and different sensuous objects as you can find for the purpose of titillating each other. Take turns dipping in (without looking) and using what you find on your lover (who should have his or her eyes closed, to heighten the surprise).

Tape Trips

Does love poetry turn you on? Do you enjoy reading it aloud to each other? Tape your next poetry-reading session and some other time play it while you're sexing. You can also sing love songs to each other for playback—an intimate serenade.

Another tape trip is to turn on the recorder before you start sexing so that all the sounds are taped for future enjoyment.

For Marrieds

Remember all those romantic things you did *before* . . . ? Like necking at Inspiration Point, going dancing, skinny dipping, writing love notes. Make a list of things you used to do and enjoy. Then do them.

Marijuana

There is never a seminar in which I am not asked about the value of marijuana in love making.

Because it is still an illegal drug, I do not feel justified in recommending it to anyone. Because its use has become so popular with so many, I do not feel justified in ignoring the issue.

There is no accounting for taste, and we're all entiteld to our preferences so long as they harm no one else. If you enjoy sex atop a flagpole or under the influence of pot, I think that's your private business and neither I nor the law should say nay. Nevertheless the law says nay, and that is a serious consideration, if not a deterrent.

Is marijuana an aphrodisiac? There are substances that temporarily remove some repressions and inhibitions blocking our desires and senses. Alcohol can remove mental inhibitors of our sexual *desire* but it *dulls* the senses.

My understanding of marijuana is that it is primarily a relaxant, without the dulling effect of alcohol and tranquilizers. It removes tensions that ordinarily dull or distract us from our sensual inputs. Therefore, while it *seems* to sharpen perceptions, in actuality it merely *releases* certain primal perceptual potentials that are ordinarily repressed. *Which* perceptions and the degree to which they are expanded depends on the person's mental set and setting.

The consensus among the pot smokers in my seminars is that it *seems* to slow down time. Anything savored more slowly is savored more fully. It also allows the smoker to focus more completely on whatever is happening. Habitual pot smokers agree that it usually has the effect of an aphrodisiac. My guess is that this is particularly so with those smokers who are usually tense and ordinarily do not focus *fully* on here-and-now sensations. When used for that purpose, they smoke a small to moderate amount immediately before sexing.

Some men report that it can inhibit or delay their orgasm by keeping them so interested in what they're doing *now* that they forget about the goal (orgasm).

Those who are normally relaxed and sensually tuned in can be naturally high and do not *need* pot to enhance their sexing, although they may use it for occasional variety.

Thus, in absence of reliable data on the drug, it would seem that marijuana elicits a wide variety of responses, or nonresponses, even in the same person, depending on his or her emotional-physical state, the particular sample and dose, plus other variables.

Surroundings

Although you may want to use other parts of your home for lovemaking sometimes, it's a good idea to introduce a change in your bedroom, from time to time. One couple I know have photos they enjoy on their walls, and they change them from time to time.

You can choose exciting colors and patterns for your sheets, now that we have overcome the antiseptic white plague. (Black silk or satin sheets are favored by those whose pocketbooks match their sensuality.) A furry, fuzzy, or velvety spread can also induce a primal sensual feeling.

Lighting can be varied with your color scheme and mood. In addition to candlelight, there is a wide variety of soft lighting in many colors, not forgetting lava lamps and fiber optics.

For those who enjoy the sound of running water, there are a number of inexpensive indoor fountains available at department stores. (They are actually refreshing and healthful to have in your room.)

You can also play tapes of natural sounds that please you, such as ocean sounds, rain, a storm, crickets, water lapping at a creaking boat, etc. Just make sure that what you think is a babbling brook tape doesn't turn out to be a leaky waterbed. I think waterbeds are marvelous—for sexing and sleeping. If you haven't tried one yet, check into a motel that features them.

Soon you'll be able to try various other exotic beds now appearing on the market. The days of lumpy, squeaking mattresses may be numbered, but you'll probably be able to get the sounds on tape, just for nostalgia.

The explorations in this chapter and the rest of the book, when integrated into your sensual life, can keep it exciting and varied for many years. I believe that those who do this will be the ones who are least likely to be bored, in any case, because they are people who are open-minded, intellectually as well as sensually, and therefore constantly changing.

12

PLEASURE BLOCKS

TO BE aware of having sexual desires and feelings is one thing.

To genuinely *accept* these feelings is quite another; only then can you realize your full sensual potentials. And this frequently involves breaking our parents' sensual/sexual taboos—*without feeling guilty.*

Guilt is an insidious, convoluted sort of thing. A powerful insight into its nature was given me by Fritz Perls when he said, "Guilt is resentment turned inside out."

For example, if mother tells you not to play with yourself, you resent her for interfering with your fun. You do it anyway, and feel guilty—which also spoils your fun. Then you resent *that.* Resentment is akin to anger. But anger is another no-no, especially at Mommy or Daddy, who must be right.

So you feel guilty.

The dynamics are similar for other sexual don'ts, and also for shoulds. If you are told that you *should* satisfy your lover, you may resent that heavy should. You may believe the should is correct, but unconsciously resent having it imposed upon you. If your lover is not satisfied, you feel guilty. And we resent anyone who "makes" us feel guilty.

The guilt-producing do's and don'ts are programmed into us

at a tender age, when our absorbent minds seldom question their merits. The programmers are our basic institutions: home, school, and church.

The voices of our programmers may stay with us the rest of our lives, even though we rebel against them later. You don't have to rebel against something that holds no power over you; when you are really free of a taboo, you can calmly ignore it, without resentment, without trying to prove anything.

The Tyrant Within

As adults we are frequently unaware that parents, clergymen and others may still be dictating to us. I call it "the tyrant within." It's the uninvited guest, sharing even your bed. It may be your mother, father, priest, or teacher. . . . Once you recognize which voice is issuing which shoulds, and that it doesn't *belong* to you, its power is diminished.

A psychologist told of a patient who had moved away from his mother's home and now had an apartment where he could entertain a girlfriend. Instead of freedom, however, he encountered impotence. After much probing, the therapist discovered the patient had twin beds in his bedroom, and although he was alone, he put on a robe whenever he got out of bed. Eventually the young man realized that he was putting on the robe because unconsciously his mother was still with him.

Is there an invisible guest in your bedroom? If it's a parent, there's a place for him or her in your heart. *But not as a tyrant and not as a substitute for your lover.*

Guilt is bad enough; but guilt and resentment you don't even recognize is even worse. That had been the case with Jill, who related the following history:

JILL

"As an adult, I came to realize that my parents were very prudish. They never let me know by word, sound, or action that sensuality and sex were anything to relish. (Fortunately I did get the idea after I moved away from home.) But when I was a young girl, without anything ever being said, I knew that I'd better not get caught masturbating even though I had never heard of it. I mean, I didn't really know what I was doing.

"So I used to keep my knees drawn up in bed when I did it, so that when my mother came in the room to check on me I could just freeze, leaving my hand on my pussy, and she wouldn't be able to tell anything under the bump of my drawn-up knees.

"I didn't know anything about lubrication, but I could get the slipperiness by putting my panties between my finger and my vulva. It felt so groovy that when I got too close to orgasm, I would switch to my other labia. Naturally I didn't know from orgasms, but I knew that when this thing happened, the good feelings ended and I would soon fall asleep. So I dragged it out as long as I could.

"I had a friend, Marcie, whose mother told her sex was something men needed, like a bowel movement, and you did it for *them*. She gave me some pulp sex magazines with weird stories and drawings about awful things men did to women, like rape. One of the ones I used to think about while masturbating was a story of a woman being kept prisoner by a man who used her sexually and beat her. And the other was about a man who captured women and did all kinds of weird things to them like freeze them in a block of ice from the waist down and turn them into mermaids. Wow, Freud would have loved that one!

"Then my mother found the magazine and there was an awful scene. I never got any more magazines, but I sure remembered the ones I'd seen.

"When I developed breasts, I'd strip and tie scarves loosely around my breasts and hips. Then I'd stand in front of the mirror and pretend I was in some kind of white slave ship and there was a contest to see who could get the scarves off fastest by wiggling, and the winner got the most important man. I always won, of course. In all my fantasies I was forced into sex one way or another.

"When I finally lost my virginity at a comparatively late age, it was because all my friends already had, and they would make cracks and jokes and I didn't know what it was all about. I felt left out, and I wanted to know what I was missing.

"I was so embarrassed at being a virgin, I didn't let Harry know; and it was terribly embarrassing when he found out. He had never made it with a virgin before and I'd been so hung up that the only reading I ever did on the subject was a tiny pamphlet put out by some family institute—which was no help at all.

"It took Harry quite a few dates to break my hymen, and intercourse was painful until a friend of his suggested he go down on me before he put it in. I didn't ever come while he was in me, only afterward.

"It was a month before I was bold enough to take a good look at his cock, and much longer before I could say the word. I thought both male and female equipment were pretty unaesthetic, not enjoyable or exciting to look at. Actually I thought mine was rather ugly. Then I got a vaginal infection that kept recurring, and it must have triggered my guilt because I became sort of compulsive about having both of us shower just before sex.

"We moved in together and I got my old roommate to help me pretend I was still there, for my parents' sake. When a close girlfriend from my hometown visited me, I let her know what I was doing and made a point of telling her I didn't feel guilty. Now I realize that I was kidding myself and covering some pretty heavy guilt.

"Since I became aware that the grownup part of me has one set of standards and my parents' voices within me have another, the voices have gotten much weaker, and sometimes I can laugh at them. I also find that my fantasies are changing to more

voluntary things. No more being frozen in a block of ice. I feel
more now when we're balling."

The negative feelings Jill expressed about genitals are typical
of people who were brought up to feel that those aspects of
ourselves are "not nice" or "dirty." As she was able to reevaluate
those childhood impressions and change her feelings, she was
able to explore and accept her sexual self, resulting in greater
pleasure during sexing.

When she experienced her lover's genitals as a source of great
pleasure, they became beautiful and exciting to behold. Her
liking for her vulva/self also increased considerably.

Jill's history had caused her to unconsciously expect pain when
she became sexually involved, and she was not disappointed. It is
not uncommon to perceive pain or unwanted pregnancy as a
punishment for sexing.

Is It Love or Lust?

Rigid adherence to religious restrictions is cited by Masters
and Johnson as the single most common factor among impotent
men and nonorgasmic women.

Men and women from the sex-is-sinful sort of background in
particular tend to interpret as love any stubborn remnants of
their natural sexual lust. Substitution of acceptable love feelings
for unacceptable lust is quite prevalent among both sexes,
although somewhat more so with women.

In describing his first sexual experience, Tom recalled:

"We had reached the heavy-petting stage and I was really
excited. Suddenly the words flashed through my head, 'I love
you.' That never happened to me before, but I didn't say it out
loud because I really wasn't ready to commit myself that far."

Once he got physically involved, Tom's puritanical upbringing
caused him to commit himself to an early marriage, which was
later dissolved.

Learning to distinguish between lust and love can save a great deal of heartbreak. It can also help you toward a relationship that has a healthy portion of *both*. That involves the ability to accept and enjoy lust without having to drape it with "love."

Unfortunately, many people think love and lust are antithetical, not to be experienced with the same person: Love must be spiritual, pure, romantic; lust is evil, dirty, and bad. Therefore, anyone who lets you know that they lust after you is automatically "bad." Such a man can only allow himself to feel lust with a "bad woman." A "good woman" can't allow herself to feel it at all or hides it, and represents it as love.

Lust comes and goes more easily than love. Lust can easily be turned off by the anger and resentments of an unfulfilling relationship. Yet many people's insecurity makes it as difficult to let go of a bad relationship as to let go of their control.

Recreation Not Procreation

Certain religious teachings have been quite effective in disseminating the idea that sex is only *proper* when there is a possibility of impregnation. Therefore, it was tolerated *for the purposes of procreation only.*

Many men and women absorbed this idea when they were young, without being fully aware of it. Once past their childbearing years, they begin to consider themselves "too old" for sex. If that thought takes hold of a man, impotence is around the corner. He becomes what he thinks.

Parental Models

Children tend to model themselves after their parents—or just the opposite, depending on the relationship. Parents' sex roles and stances are absorbed and accepted or reacted against in the same way.

More is learned about parents' sexual feelings from their nonverbal body language than from the phony "right" things that they may say. (Sometimes children are also able to overhear or see their parents making love.)

Neither aping their parents nor taking the opposite stance is true independence or maturity. Either way is locking oneself into a role. The person who makes love silently in reaction against "noisy" sexing on the part of parents is robbing him or herself of tremendous pleasure and spontaneity.

You can *decide* whether or not you want to be locked into your parents' role or antirole for the rest of your life. The intellectual decision is important but not enough. You can free yourself *emotionally* by fully experiencing and expressing your *original feelings* when you first perceived their attitudes and roles. You can do this through the *ice cube* exploration later in this chapter, and also by sharing your *feelings* (not ideas) with your lover.

Emotionally turned-off people, when asked to express feelings, merely substitute the *words*, "I feel" for "I think." For example, when Tom first tried to express his feelings he was analytical: "I feel that she's trying to manipulate and trap me through sex." That was really an "I think" statement. Later he got into *feelings* like, "I'm scared . . . feel trapped and sort of helpless, like a puppet being signaled what to do." Now he wasn't trying to lay the whole trip on his girlfriend and she was able to respond to his feelings.

Obsolete Responses

Human beings have a tendency to take one experience and assume that others will be similar. There follow generalizations and stereotypes: "All men are unfaithful" or "All women are golddiggers," ad infinitum.

People tend to do this after a disappointing love affair or marriage, frequently without realizing they are relating to a new lover in some ways as though this were the former one, carrying over anger and resentments that belong elsewhere. They may choose new lovers because there is something about them that is similar to the old one even though superficially they may seem quite different. Although they *want* them to be different, they *expect* them to behave similarly. Since the last one ended badly, there is a lack of trust—the vital ingredient of any good relationship.

The less deeply you know a person, the easier it is to superimpose somebody else's picture on him.

Thus, Rick, who was traumatized by the insulted beauty queen, not only worried about being unable to "produce" for someone else, but about getting the same kind of violent reaction. He was stuck in the repetitive groove of *then, when* and *if.* Every new woman was a beauty queen for whom he *should* produce an erection.

Taking the behavior of one person and generalizing it to an entire sex or group can be a consequence of not having completely experienced and *resolved* the pain of the last relationship. (That numb feeling after losing someone you love is a shutting off of pain and grief that needs to be fully felt in order to be finished—resolved.)

Treating men or women as sex objects, for example, may have its genesis in one's relationship with Mom or Dad.

Stereotyped sex roles are such a formidable pleasure block that I have devoted the entire next chapter to that subject.

Nonsexual Sex

When "making out" is the name of the game and sex is used as a barometer of interest, people tend sometimes to rush into sex or allow themselves to be seduced or pressured into it before they are ready for that much intimacy. The result is less than satisfying.

Sex may also be used as a *substitute* for intimacy:

"I'll give you my body, but I don't trust you with my *feelings*," was the attitude of Janet, who treated men as discardable sex objects.

Psychologist Arthur Janov gives some interesting examples of nonsexual sex in *The Primal Scream* (G. P. Putnam's Sons, 1970):

A thirty-year-old male patient suffered from impotence. He lost his erection whenever he entered his wife. The man grew up with a cold, demanding, "bitchy" mother who gave him no warmth, only orders. Since it was beyond the realm of his understanding that he deserved warmth from anyone, he denied or did not recognize any need for warmth. He married a woman who was very aggressive and demanding like his mother but someone who also took charge of his life and allowed him to be passive. When it came time to enter her, it was no longer a matter of having sex with a woman: It was the little boy being loved symbolically by Mother. The symbolic aspect of the act (incest) prevented him from functioning as an adult. This man had denied (did not recognize) his early needs for warmth and sought this motherly affection from other women. Women were symbols of mother love, and the sex act with them was symbolic; functioning was thus impaired.

A similar sexual impairment is suffered by the woman who seeks or marries a symbolic father. Both men and women can go from one partner to another seeking but never finding what they really want. When the real need is *only* to be held and to feel loved (by Mom or Dad) the experience is infantile, not sexual, Janov points out.

However, there most certainly is a place in normal, healthy sexing for being cradled and pampered like a baby, using nonsense syllables and other childlike types of play that are part of the spontaneity and delight of lovemaking. It's not *what* you do but *why* you do it that counts in this case.

Jealousy and Possessiveness

A good way to put out a fire is by smothering it. That's what jealousy and possessiveness can do. Yet our culture encourages these qualities and makes us feel that they are normal and expected of us. (Listen to our "love" songs.) They are normal only in our culture, not to human beings universally.

The more secure we are in our own self-worth and intrinsic value as humans, the less worried we'll be about someone else "taking away" a lover. No one can take away your lover unless she/he is ready to leave. And when you feel good about yourself, you don't think you're a horrible failure and it's the end of the world if it happens.

The most extreme case of possessiveness I know was a middle-aged couple whose children were grown and gone. They were together day and night (they ran a business), but their conversation was pared down to the minimum banalities of home and business. "He won't talk to me," she complained. She also complained that they had no sex life, never kissed or even held hands. No touching. No contact.

Yet this woman literally could not bear to have her husband gone for even an hour. This is not love. Small wonder he became impotent with her.

THE PERFORMERS

When parents make their "love" contingent on the performance of the child, withdrawing it for unacceptable behavior, the message is, "Perform—or else."

This message is duly absorbed by the child: "To get love I must perform." It means being what *they* want and suppressing unacceptable feelings, such as anger, fear, etc.

Performing then becomes second nature, below the level of awareness.

Later, when we want love from others, we also feel that we must earn it by performing. In other words, we can't just be real—ourselves, doing whatever comes naturally.

Performing is antipleasure, antisensual. It is phony. What kind of love can you buy?

ORAL-GENITAL LOVING

An unhappy strain is put on many relationships when one

partner views oral lovemaking with distaste, either doing it with that feeling or refusing entirely.

Oral sexing is not immoral or perverted.

It is a perfectly normal, healthy part of sexing that was an *accepted* part of the great civilizations of history, crossing all cultures and religions in its universality. In most parts of the world a taboo on such sex play is nonexistent. (Alfred C. Kinsey, pioneer sex researcher and biologist, has pointed out that oral-genital stimulation is part of the courtship of most higher mammals, which includes us.)

The idea that oral-genital contact is unhygienic is merely another way of saying that it's dirty and abnormal (the residue of Victorianism). I do not think it is possible to have such ideas without the sneaky feeling that sex in general is dirty business.

Negative genital feelings may also be entangled with the proximity of the urinary and anal excretory functions.

Urine itself is sterile, *as are the secretions of healthy genitals,* which are normally free of harmful bacteria. The same cannot be said of the mouth, whereas the throat of the healthiest person is likely to contain unsavory bacteria. So if it's *really* hygiene you're after, you'll avoid deep kisses at all cost.

Women handicapped by the sexual double standard have frequently refused their husband's desires for oral-genital stimulation. It has been estimated that some 75 percent of a prostitute's clients are those husbands, coming for what they can't get at home—oral sex. (However, the percentage of such deprived husbands is fast declining as more and more Western women accept oral-genital loving for what it is—a natural, exciting part of our primal sensuality.)

Betty was typical of some women who associated the practice with prostitution and homosexuality. She expressed fears that it would demean her, that her lover wouldn't respect her if she allowed it. Once she tried it, she discovered her fears were unfounded. With the man who really excited her, she could enjoy fellatio.

Only a Victorian would think less of a woman for making love wholeheartedly. The better educated, the more intelligent and enlightened the man, the more he expects and appreciates total sexual response in a woman.

One might regard oral-genital lovemaking as no different from kissing, licking or sucking your lover's nipples or any other part of the body. It is also possible to achieve orgasm from stimulation of other parts of the body, and one could correctly say that such lovemaking is normal and natural.

Guilt (to which negative feelings and fears are linked) is irrational, and therefore not dissipated by rational argument alone. However it does respond to a sharing of those guilt *feelings* (with your lover perhaps), to *experiencing* them as fully as possible—*together with their origins*—producing a gut-level understanding of the forces that produced the guilt.

Feelings about your own and your lover's genitals are clues to any hidden guilts or fears you may harbor. You can explore this territory if you wish, through the following exploration.

PRIMAL IMAGES—AN EXPLORATION

Choose a time when you will be alone and uninterrupted. A good time might be just after you awaken, before you get out of bed. Take six deep breaths and visualize your genitals in the greatest detail possible. Then allow another image to appear. This one will symbolically represent your sex organs. Repeat the same process, visualizing the genitals of the opposite sex, followed by a symbolic image.

Do not reject any image, or try to force one intellectually. You may get several images in succession which, if spontaneous, may represent various levels of feeling.

Details and feelings about the image change its character. For example, two people may visualize a woman's genitals as a pool of water. For one it is clear, inviting, thirst-quenching. To another it may be fetid, deep, dark and dangerous.

In the symbolic image for the male two people may see a mountain. For one it may loom frighteningly large and foreboding, stony and barren. The other person may see it towering majestically, breathtakingly beautiful and exciting.

If you make an *effort* to *produce* a "good" picture, you are defeating your purpose. This is for *yourself.* No one else need know your images if you do not wish to share the experience.

Should you get an image that is unpleasant or frightening in any way, try to *stay with the feeling* it produces rather than shutting it off, which you may have done in the past.

You need not get into both male and female primal images at the same session or necessarily begin with your own.

Close your eyes, turn off your computer, and let it happen.

(Stop here if you are going to do the exploration now.)

Later it would be helpful to discuss your feelings about genitals with your lover or with some other friend.

Be aware that mind and body are one entity; your feelings about your genitals are not divorced from your feelings about yourself. The same is true of the opposite sex. For example, if there is an element of fear in your image, see if you can get in touch with any other (nonsexual) fears you may have of men or women. They are best dealt with out in the open where they can be seen for what they are.

GENITAL RECONDITIONING

You were probably brought up to view all your bodily functions negatively. *Now,* find all the positive, enjoyable aspects rather than the negative. Emptying your bladder feels good. A healthy bowel movement feels good. *Human elimination is primally sensuous.* It is natural to enjoy your own odor when you pass gas (even though you may not like another's). *Enjoy* your functions and odors.

Rub your finger on your genitals and enjoy the odor. Do the

same with your lover's genitals. The next step is to taste the secretions. You can start by tasting them off your finger.

(Any activity that is difficult can be supported and reinforced by combining or following it with other things that are already pleasurable, such as a favorite snack or drink, being caressed, spoken to lovingly, etc. It can also be followed by an especially enjoyable activity such as a loving massage, a gourmet dinner, etc. Special attention and encouragement is called for. However, any eating or drinking should not mask or interfere with the primary reconditioning activity.)

If you have not been able to bring yourself to engage in oral-genital sex play and wish to take that step, the reconditioning of attitudes toward your bodily secretions (above) should precede it. If you are (over)concerned with cleanliness and have difficulty making the genital contact, you may find the first attempt more pleasurable in the shower, after you have soaped and rinsed the area and it is still wet. Leave the water running if you like. Next time try it *after* bathing and when your lover has been well aroused, see if you can detect a genital odor to enjoy. Gradually increase the amount of time between bathing and sexing, from immediately, to an hour, two, etc.

(Women who have residual fears about fellatio and semen are directed to the section on Fellatio-Play in Chapter 17.)

An important reconditioning dynamic is choosing sensual names for the secretions as well as the genitals. For instance, the erotic Hindus refer to secretions as "love essence" or "love water." You may prefer something like "nectar" or "joy juice." Endearing names for genitals, translated from other sensuous Eastern cultures are (female) "lotus," "little clit"; (male) "sugar stick," "magic wand" (or "rod"), "reed" and "prickle." In India the words for vulva and penis are "yoni" and "lingam," respectively.

Humor

Humor is a powerful ally in overcoming hangups. For example, a couple who had been repressing feelings about sex being dirty reported that after the feelings were acknowledged, private jokes such as "Let's have a dirty" were helpful and releasing for them.

When you can laugh at a problem, you're over the hill with it.

In another instance, Phil told Donna his fears about being trapped into fatherhood. They were then able to joke about babymaking, and tension was reduced. A trap is something *hidden*.

Holding Your Breath

Under fear (which may be unconscious) or in stress situations, there is a strong tendency to hold your breath. Not until blue, of course, but enough to cut off unpleasant feelings. To breathe is to feel. To breathe less is to feel less.

Holding your breath is an effort to avoid feeling the intensity of anger, sadness, pain—and pleasure such as genital excitation.

Most people think of shallow breathing as insufficient inhalation. This is true of some persons, but even more common is insufficient exhalation.

To exhale deeply is to let go (sigh). This sort of expiration brings about the bodily expression of sexual surrender. In *The Function of the Orgasm*, Wilhelm Reich points out that those unable to surrender control hold their breath as they approach orgasm, thus inhibiting the intense sensations. In such people, releasing air is symbolic of giving up control—which they fear. Men sometimes inhale and retain the breath, to keep from ejaculating.

Increased breathing (especially exhalation) during sex can intensify your enjoyment and orgasm. A change to fuller breathing usually happens *involuntarily* when you learn to let go.

A very simple experiment with *voluntary* change in breathing was attempted by Dan, a sexual sybarite in his thirties, who later reported to a seminar group, "I just decided to breathe like crazy and it worked, I thought sex was good before, but wow!"

For many people, having to *think* about breathing could be a distraction that would bring them down, so I have combined deep breathing with pelvic movements used in sexing as part of my sexercises (Chapter 16). With practice it can become something you do naturally during lovemaking, without stopping to think about it.

Armored Against Pleasure

It is well known that some people feel more or less intensely than others. But there are some who are so closed off sensually that they are effectively numb to sexual pleasure stimulus. Since they are not aroused by pleasurable means, such persons may substitute artificially induced feelings over which they have less control: extreme pain, fear, anger (which induce tachycardia and increased adrenalin as does pleasurable sexing). It requires any one or a combination of these to penetrate the numbness and arouse them in some way. To them these alternatives are preferable to feeling nothing. (I do not refer here to biting, scratching and other kinds of moderate pain that might be a normal part of lovemaking.)

BLOCKING OUR FEELINGS

Our emotions form a continuum.

What affects one emotion will affect the entire spectrum of feelings from joy to grief.

Many of us learn at an early age to turn off feelings that are unacceptable to our parents/culture and those that are too painful for us. What happens to those feelings?

Every emotional state has a physical manifestation. (We tighten up against pain, for instance.)

To the degree that you turn off anger, sadness, feelings of being unloved and alone, to that degree you will lose the ability to experience the *good* feelings. *They are all interconnected.*

In your efforts to avoid the agony, you lose the ecstasy.

That is why tranquilizers, alcohol and other drugs that dull painful feelings will also dull your primal sensuality.

Because they are interconnected, the release of dammed-up anger often releases dammed-up eros and sexual feeling. For this reason some therapists will provide clients with Batacas, padded cloth "clubs" with which they can strike each other without the danger of injury. ("Sex is so good after a fight.") They are sold as a game (Batacas) at sporting-goods stores, and have aided impotence problems.

Anger is especially difficult for many people to express. During a seminar at Esalen Institute, Alexander Lowen asked each of us to strike a mattress as hard as we could with a tennis racket, shouting, "I hate you." It was very sad to see the number of people who smiled incongruently as they did it.

In several of my explorations (elsewhere in the book), I ask you to engage in mock-fights. Although you may find it difficult at first, try to get into the spirit of it. At my seminar most people do let go and end up laughing and enjoying.

PRIMAL ICE CUBES: An Exploration Into Your Self

This exploration was inspired by Laura Huxley's book, *You Are Not the Target* and Arthur Janov's *The Primal Scream*. It can be highly effective in unblocking long-buried feelings (and nonfeelings) that remain "frozen" within us because we split ourselves off from the experience and the pain.

Make your basic preparations and allow two uninterrupted hours from the time you finish your preparations. Keep the lights dim, lie down, get comfortable.

Begin with six to eight slow, deep breaths in the Yoga style described in Chapter 16.

Picture a flowing river, deep blue and tranquil. As you gaze at the river you see ice cubes floating along. You pick one up and it becomes transparent.

What do you see inside?

Whatever scene you see, relive it, allowing yourself to experience the full emotional impact. It was frozen because some feeling(s) of yours—anger, fear, whatever—had to be denied.

Feel those original, primal feelings now!

When you are through, go back and experience it again, giving full expression to your feelings. Yell, scream, sob. Let go with your body. Kick your legs or pound the pillows if it feels good. Say (or yell) things you couldn't say at the time. Tell the person or persons involved how you really felt.

"You hurt me!"

"I hate you!"

"Why did you leave me?"

"Don't hurt me!"

"I need you. Help me!"

"Please be gentle."

"I am *not* a whore!"

"I'm frightened!"

"I need you to love me!"

Whatever the feeling—helplessness, terror, hate—abandon yourself to it, sink into it. Feeling the pain *completely* will get rid of it—and its influence on your life. Relive it again, telling the person(s) what you needed and didn't get.

Relive the experience over and over until the emotional charge is gone—no more terror, anger, pain. Only release and relief. The ice cube is melted.

Some other time you can melt another.

It is not advisable to have anyone with you unless you are sure that he or she will not inhibit the material you bring up and your *full* expression of feelings (such as crying, cursing, screaming, stomping, etc.).

Such a person, if you are sobbing copiously, should not rush in to stem the flow, to embrace you, or comfort you verbally.

The support is in being there, caring, sharing and *encouraging* you to *stay* with your feelings.

Do not decide in advance what experience you will relive. Be guided *only* by what you see in the ice cube because your psyche is the best judge of what you are ready to experience.

Often the ice cube you fish out is something you had "forgotten," or the significance of which you had not realized.

The experience will frequently be followed by spontaneous insights (Aha!) about how the incident affected you emotionally and sensually later in life—"That's why I've been so insanely jealous. . . ."

You may have in mind finding something that bears on a specific problem. At first glance into the ice cube the scene you see may seem not to have any connection with that problem, *but stick with it.* The connection is a process that will come later, after you have confronted your primal feelings.

Later you may wish to share the experience and insights with your lover.

Occasionally a person is not able to let go enough to *see* what is in the ice cube. Obviously you would not attempt this exploration if you did not feel you have some emotional ice cubes to melt. Therefore, if you don't see anything, you are holding back for *fear* of what you will see. Then let yourself feel this fear and merge with *that.*

This exploration can be repeated as often as you like, allowing yourself time in between to gain insights and integrate the experience.

HELPING EACH OTHER CONNECT

Exploration I

As you are sexing you can help each other connect some of the voluptuous feelings from the genitals to other parts of the body and vice versa. Caress (with hands, tongue, feathers, etc.) your lover's most sensitive nongenital erogenous places and then move across his/her body to brush lightly across the genitals and perineum; then *without breaking contact* move back to the same or another erogenous zone and again across the genitals. (Do not ignore your lover's face and head.)

Repeat as often as you like, whenever you like.

Exploration II

A mutually planned connection experience involves choosing a particular nongenital erogenous zone, preferably one you can reach and play with during coitus when you wish to increase your lover's excitement. Stimulate that spot while you manually or orally stimulate the genitals in the way your lover likes best. *Use lubrication*—for both places, if necessary—and synchronize your movements. You can go on to other kinds of lovemaking or continue until your lover climaxes.

The ability to climax from stimulation of the nongenital area alone is best accomplished by oneself, following the directions for Experience F, Chapter 3. Once that is achieved, you are connected, and well on the way to experiencing any part of your body as an erogenous zone.

Exploration III

With the fingertip of one hand make a small circle at the center of your lover's perineum. Simultaneously describe a coin-size circle at the top (middle) of his or her head, using the corresponding fingertip of your other hand. Synchronize your movements.

Experiment with different degrees of touch—light, firm, firmer—checking with your lover to see which is best.

This can be integrated with your lovemaking.

Focusing

If I were asked to state in one word the major block to one's primal sensuality, I would say "anxiety." The reasons for anxiety are myriad, but the result is the same. It distracts from the vital component of sexual pleasure—sensate focus (focusing strongly on your sensual stimulation). If your mind involuntarily wanders from the here and now, it's not that you're flighty, you're anxious.

Perfectionists are most vulnerable to sexual anxiety. They cannot allow themselves ever to stray from their tightrope high above the ground. When they fall, it's not a question of jumping up, brushing oneself off and saying, "That didn't work out too well but—tomorrow's a new ball game." Perfectionists don't absorb shock very well. Rigidity is brittle. It snaps under pressure.

Flow with the now and *let it be.*

> We who run from
> emotional pain
> will feel it in our bodies.
> Pain will out
> It will not be denied!
> Take me then,
> I am yours.

13

SEXUAL STEREOTYPES AND
PRIMAL SENSUALITY

Stereotype: . . . a set form . . . ; Sociological definitions: A simplified and standardized conception or image invested with special meaning and held in common by members of a group: *The cowboy and Indian are American stereotypes*—The Random House Dictionary of the English Language, unabridged edition, 1966.

Sex stereotyping is the enemy of primal sensuality.

Suppose this country designated one set of personality traits as normal, proper and representative of all its people, male or female, and those who deviated were considered maladjusted, neurotic and un-American.

To be accepted and a citizen you would have to be aggressive, tough, unemotional, decisive, authoritative, consistent, strong, practical, highly responsible, logical, rational, financially shrewd, and be able to hold your liquor. Most men are familiar with these expectations, but if you are a woman, picture having these *demanded* of you *to the exclusion of all other traits.*

Now suppose instead that everyone were required to be gentle, emotional, passive, changeable, gracious, giving, permissive, artistic, sensitive, free-spending, shy, modest, illogical, irrational and soft-spoken. Men, pause for a moment and imagine that you're *expected* to display each of these traits and suppress the first group.

If you were raised in such a way that your entire identity depended upon being accepted as an American, you would strive mightily to fit the mold lest you become an outcast.

In order to fit yourself into the mold you would have to negate the unacceptable aspects of your human nature and pretend, even to yourself, that they weren't there. But you couldn't fool yourself all the way; underneath you would know that there were these un-American elements within you. So you would strive all the more to hide the awful truth, by loudly belittling anyone else who possessed these undesirable traits and zealously demonstrating your Americanism to all—especially yourself. You would have to see yourself (and others) as an American first and human second.

To label a single set of human traits as American and all others as subversive would make as much sense as it does to label one set masculine and another feminine.

The reality is that *all* traits belong to *all* people because they are *human traits* and not limited to any one group or sex. Human beings have a capacity for all these characteristics. The more human we are the more we can express these varied facets of our *selves*.

After a lecture I gave one night, a virile man, short, small-boned, lean and muscular, came up and asked me what I thought of a counselor who, many years ago, informed him during college testing that he had marked feminine characteristics or tendencies. He was a sensitive, intelligent, creative and sensuous human being. But that thoughtless statement demolished him and he spent the next twenty-five years desperately trying to prove his masculinity. In the course of this quest, as I discovered when he and his wife took my seminar, they became swingers, an activity they had been pursuing for more than a year. And the quest was not over yet.

If there were no phony masculine and feminine criteria to live up to, people wouldn't have to waste all that energy trying to prove an illusion. They would be free to pursue human values that have synthesized the best of the feminine and masculine mystiques. Nurturing qualities like tenderness, compassion, sensitivity and emotional involvement were for many years labeled feminine—and culturally devalued. The more we can now integrate the positive, so-called feminine traits into our societal goals and value system, the better we shall be able to make love, not war.

Nobody should have to prove one's masculinity or femininity. One is male or female by virtue of one's physiology. What *is* important is to accept *that* aspect of oneself along with the rest.

A cultural stereotype applies general and superficial characteristics to a group, does not allow for originality or individuality and would hardly characterize any single member of the group. It is a process of dehumanization, a put-down, in an unconscious effort to make the others feel superior. When someone says you are behaving like a typical man, woman or ethnic group member, it is hardly a compliment. Stereotypes can also be used to avoid making the effort to *personally* find out what other people are really like.

The common destructive element in stereotypes is that they are removed from reality.

Most of us have run into stereotyped attitudes equivalent to "All men are brutes" or "All women are the same in the dark." These are blatant, but the subtler ones are with us constantly.

Role Training

When a child is taught his/her early word concepts, he/she is first taught that he/she is a boy or girl, not simply a person, a human being. He/she then learns to divide others into boys and girls. *Emphasis* on the difference between sexes makes the "other" group suspect. The division is deepened when they are encouraged to pursue different activities and play with different toys relating to the different roles they will play as adults. Is it any wonder that during primary school they have no use for each other and have already declared war? During adolescence the sex drive initiates a degree of rapprochement, which may be limited to "making out" or "ripping off a piece." Or the fortunate may develop mutual affection and feelings of self-worth.

If they grow older but not wiser, they are not able to cut through the distrust and fear of that alien Other and continue to see each other not as human beings but as "a piece of ass" or "a meal ticket." This is reinforced by the dating ritual in which the male pays for the female. He has bought himself the one-up position and put her one-down.

The male-female roles of traditional marriage can distort and petrify a relationship that was previously flexible, loving and undemanding. Once married, the couple is drawn into a maze of expectations for a Husband and His Wife that are unrealistic and dehumanizing. In time, cracks appear in their role-playing masks. Faced with a person who is different from the carefully posed wedding picture, each spouse may feel disappointed and cheated.

Masculine and feminine as they have been defined in our culture are nothing but *illusions* presented to us as models of what we *should* be. Since these illusions are unreal and unattainable, it is small wonder that when recent generations were allowed to develop more freely, humanly, they became more confused and insecure in masculine and feminine roles. Until, finally, the myth has become a farce, to be openly mocked in the streets by the long-haired, unisex young who shout, "The emperor is wearing no clothes. The emperor is naked!"

When one is presented a role that is *considered* reasonable and attainable but in reality is *not,* he can spend a lifetime trying to prove the impossible, all the while feeling that he has failed. The resulting insecurity deeply pervades one's primal sensuality, sexuality and humanity.

Because of the different expectations with which they were

raised, the average man grew up more *sensually* inhibited than the woman, while she became more *sexually* inhibited than he.

The boy, while still in his childhood years, was conditioned to give up many sensuous feelings and pleasures that his sisters enjoyed freely. Cuddly playthings became inappropriate. To enjoy the fragrance and beauty of a flower was to be a sissy. Sooner or later he learned "Boys don't cry" and suppressed an entire range of emotions.

The *no touch* taboo descended on him at a much earlier age than his sister, who was allowed to climb into her parents' laps for loving and comfort even in her teens. She could hug, kiss, or put an arm around her girlfriend while her sensually deprived brother dared to touch his friends only in sports, wrestling and fighting.

As he grew up, he did not learn fully to enjoy the sensual aspects of love play. Sexuality was just another competitive sport.

And still he felt the need to prove his manhood.

He did not have a rite of passage (from boyhood to manhood). In older cultures this puberty rite firmly established him in the appropriate manhood role in his eyes and those of the community (by feats of strength, scarification, courage, or endurance, divorced from sexual performance). Those Judeo-Christian religions that retain the remnants of a puberty rite have reduced it to a ritual devoid of its original significance.

What he has, instead, is a masculine image that is supposed to prove that he is a man. But the veneer is rather thin, so he uses sex and/or money to keep it hard and shiny. That may work for a while, but sex was not meant for proving anything. Quite the contrary. The more he uses sex as a goal, the less it will work for him.

Sexuality will not allow itself to be manipulated with immunity. Eventually he orders a command performance—and gets a flop!

When it was believed that women were not supposed to enjoy sex, men did not concern themselves with pleasing or satisfying them. They did not have to perform and were able, without guilt, to be selfish.

Once knowledge of female responses was rediscovered—like finding a voluptuous Rubens hidden under a Victorian land-scape—the more sophisticated man did a complete turnabout. All of a sudden the woman was *supposed* to respond orgasmically and it became terribly important to the man. To prove her femininity, a woman was now expected to: (1) reciprocate his desires; (2) have "vaginal" orgasms.

But although the expectations changed, the stereotypes re-mained basically the same, with the pernicious addition of exacting performance standards for male and female.

In the sexual stereotype the aggressive male penetrates, thrusts, pushes. The female is deflowered, violated, invaded. Considered otherwise empty or incomplete, she receives, she is filled.

Receptivity is not the same as passivity, but one is mistaken for the other. Receptivity and activity are life-seeking; passivity is closer to Thanatos, the death instinct. A woman who binds to the stereotype may confuse responsiveness with aggressiveness (for-bidden to her) and reject both.

A viable alternative to aggressiveness for both men and women is assertiveness, which is outgoing but includes consideration of another's sensibilities.

Sensuality

Another factor that reinforced the tendency of girls to be more sensually oriented than men is that when a "nice girl" used to neck and pet, she desired only to enjoy the sensual aspects of what was going on. Then if her sexual feelings became too intense, she would shut them off.

But for too many boys the sensual pleasures were not an end in themselves. Their pattern was already set on "making out" or seeing how far they could get; the hike was lost as they strained to reach the waterfall.

PERFORMANCE STEREOTYPES

The average man's concern about his lover's orgasms (or lack of them) is simply that—a concern for her. But there is another component too often overlooked. That is the involvement of his masculine image in her orgasm. The more concerned he is about proving himself (often unconsciously), the more important her orgasm becomes to him because the stereotype dictates that a "real man" satisfies a woman during intercourse. From that standpoint it is no longer her orgasm, but *his* to give.

Perversely, or so it may seem, the harder he tries to *give* it to her, the more anxious he gets about it, the less likely she is to have it.

The dynamics are similar to a man's struggle for erection when he is under too much pressure to produce.

The woman's role preparation, from infancy on, stressed the importance of pleasing the man in her life. The desire to please him became terribly important, a major source of gratification (and frequently of survival). Her status in society was dependent not on her own accomplishments but on winning and keeping the right man. She must assume the feminine role to help him feel successfully masculine. She must play hard-to-get so he can make his conquest; let him beat her in chess so she can look up to him; be passive so he can be aggressive; *and have one or more orgasms during coitus so he can be a successful lover.*

An orgasm, however, is a highly selfish response. When called upon for a command performance it becomes maddeningly elusive. The more she desires to please her man with an orgasm, the less likely she is to have it. *She can only have it for herself. It is her orgasm and she cannot have it for anyone else.*

A man does not even have to ask whether she had an orgasm before she picks up his concern. The message may be sent and received unconsciously. *But it gets through,* sometimes without either of them realizing it on a conscious level. Similarly, when he is relaxed about it and his ego is not involved in her orgasm, that message can also get through and give her the freedom to please *herself.*

Unfortunately male expectation of female orgasmic response has become so common that many women, when they are unsure of themselves, automatically anticipate it and resort to faking.

A man does not have the option to fake when he feels called upon to perform. His curtain call may be initiated by either his or the woman's insecurity.

Because society has raised her as a sex object, a woman's ego is tied up with how sexually attractive she is. Her inner (unconscious) dialogue may be, "If I am not sexually attractive, then I am nothing." Therefore *her ego* gets involved with *his erection.*

The fury of the Miss Universe contestant when Rick couldn't perform is a perfect example. Her physical/sexual attractiveness was the prop for her fragile self-esteem and feminine identity. She was furious because Rick pulled it out from under her. If she could not arouse him, how much of a woman could she be?

Passivity Loses

One of the factors that makes it more difficult for passive women to achieve orgasm during coitus is that it is usually necessary for her to let a man know, verbally or nonverbally, what she enjoys most and what she doesn't, in terms of positions, types of stimulation and rhythms. This requires a considerable amount of assertiveness, plain old gutsiness lacking in the passive person. If she has assumed the female stereotype of reluctance to express her ideas and desires, it will logically extend into the sexual arena, and both will be the losers.

Ben, who wants a woman who is quiet and demure but a free and active wildcat lover, may think he has found his dream girl but each time discovers that one or the other (and possibly both) of those personas is phony.

Behavior in the bedroom cannot be divorced from behavior in the rest of the world without splitting or compromising one's *self.*

Only when mind and body function as a whole do they fulfill their potential.

Marital Roles

A woman's stereotyped expectations of her husband may demand that he be the sole provider for the family and responsible for her sexual pleasure and orgasms. If a man resents all that unshared responsibility, the sexual provider could become another role he just doesn't feel up to. It is a difficult problem to bring into the open with his wife, especially when he is trying to accept his traditional gender role. The communication aids and explorations in Chapter 9 are designed to help.

Until a woman can accept responsibility for herself, her pleasure and satisfaction, she will be placing an undue burden on the man.

A man's expectations of his wife used to end at housekeeping, child rearing and sexual submission. Now she's *expected* to be a red-hot lover. In addition she frequently shares financial support of the family. If she is suffering ennui or resentment at a role that makes the household drudgery her responsibility alone, it is bound to contaminate their loving.

Chances are she will not have the courage to state her grievances; she may be afraid he will not accept them and therefore choose not to rock the boat; she may speak up and indeed find him closed, leaving her even more turned off; or she may find him willing to change, albeit reluctantly, and so discover new passion beneath the shards of her old role. This may not happen easily; she may have to undergo a painful struggle to initiate change* (as I did). But once they begin seeking *mutually agreeable* solutions *together,* they will switch from *blaming* each other to *helping* each other. That difference is enough to nourish all aspects of the relationship into blossom.

* Growth is painful but *The Intimate Enemy* by Bach and Wyden can help; also the RDS communication technique (Chapter 9).

STEREOTYPING YOUR SEXING

Because we grow up with the habit of labeling and stereotyping others, we tend to do the same to ourselves. With the help of others (bless them) we decide that we are smart, lazy, good, bad, nice, crummy, dumb, talented. . . . Actually we are probably all of those things some of the time and none of them all of the time.

We change, depending on circumstances, our moods, interaction with others, state of health, growth. *Nothing is constant.* Moods and desires fluctuate.

Sex is no exception. Yet there, too, we tend to stereotype ourselves (again, possibly with a little bit of help from our friends). We get a picutre of ourselves as passive, aggressive, passionate, low libido, good, average, mediocre or lousy in bed, conservative, adventurous and so on.

Once you decide, for example, "I am passionate and have a very strong sex drive," the tendency is to fulfill that stereotype. Now that's perfectly fine as long as you feel passionate and horny. But since your sexual appetite is bound to change with circumstances—the interaction with your lover, your health, maturity and any number of intangibles—it may not always be possible to live up to your stereotype. If it is important to your self-esteem and you don't live up to the stereotype—you're in trouble.

Part of the problem is in our language. "I *am* passive" has a static, constant finality to it. This *is.* You *are.* These are present tense conjugations of the infinitive "to be." *I am* is *to be.* We do not separate a particular behavior at a particular time from what *we are.*

Thus, a parent responds to a particular behavior by saying, "You're lazy." If he hears it often enough the child will believe it—and act it. But everyone *feels lazy* sometimes, and behaves so as well.

Everyone feels sexually passive some of the time. But someone who has an opposite picture of himself will not admit it.

Conversely, the person with the passive self-image tends to repress more active feelings.

You can make a list of the ways that you experience yourself sexually. Instead of writing "I am," substitute (with the knowledge that it is transitory) "Here and now, I *feel* . . .".

Spontaneity

When you are locked into a role—be it femme fatale, passive-dutiful-wife, faithful husband, irresistible lady-killer, virile he-man, guru or crusader—you are tied to a tight little script. (If you're hanging on to a role for security, you can't try on your lover's role to understand him or her better, because that would mean *letting go of your own.*) "Anything goes" goes out the window, and with it, spontaneity.

Spontaneity is the most delicate of life's treasures, the magic brush that can color your canvas with joyous movement. It has myriad enemies: guilt; control; fears of intimacy, hurt, pregnancy, rejection; make-out games and roles that grip tightly about the neck. Many "nice girls" allow themselves to be seduced (they'd never admit they wanted it just as much) but they continue to exercise restraint during sexing.

A lovely twenty-two-year-old woman said during a seminar, "Sometimes I feel like letting go and being really wild, but then another part of me says, 'My God, what will he think of me if I do that!' and I don't." The feeling was hers, but the voice in her head belonged to Mama.

Most of the explorations in this book encourage releasing of inhibitions, spontaneity and abolishing stereotypes. Here's another.

Role Reversal

Reverse masculine-feminine roles with your lover for a day, a night, a weekend—as long as feasible (including sexing, picking up the tab when you go out, household duties if you live together). If you have children, tell them Daddy's gonna play Mommy and vice versa. They'll enjoy the game and help out by reminding each of you how the other does things. You'd be amazed at the things they notice!

HOMOSEXUALITY AND STEREOTYPING

Sex stereotyping leads to labels that force people to define and think of themselves in fixed ways.

In many so-called primitive societies, especially in those that are relatively sexually free, sexual encounters within one's gender (more common among adolescents and infrequent among adults) is simply accepted as a normal variation. Without the label, shame and social stigma, there is no issue. Nobody is branded. People are not *forced* to make a conscious choice between men and women. It's not either-or, although among those cultures studied, the extent of homosexual activity is minimal. (And there was no real sexual privacy among them, making secret liaisons all but impossible.)

The power of labels is great; a concomitant of black and-white thinking, labels allow no shades of gray. If people were divided into carnivores and vegetarians, and if eating both meat and vegetables were taboo, a meat-eater who at some time fancied vegetables would be forced to label him or herself a vegetarian. Once accepting the name, people would tend to live up to it.

Intellectually independent and creative people reject labels and categories for themselves and *less often label others*. If a women's liberation leader states that she is bisexual, I do not automatically assume that means she has sex relations with both men and women (that issue does not concern me), but I can be sure it means she feels love for both genders. I would reject the label heterosexual for myself, although if someone were to categorize me, my experience would fit that label (pubertal sex play excluded). Neither would I *label* myself bisexual, although I have come to accept my androgynous nature. For myself I accept only two biological labels. In order of importance they are: (1) human; (2) female. Those will not change in my lifetime, whatever else may.

Bisexuality can simply extend the expression of one's androgynous nature to include sexual lovemaking. It is less likely than exclusive homosexuality to be motivated by fear of the opposite sex. When homosexuality involves guilt, resentment and anger that mask a fear of men or women, that saddens me.

I am equally saddened by the not uncommon phenomenon of obsessive *hetero*sexuality *out of fear of homosexuality.*

High school and college-age people are particularly vulnerable to fear of homosexuality because it presents the greatest threat to those who are sexually insecure and immature. They hear their friends boasting and prevaricating about their heterosexual adventures and think there is something wrong with them if they don't go out and do the same. Someone who does exhibit a few of the stereotyped traits that are supposed to belong to the opposite sex begins to wonder. Then if he or she feels a perfectly natural warmth and caring for someone of his or her own gender, the suspicion of homosexuality seems confirmed. Natural expressions of affection among people of the same sex, accepted in other cultures, are considered perverted here. Sexual insecurity causes negative overreaction to anything remotely identified with homosexuality.

In a sexually secure society the gender of one's sex partner is not a matter of concern.

The gay liberation movement is now making it easier to express homosexual desires. I am concerned, however, that homosexuals not feel compelled to step from one stereotype into another.

Just as I am unhappy about the sanctions against any deviation from heterosexuality, I am unhappy about the appearance of similar either/or attitudes among some men and women who have chosen to limit their sexual expression to their own gender. This can result in such psychological pressure as the argument, occasionally encountered, that in order to be committed to one's own sex, one must reject the opposite sex. Such attitudes are narrow distortions dangerous to humanity.

The person who can truly love finds it possible to cross sex, race, religion, nationality—all artificial separations among our species.

As long as people feel they must make a clear choice between the sexes, they will continue to be locked in by one label (stereotype) or another.

Heightened awareness of stereotyping and high-handed treatment by men has in recent years helped to turn a greater number of women away from men and toward their own gender for emotional and sexual nourishment. Many women have recently "come out" and labeled themselves lesbians. Some have cited the subservience, the imbalance of power in their previous relationships with men as reasons for becoming gay. Certainly these are realities to be reckoned with. In addition to these reasons I find others, less clearly expressed.

An example is Pam: A big-boned, strapping girl who matured early, Pam's Calvinist parents repeatedly warned her to be wary of strange men. But she was more scared of the boys at school who would grab for her in the cloakroom and sometimes band together to knock her down and "cop a feel." One day she was chased across an open field by a grown man with an "enormous erection, pointed at me like a weapon." Fortunately she managed to elude him.

In spite of the early and generous development of her breasts, Pam recalls she was never able to feel "feminine," to fit herself into the stereotype. Although she felt unlovely and graceless, one thing she could do to identify with her gender was "act sexy." However she was never able to relate authentically to men.

She had been taught that women have to perform for men.

"I could never really relax and just be myself with a man," she said. "When I got married I was *afraid of being frigid* because I didn't come like I was supposed to when he was in me. Then one night a close girlfriend and I ended up sleeping in the same bed and finally she made love to me. I never knew I could have such sensual feelings before. I had never been aroused that way with a man. And my fear of frigidity was gone!"

It certainly is difficult to get fully aroused by something you fear, especially when that fear has been repressed in an effort to be "sexy" and prove you're not *frigid*—two more insidious labels.

I believe that our cultural climate is gradually becoming more receptive to changes in relationships between men and women that would remove much of the fear and the power struggles between the sexes.

A beginning has been made in the areas of child education and job opportunities. A much smaller beginning is being made in changing the stereotyped boy-meets-girl game-playing contest.

Obsolete Dating Rituals

The traditional dating ritual is as conducive to sensual/sexual spontaneity as the knowledge that you're on Candid Camera.

Love, post-Victorian style: It's a magic night. Their eyes meet. (Or was she looking at that other fellow?) Anyway, it's love at first sight. (I think. . . .) He fidgets. The next move is up to him. (What if it was that good-looking guy she smiled at? Probably. Better cool it.) That would have been the end for this shy one, but somehow they end up at a coffee shop with several others and he manages to get her phone number.

(In order to get a date the man must put himself on the line. Each time he takes the risk of being turned down. It's not easy or fair. On the other hand, woman's fate is to wait. He can approach those who *appeal* to *him;* her choice is limited to those who *approach her.* Like a Victorian child, she must not speak until spoken to. She's gagged and bound to her chair, waiting for the phone to ring. If she manages to free herself and phone him for a date, she takes a greater risk than the man because many a male who would otherwise find her attractive is frightened by her advances. She may not have lost much, but she still hurts.)

Back with our hero and heroine: He calls and gets a date, but he's not really sure whether she's interested in his company or the free treat. To a great extent he judges her degree of interest in *him* by how far he gets with her sexually. If she doesn't go to bed with him after several dates, he'll get pretty uptight because: (1) He still doesn't know how much she likes him. (2) It's costing him real money to try and find out. (3) He doesn't want to waste his time and money on a "frigid chick" who isn't that interested in him. At this point, if not before, he will pressure her. The nonverbal message is, "If you don't, I won't ask you out again."

Meanwhile, she too may have felt uncomfortable about the money he's been spending on her, especially if he doesn't have much. If she feels guilty or apologetic about the expense, this adds to the pressure.

If she succumbs to the pressure because she wants to keep dating him, the result is as spontaneous as a final exam—and each knows they'll get graded.

Long before the women's liberation movement took off, an actress friend of mine spontaneously confronted a man who took her to an exorbitantly expensive restaurant on their first date; after dinner he got quite sexually pushy.

"Oh, you want me to pay for my meal!" she exclaimed, contemptuously flinging off her dress. He couldn't get the dress back on fast enough and took her home posthaste.

Eventually they became friends—and lovers. A couple who could have such an out-front confrontation and go on from there had something going for them.

When a woman is seduced by a man—when she is pressured or goes to bed with him for any reason *other than her own consciously accepted desire* and then does not get what she wanted—she may feel sexually used. That is not possible when the sex is something she honestly desires. However, either person can be used when the involvement of one is emotional while the other's is merely sexual. This is much easier for a man to do when he is paying her way on dates, with a gift thrown in now and then. He can therefore delude himself that he is giving her something in return for her involvement, and not just taking.

Money is a common substitute for involvement, love, sex. That sort of barter arrangement is not possible under "dutch treat" dating, although it is certainly no guarantee that one person will not become more emotionally involved than the other.

The New, Open Dating

Those who have been able to discard the old courting rituals have a much greater opportunity for spontaneity, openness, security and genuine friendship.

1. If she calls him, he knows she likes him.

2. If he calls her, and she pays her own way, he knows she wants his company, not a free ticket.

3. Either way, they begin on the basis of two people who enjoy each other and wish to invest time and money in doing things together.

I do not mean that they should necessarily split all costs equally down the middle. One may earn more money than another. Friends of the same sex frequently treat each other. And there are so many ways of reciprocating a treat. Some women prefer to let the man pay the bill, if he prefers it, but find ways of treating him, such as cooking a dinner for him.

I have discussed this idea in seminar groups and have found a small percentage of single people who do this and many women who say that when they like someone, they would just as soon go to parks, hiking, the beach and other places that do not involve much expense. One couple said they take turns inviting each other over for dinner.

This kind of dating removes many of the artificial pressures so deadly to primal sensuality. Two people can get to know each other in a more relaxed, game-free, unstructured setting, free from conventions, which are not meant for real lovers. Sexual pleasure can be built on mutuality rather than barter.

The relationship can be one of equals, without the man's being responsible for the woman, as though he were a substitute father. Sometimes she can call for him, or they can meet halfway when they live far apart.

The new dating is gaining a foothold among the younger generations and will become more popular, I believe, as women achieve greater equality of earning power and job opportunity, eliminating several major reasons for the dependency on men and their own stereotyped roles.

My own assessment of the nongame dating situation on the West Coast is that women will accept a man's desire for open dating more easily than men will accept a woman who initiates efforts in that direction. In the under-forty age bracket, roughly two out of three women would not resent paying their own way unless they really don't have the money.

When asked, men and women in their forties and up are more likely to prefer the traditional dating ritual, but many men will go along with the "dutch treat" preference of a woman. Those people who have not been conformists during most of their lives are more likely to embrace open dating at any age.

However when it comes to the aspect of open dating in which the woman approaches a man for a date, she is still likely to encounter more rejection (overt and covert) than acceptance unless she is *highly* selective and waits until she has reason to believe he would not feel threatened by her initiative. And if she is open about her sexual desires, he may treat it more casually than she meant it.

In general the great majority of men and women still seem reluctant to give up their gender roles. For each there is an illusion of security in these roles.

The woman does not have to risk rejection—at the outset. But it's more painful to be rejected by someone you've dated (or married) than by a relative stranger you asked for a date. Women enjoy being courted but pay dearly once they are possessed in marriage or its facsimile. Then the tables are turned.

As more rewarding jobs open up to more women, they will be less tempted to plan their lives around being dependent on men.

Once the false feminine and masculine stereotypes are broken down, it will also be easier for men to give up their "top dog" role, for which they, too, pay dearly. Then responsibility will not be so heavy. They will no longer have to prove how manly they are by the amount of money they spend on a woman, how many orgasms they "give" them, how much sexing they do, how much . . . how much . . . how much. . . .

True friendship is only possible among equals. This has been a factor missing in many male/female relationships. However it is happening more and more among the young men and women exploring their new maturity.

Friends make the best lovers. They are truly together.

A *genuine* sexual revolution is in the making, and it basically involves more *human* ways of relating between human and human.

14

HER ORGASM—WHAT YOU CAN AND CANNOT DO ABOUT IT *

DESPITE the marked increase in sexual freedom during the second half of the twentieth century, a great deal of potential happiness is marred by sexual problems.

In 1972 sex researchers Masters and Johnson, addressing the American Medical Association's Committee on Medicine and Religion, estimated that one or both parties in half of all U.S. marriages considered his or her sex life inadequate. They stressed the importance of considering sex a natural function like eating and breathing.

If you force a child to eat when he has no appetite, he is likely to regurgitate. An adult in the same situation will have some type of digestive upset.

Masters and Johnson indicated that sexual dysfunction arises when one or both partners force themselves to perform when their appetite is low. They pointed out that many a bride is disabled sexually by a husband who accuses her of being frigid because her desire does not meet his·at the time.

A woman who was trained to curb her sexual appetite from childhood on cannot be expected to suddenly regain her full

* Because it is an essential frame of reference for the next three chapters, anyone who skipped Chapter 12 or read it so long ago that its content has faded from memory would be well advised to turn back and read it now before going any farther.

capacity with the issuance of a license any more than a starved prisoner could eat a full meal immediately upon regaining freedom.

Any woman *can* gradually learn to accept and enjoy her sensual appetite to the fullest, when she reevaluates her sensual-sexual taboos, defuses them *and is not pressured or force-fed.* I traveled that road myself, at a time when practical methods for help had not yet been tested, and there was no forum for difficulties to be discussed freely.

"Nice girls" had to work overtime: first to armor themselves properly against their own sexual desires, then to resist the male onslaught, and eventually (when a peace treaty was arranged and ratified in a formal ceremony) to please their mates. None of these conditions is conducive to experiencing one's *own* sexual feelings, independent of another person's desires.

What You Can Do

If you (the male) are truly interested in helping your lover get in touch with her *own* sexual desire (rather than merely trying to respond to yours), you might consider coming to a mutual agreement to wait for her to initiate sex *when she feels horny.* The time period set should not be so long that you resent it but long enough for her to experience those feelings. It may take as many as several weeks before this happens. If you are not genuinely willing to wait patiently for her sexual tension to build up and be felt, skip this idea and go on to another. Any feeling of pressure or demand, however small, can cause her to feign desire, just as she might feign orgasm to please you. If you use sexual desire or submission as a yardstick for measuring her love, this idea will not work. Sex *does not* equal love, and you must be able to remove your ego from her desire in order for her repressed feelings to emerge.

If she *does not* desire you sexually for a period, you are no less lovable at that time—on the contrary she will probably find you more so. *The amount of affection you express toward each other is not limited*, only the extent to which it is carried. This is also good for a woman who may feel her own sexual desire but has accepted the passive role and waits for you to initiate sexing. In order to help her throw off the gender role, you might *mutually* agree to leave the advances and seduction up to her for a period. A good time to start is ten days or so before her menstrual flow is due.

Part of the female stereotype has been for the woman to allow the man to decide what *she* should be and feel. It used to be the good girl. Now the hip, sexually liberated woman has been molded, labeled and packaged to think that she must be able to respond and experience orgasm with anybody, any time, under any circumstances. Squeezing herself into such a package can put her in the position of doing it more and enjoying it less.

Our society is imbued with competitiveness and the idea that if one is good, two is better. We *work* for orgasms, count them like money, and anesthetize ourselves trying to keep up with the Janeses.

An increase in sensuality awareness between lovers involves shedding stereotyped *expectations!*

WHOSE ORGASMS?

You would like your lover to have orgasms more easily or more often. Why? What does her orgasm mean to you? Do you use her orgasm (or lack of it) as an index of her love for you or as a barometer of your manliness and skill as a lover? To the extent that these factors are operating, her orgasm is for *you* not for her.

When your ego is involved in your partner's sexual functions, the vibrations are picked up by that person, on some level, as a demand for performance. What the body will do naturally, involuntarily, without prompting, it will not easily do on command.

Once you have recognized the extent of your personal stake in her orgasm, you can then renounce that stake as unreal and *disown* her orgasm. This involves the realization that you are *not* responsible for her orgasm, no matter how much *she* would like that in order to evade her *own* responsibility.

That is difficult for a man to accept when he feels that *he* gave her the orgasm and is duly entitled to great-lover stamps for his masculinity book (which never seems to fill up, however hard he tries).

Larry had an exaggerated sense of responsibility and balked at giving it up, confusing his responsibility with concern.

"Wait a minute, now," he said, at a seminar session. "If I care about Judy, *I have to* feel responsible for her pleasure and satisfaction."

"You can care," I answered, "and do everything possible to facilitate her pleasure and satisfaction *without* being or feeling *responsible* for it. Responsibility involves obligation—a *should*—or as you put it, a 'have to.' I wonder, is stimulating a woman to climax part of your image of a good lover?"

"Well yes, but what's wrong with wanting to give her an orgasm? I don't feel obligated, I love Judy and want her to get the most out of it."

"It's fine to care, but are you sure you want it for her sake alone and not partly to get credit for your role in it? Actually, you cannot *give* her an orgasm. It's *hers*. Only she can give it to herself."

"But if she had it with me *I'd* be giving it to her."

"What you can give her is pleasure—and your penis to enjoy. If she is able to receive the pleasure and utilize the enjoyment, focus on it, sustain it and *let go* at the peak, she will have an orgasm. But that part is up to *her*. The idea of giving it to her goes along with the passive stereotype where all she has to do is lie back and let you do it for her. Then if nothing happens it's supposed to be your fault. Do you think you're doing everything *you* can to help her get there?"

"I've been doing everything I know of, but we're here to see if there's anything else, or anything we're doing wrong."

"You can be the most imaginative, skillful, exciting, passionate, patient lover in the world, but if *she* doesn't actively respond and then *give up control* at the edge of orgasm, it will not happen. All your responsibility won't help—it just gets in the way."

"I keep thinking that maybe she doesn't come because I'm not a good lover for her."

"Now we're back to the masculine mystique. If the criterion for manliness were to be *exactly* the way *you are*, and being an adequate lover was considered totally irrelevant to being an adequate male human being, would you be so interested in judging your lovemaking?"

"Hmmm. Not in the same way, I guess. I'd still want to see that she enjoyed it, but I wouldn't be grading my own performance."

"If you can get to that point, then you'll be able to concern yourself only with your mutual pleasure. In focusing on Judy, you become sensitive to her needs, desires and the nuances of her enjoyment. Without performance anxiety you can spontaneously utilize all you've learned about what turns her on, while she does the same for you. In addition, if you can *maintain* the rhythm that pleases her during coitus, that is the most any reasonable woman would ask. She doesn't need your masculine responsibility. She wants you to make love to *her*, not to your male image."

"Then if I do all that without worrying about whether I'm a good lover, I'll probably be a better one. Hmmm . . . when I think about it, the responsibility for her orgasm gets me pretty uptight . . . and I guess it keeps her from carrying the ball herself."

"*Right on!* You can disown her orgasm but share and enjoy it when it happens. The responsibility each of you has is to let the other know what excites you—that's part of being responsible for your *own* pleasure."

For Larry, this involved readjusting his attitude that sexing is something you do *to* a woman or *for* a woman, to something that you do *with* a woman.

The no-anxiety, no-pressure kind of caring is achieved most easily when you are convinced, at gut level, that you are as much a man whether she has an orgasm or not—and conversely, that *she is as much a woman.* The less concerned you are about your manliness, the less proof you will require that she is a "real" woman.

Examine your feelings. Do you think there is something wrong with your lover if she does not have orgasms during vaginal-penile stimulation?

The idea, or feeling, that a woman is somehow less a woman if she does not achieve orgasm in a particular way is just as dehumanizing as the Victorian concept that there was something wrong with her if she *did* have orgasms. It amounts to flipping over the same coin.

She is woman by virtue of her anatomy. That is where it begins and ends. There is nothing to prove. Every woman's healthy body knows how to achieve orgasm and will do so when she is turned on *and free of anxiety*. If she doesn't have an orgasm, she is no less a human being. And she is no less a lover, as long as she actively *enjoys* sex. It is best for her own well-being, however, that she have an orgasm and release her body from the buildup of sexual tension. If she knows how to bring herself to orgasm she can show you how she does it, so that you may share that together. You may also discover new ways together.

An orgasm reached by means other than vaginal-penile stimulation is just the same—sometimes more intense. There is no physiological difference between one and the other. If she has not been able to reach it any other way, a vibrator can be tried and eventually replaced by your finger or tongue. Let the vibrator be the *last* choice.

When you have both read this chapter and sorted it out in your minds, discuss the various aspects together, sharing with each other where you stand *now*. Come to an understanding, if possible, about who is responsible for what.

When she is released from the anxiety of pleasing you, she will be free to have her *own* orgasm to please herself.

Encourage her to let you know what increases or decreases her pleasure, but let her know that whatever happens is all right with you (if it really is). If she has difficulty reaching orgasm, even occasionally, assure her that although you will do your part to arouse her to the peak necessary for orgasm, whether or not she has one will not change the way you feel about her *or yourself.*

An Orgasm Is an Orgasm Is an Orgasm

Unfortunately there has been an unwarranted status attached to a woman's orgasm reached during intromission. This has spawned an anxious breed of orgasm watchers, which in turn inspired women to put on virtuoso performances worthy of Sarah Bernhardt.

Why all the fuss?

Women who had been brought up with the Victorian idea that it was not normal for them to have orgasms awoke one morning to find that they were labeled frigid, because suddenly they were supposed to. Not only were they expected to have orgasms but they had to be achieved not before or after but during penile-vaginal stimulation—intercourse—in order to qualify as truly adequate and womanly. This was called a vaginal orgasm (because it supposedly took place and was triggered within the vagina) and differentiated from a clitoral orgasm.

This time the man whose theories were turned into a new bible for how women *should* function sexually was Sigmund Freud, founder of psychoanalysis. It is true that he risked professional rejection and contempt by proclaiming to a shocked Victorian medical profession that females had a strong sex drive and its repression was harming them. In this he did women a great service. However, the eventual codification and application of his concepts about the sexual development of the female was a disservice.

Freud postulated that in childhood a girl's clitoris played the role of a penis; therefore its excitation was immature and part of a masculinity complex. (Is this not the Victorian masturbation taboo given a new rationale?) "For a girl to become a woman," he said, "depends very much on the clitoris passing on this sensitivity to the vaginal orifice in good time and completely."

It is possible (as suggested by one analyst I know) that in speaking about passing the sensitivity to the vagina, Freud was speaking not physiologically, but psychologically, i.e., that maturity involves the ability to experience the same pleasurable feelings during penile-vaginal stimulation. However, his emphasis and use of the word "completely" gives the impression that he felt the woman must give up clitoral pleasure completely. (Again the masturbation taboo.)

Freud's statements led to the eventual popularization by Freudians of the vaginal orgasm myth. Two distinctly different types of orgasms were postulated by this myth: the right one, a vaginal orgasm, mark of a real woman; the wrong one, a clitoral orgasm, considered inferior and immature.

Thus, a *single* orgasm was *split* in two by *words* and its *center*—the clitoris—was devalued.

This new criterion for sexual maturity plunged untold numbers of women into a desperate struggle to prove their femininity. Anxiously pursuing the elusive vaginal orgasm as a goal, they defeated their own purpose while eschewing satisfaction from clitoral stimulation.

(Albert Ellis tells a poignant story of a psychologist who came to see him for therapy because she was not having vaginal orgasms. After a number of sessions she revealed that she was having orgasms during coitus but, she said, "They're exactly like my clitoral orgasms, they're not vaginal," and this had been causing her a great deal of distress. Ellis, by the way, poohpoohed the vaginal orgasm long before Masters and Johnson started their research.)

Clitoris Vindicated

Fortunately for all women, the vaginal orgasm myth was scientifically debunked with the publication of the distinguished research of Masters and Johnson in 1966.

Over a period of eleven years, they conducted controlled direct observation of thousands of sexual-response cycles, using highly sophisticated scientific instruments to determine (among other things) whether vaginal and clitoral orgasms were *actually* separate anatomical and physiological entities. No one had ever done this before. Not only did they conclude that the two were *not separate* but that regardless of *where* the direct stimulation occurred, the physiological response leading to and including orgasm was the same. Moreover, they stressed the fact that their exhaustive research showed the *clitoris to be the primary focus for female sensual responses.*

With the aid of colposcopic magnification, Masters and Johnson found that the clitoris always swelled during the preorgasmic stimulation (which they labeled the excitement phase) whether the sensual feelings originated from stimulation of the breasts, clitoral shaft or surrounding area, vagina or from psychogenic arousal resulting solely from fantasies or suggestive literature.

Clitoral response to all the different methods of physiological and psychogenic stimulation varied only in rapidity and intensity of reaction.

In other words all sensual roads lead to the same place in the female—the clitoris. Its concentrated mass of nerves are connected with the central nervous system. Therefore, when sexual stimulation is felt mainly on the breasts, for example, the nerves that go to and from the spinal cord transmit the impulses to the clitoris—unless they are inhibited by a no-no in the mind.

Our sensual-sexual don'ts, shoulds, myths and expectations can short-circuit the message transmission so that sensual feelings may end up as spasms in inappropriate areas and manifest themselves in physical disorders such as the proverbial headache.*

Although few coital positions offer *direct* stimulation to the clitoral area, sensations are both sent and received in a variety of

---

* To reestablish the connection between stimulation of other areas and the clitoris or penis, I suggest Experience F, Chapter 3, which is meant for that purpose.

ways. Not only does the clitoris respond to sexual stimulation anywhere, any way, but any stimulation it receives spreads through the entire sexual apparatus.

As a woman becomes sexually aroused by *any* means, the inner labia of her vulva swell until they have at least doubled their thickness and they protrude through the outer labia. This has the effect of lengthening the vagina, so that penile thrusting stimulates and pulls on these sensitive inner lips which enclose the vulva and *join at the clitoral hood*. This in-out movement exerts *traction* on the clitoris in every position that allows full penetration of the vagina by an erect penis.* The voluptuous feelings that result may merge with the exquisite sensations that can result from adequate pressure of the penis against firm vaginal walls.

Although the vagina itself is relatively insensitive, containing no nerve endings, the musculature beneath the vaginal lining is rich in proprioceptive nerve endings that primarily react to stretching and firm pressure. (Therefore a badly stretched vagina will not allow adequate pressure, nor will very rapid friction.) Any sensation from the proprioceptors surrounding the vaginal walls will be intensified during the phase just before orgasm. At this time the outer third of the vagina becomes grossly engorged, which narrows it considerably, thus increasing pressure on the walls. Masters and Johnson call this distended area the orgasmic platform; it is the section of the vagina that experiences the series of contractions that identify an orgasm.

All these sensations, although experienced as vaginal, result from stimulation of nerve endings *without* the vagina, which are normally transmitted to the clitoris in the same way as excitations of the breasts and other erogenous zones.

Thus, penile-vaginal thrusting *when the woman is well excited* causes indirect stimulation of the clitoris in addition to any pressure upon her mons pubis area or direct pressure in the woman-on-top position. This stimulation may be combined with

* The only exception occurs when the vaginal outlet is too expanded from childbirth or other injury. The physiological reactions to effective stimulation described above were found by Masters and Johnson to be universal for women.

sensations resulting from pressure on nerve endings surrounding the vaginal walls and within the sensitive inner labia. When any of these sensations continues uninterrupted, *without anxiety distractions*, an orgasm results—an orgasm that is neither vaginal nor clitoral alone, but is, as Masters and Johnson put it, an "explosive physiological *entity*" (my emphasis).

The clitoris is the only human organ that has as its single purpose the reception and transformation of sexual stimuli and tension. Thus in an orgasm resulting from penile-vaginal coitus, the preceding sensations are subjectively felt to be in the vagina although technically they are not.

The contractions of the orgasmic platform (the consistent factor in all female orgasms) are experienced within the outer third of the vagina *regardless* of whether the stimulation was directly clitoral, vaginal, or in another part of the body. Therefore, a male could feel these muscle spasms while his penis is within the vagina, and feel that they were proof of the illusory *vaginal* orgasm, not realizing that the *same* contractions take place when orgasm is reached any other way.

The Sex Muscle

Involved in the *involuntary* contractions of orgasm is a deep ring of powerful muscle just beyond the vaginal entrance that runs between the legs from the pelvic pubis to the spinal coccyx. It is called the pubococcygeus and has been referred to by other names. This muscle can be contracted voluntarily and is referred to in Indian erotic instructions for heightening sexual pleasure. In the United States the muscle was used by Dr. Arnold H. Kegel to treat urinary incontinence. After exercising this muscle for two months, many women reported having orgasms for the first time in their lives.

Various doctors have reported on the proprioceptive nerve endings of muscles that surround the vagina and support the other pelvic organs. If the pubococcygeus muscle is firm and taut, so is the vagina, thereby allowing the penis to exert enough pressure against the walls to stimulate the nerve cells on the other side. When the muscle is slack, so is the vagina and contact with the penis is insufficient.

The process of strengthening the pubococcygeus became known as the Kegel exercise, after the doctor who developed it. In my sexercise chapter I give an improved version. It also has value to men, as will be discussed later.

If you wish to give your lover maximum sensation from pressure against the vaginal walls (providing they're firm), thrust relatively slowly at the rhythm *she* prefers. You might also experiment with rotary hip movements.

Whatever you do to help her, let it clearly be understood between you that your only aim is to give her pleasure, *not an orgasm*—and mean it. You can manipulate her to orgasm afterwards. Of course you have to know what is good for her and only she can show you. With effective, uninterrupted stimulation, almost any woman can be brought to orgasm through manipulation. Authorities agree, however, that to build up her sexual tension and sensations to the point of climax during coitus is more of a *learned response*—although some people do learn spontaneously, many do not.

Professor Margaret Mead has pointed out that a woman's orgasmic capabilities reflect her culture. The potential is always there. Some cultures develop it, others don't. For a good portion of this century and the last, *we* didn't. In France and Samoa, she points out, men do not expect women to reach orgasm by copulation alone, and provide additional clitoral stimulation in one way or another.

Suppose for a moment that you are lying on your back. She mounts you in such a way that you cannot move and thrust freely in the way that suits you. She moves in a manner that is best for her but not for you. Would you be able to achieve orgasm by that means alone? And if so, how long and difficult would it be compared to the situation where *you* control the movement? (I address myself to the man who ordinarily is able to enjoy coitus for ten minutes or more without difficulty.)

Method Unimportant

The fuss and grim struggle for orgasm during coitus seems all the more pointless in light of a comparison that Masters and Johnson made among various methods of achieving orgasm.

Masters and Johnson's research reported that the most physiologically intense orgasms resulted from masturbation; the second highest level was achieved during manipulation by a partner; and the lowest level took place during coitus. However, when psychological factors are included, women seem to experience greater pleasure and satisfaction from orgasm during coitus. How much of this is due to the cultural input—that this is the *preferred* way to achieve orgasm—remains a matter of conjecture.

Although Masters and Johnson were able to objectively record the intensity of the actual orgasms, they gave no comparison of the intensity of sensations leading to the orgasm, among the three means of achieving climax.

I certainly know of women who find the sensations during coitus *more* intense than from other methods, and rate those orgasms as more intense. Most women report a marked variation in sensation and intensity from one time to another, so that during one coital experience an orgasm may be less intense than one achieved through masturbation while at other times it exceeds it. However, this is only the physiological aspect, which is not the major factor. The social influences are profound and inseparable. For this reason people experience infinitely more pleasure from coitus within an *affectionate* relationship than from the most intense *self*-stimulation.

Women, in particular, seem to evaluate their sexual reactions according to the emotional dynamics of a relationship.

Emotional Factors

A woman's feeling of security with her lover can be a key factor in how much she lets herself go (feel). Paradoxically, some highly seductive women feel more secure in a transitory situation in which they experience no anxiety-producing demands or expectations.

Anxiety, whatever the cause, is the greatest killjoy of sensuality.

Anxiety may be caused by anticipating that her lover will desert or betray her; by various expectations and fears—of involvement or rejection, of pregnancy, of discovery and disapproval, of failure and loss.

There isn't too much you can do about most of her inner, *irrational* anxieties. *Whatever you can do to reassure her of your love or affection will help.*

Things for the Male to Do

Avoid unnecessary belittling, corrections or criticism. Verbalize your favorable feelings about her. Relax her with massage before sexing. Remove any subtle pressure for her to have an orgasm.

You can also participate in seeing that precautions are taken to avoid pregnancy. It's not her responsibility alone. If she takes the pill and is absent-minded, be a gentle reminder (not a nag) or suggest another method. Be relaxed about it, however, because any anxiety of yours on that score will only exacerbate hers. Responsibility and anxiety are not the same.

Discuss all aspects of your sex life together. Explorations in communication and your aggression–gentleness profiles (Chapter 9) are particularly important to such discussions.

Make time to perform the experiments and explorations you have been reading about. If she is shy, you may have to be lovingly aggressive about finding out her likes and dislikes. You may have to ask her, gently, more than once, if there is anything *you do* that she *doesn't like*, for she may be reluctant to tell you. Many women will bear actual pain rather than let a lover know that he is doing something displeasing. Inquire, also, whether there is a particular position she prefers.

During coitus, make sure you're not thrusting so hard or so fast that you frighten her. Err on the side of gentleness; unconscious fear of injury from thrusting (especially when the penis is large) can inhibit her ability to relax and surrender to what's happening. If she wants you to thrust harder, ask her to indicate this by pulling you toward her. When you thrust, hold and press for a second or two before withdrawing for the next stroke. While thrusting, when possible, you might stimulate her clitoral area or other especially sensitive places. Find out *from her* whether that is a plus.

If you have learned to contract your pubococcygeus muscles, you can hold your glans just inside her vaginal entrance and work those muscles so that your glans quivers. That can also be pleasurable at the end of a thrust, or outside the vagina by holding your glans against the clitoris or other parts of the vulva.

When you use any of these suggestions, keep in mind that your purpose is simply to heighten her pleasure and sensations, *not* her orgasm. I make one exception: If her feelings are unusually intense and she is not accustomed to having an orgasm during coitus, she may try to make you stop because "It's too much" (of a good thing) and she "can't stand it." Say, "Just a minute," and keep going *without changing rhythm* because she is probably on the verge of orgasm and afraid of losing control.

Because a man usually speeds up in order to climax, it is common to assume that this is best for the woman as well. There you are, going along nice and easy, when she starts breathing hard and moaning. So you think, "Wow, I'm really gonna send her over the top." Or you get more excited because *she* is, and you want to come with her. So you speed up. Then, if you're not too far into your own orgasm, you notice that her moaning drops several decibels or stops. And her breathing slows down. If she doesn't look annoyed, she probably is, inside. Because unless she informs you otherwise, a woman usually requires a *constant* rhythm; any change can drop her way down, even if she was very close to orgasm.

Separate Is Satisfying

The myth of the simultaneous orgasm, which used to be stressed by marriage manuals, is just that—a myth.

For many women it is better if you ordinarily postpone your orgasm until after she's had at least one. She can feel secure that you will not come before she does (that's a big anxiety producer). She can have more than one and you can enjoy each other's orgasm more fully than when you are of necessity each absorbed in your *own*. A combination of skill and mutuality is involved in doing it her way first and your way later.

She also needs reassurance that she is not tiring you out physically by "taking too long." That, and anxiety over whether you can hold out, are real turn-offs. However, when she knows you will stick to her rhythm (which is usually not the best for you), she can feel more confident that you will not come too soon. *Discuss these things together.*

Some women discover that it takes two or more orgasms to satiate them. There is no more status in this than if one person requires more food than another. Such women, however, do appreciate the lover who is able to maintain the combination of excitement and control that is required if she is going to climax at intervals during the same coital experience.

You are likely to hold out longer if you stay away from your best rhythm and relax your buttock muscles as much as possible in addition to relaxing your pubococcygeus muscles (see sexercises).

If it is not too difficult for you and she is *accustomed* to having multiple orgasms, you can wait until her contractions die down before resuming active thrusting (unless she desires it sooner). Have her let you know when to stop moving and when to start again. She can signal you to stop with a simple touch or motion of her hand.

If she is not accustomed to having more than one orgasm and you're experimenting to see what happens—don't expect anything, but resume thrusting before her contractions stop (i.e., if she usually has four or five contractions, start after two; if she has a half-dozen or so, start at four, etc.). Should it bother her, don't.

Did She Come?

There are times when you are not sure whether a lover has had an orgasm. Asking whether she came (so as not to leave her frustrated) can be quite relaxed and simple, or it can be anxiety-producing for one or both of you. *Your* attitude can make the difference, even if hers is defensive.

A woman who is defensive about not having orgasms the way men expect or want her to will react negatively to being questioned about it. The more concern you show, the more she will react. The more relaxed you can be about it, the better. Instead of "Did you come?" which is a *you* message putting the "onus" on her, you might try an *I* message.

If you feel awkward about asking, you don't have to hide that from her. It won't work, anyway. An *I* message can be right out front, like, "I feel as though I should know without having to ask whether you came, but I sort of lost touch with things just before I came. I thought you were pretty close the last I remember. . . ."

With a couple who know each other well, it should be simple. You should be able to tell without asking. Ask yourself if you really want to know for *her* sake or because you're not sure of your*self* and want some masculinity stamps. A woman who has a good, strong orgasm may feel your question makes as much sense as if she asked you, "Did you have an erection?"

If you don't know her that well yet, and didn't feel any vaginal contractions (coinciding with any other orgastic symptoms such as rapid breathing and extreme muscle tension or twitching), you can assume she didn't. Then you can hold her in one arm, and gently rub her mons with your free hand. If she doesn't want any more, she'll probably stop you. If she responds, use whatever information you have about the kind of genital stimulation she likes.

If you don't know her preferences, keep in mind that the nerves of the clitoris spread all the way down to the vaginal entrance including the inner lips and the area they enclose. The nerves of the perineum (the area between the vagina and the anus) reach to the vaginal entrance and that area too is quite sensitive but not usually as conducive to orgasm for the woman as the area between the clitoris and vagina.

Some kind of lubrication is necessary because the touch should be light, and slide along. You can use her own vaginal lubrication, but unless your strokes run right into the vagina, you'll have to pause for refills. The most consistently accessible lubrication is your saliva.

Soft and sensitive as it is, even the tongue can press too hard. It is very easy for your touch to become uncomfortably hard or painful, but difficult for it to be too light. Sometimes it can be helpful if your lover uses her hands to part her vaginal lips, leaving one of yours free to stimulate her elsewhere. When her labia are parted and she is excited, you may see her erected clitoris protruding under its hood. Its sensitive shaft angles up toward the apex of the outer lips. With your finger you can feel it move under its thin, fleshy covering. With a fingertip you can stimulate the shaft, up one side and down the other, or play with the hood. All this may be combined with cunnilingus.

If you have not yet been able to find out what kind and rhythm of stimulation is best for her, do not expect her to climax. What was good for somebody else will not necessarily do for her.

Because the variety of preferences is so wide, it can take you years to discover them by trial and error. It's like trying to make your way blindfolded through a sandpaper maze—rough. So sexcommunicate!

Cunnilingus

The licking and sucking of a woman's genitalia can vary in enjoyment according to the person, but if there is no lover with whom you have been able to enjoy this pleasure, you may have some irrational feelings that you have not challenged. (See the section in Chapter 12 on oral-genital loving.)

I like to think of vaginal secretions as nectar or love juice. Make up your name if you like—and choose a pet name for her vulva. Speak to it lovingly; how beautiful it is. (This is especially important if a woman holds her own genitals in low esteem.)

As a part of your lovemaking it is important to ascertain your lover's unique preferences regarding cunnilingus.

Some women climax quickly when the clitoris is sucked; many find it unpleasant. Some enjoy the lightest of flicking with tongue tip on the clitoris; many find any direct contact too much.

Other parts of the vulva are not as touchy when it comes to experimenting. Some women may respond well to a slow insertion and withdrawal of the tongue in the vagina. Others may prefer quick flicks of the tongue around the entrance and the entire area between the clitoris and the anus—or slow strokes along the inner labia from clitoris to vagina.

Cunnilingus is worth *experimenting* with, because unless she is a contortionist, it is something she cannot have discovered by herself. She can only guide you by showing you her most sensitive areas and letting you know whether to lighten up, slow down or speed up while you are exploring. It is also one of the best methods for arousing a woman to a high pitch.

She can be almost at the point of orgasm, yet drop considerably in excitement when you pause for intromission. She will not, however, drop as far as she would if she were less stimulated beforehand. The higher she is when you enter, the more easily she will climax.

Intromission

A good time to enter is when her vaginal opening becomes *well* lubricated and she is *breathing heavily*. However, when this sort of response happens very soon, she may prefer more love play to prolong the pleasure and the emotional satisfaction of making love.

If you stimulate her to orgasm just *before* entering, she'll still be very high right afterwards. If you thrust in *her* rhythm, she may come again.

Another method is to agree that you will wait for her to let you know when she is ready for you to enter. You can also let her indicate when she would like you to start thrusting, which may not be immediately upon entering.

The best position for a woman just learning to intensify her pleasure during coitus is seated above you, with her knees somewhere between your nipples and armpits. Let her do the moving. If she seems close to orgasm but unable to break through, try moving with *her* rhythm. That will put added pressure on her clitoral area. If she stops and seems unable to continue moving, pick up her rhythm and do the moving for her. *A pillow under your hips* can provide the extra pressure needed to arouse voluptuous feelings where previously there were none. The same is true for a pillow under her hips when she is supine.

Once you have entered, love play need not cease. *Its continuation can greatly enhance your lover's pleasure and orgasm*, especially when you pick her most erogenous zones accessible to your hand or lips. See what happens when you massage her scalp. You might even stay quietly connected and stimulate her only in nongenital ways for a while.

A lubricant such as vaginal jelly may be advisable in the case of a tight vaginal opening or a woman whose lubrication may not be so plentiful. Insert it *sensuously*, as part of your love play.

The quantity and quality of love play before you enter are major determinants of her subsequent enjoyment. Quality, however, is much more telling than quantity. By quality I mean tenderness, passion, sensitivity, spontaneity, imagination. It also means remembering the various things that turn her on and doing them—but not *all* of them *all* the time—in other words, variety. If you memorized her entire list of turn-on places and covered them methodically from head to toe *each time*, the eventual result would be a deadening sameness, which is what happened to George and Marge:

His favorite kind of stimulation before coitus was fellatio and he therefore assumed that cunnilingus (which he also enjoyed greatly) would be most effective for Marge. At first it was highly stimulating, but as it became repetitive and unrelieved by other forms of arousal, it took longer and longer for her to get excited. One night they came home from a party feeling mellow and affectionate and started making love before they got to the bedroom. Before he even touched her genital area, Marge urged him inside her.

"Aha!" thought George. "This is the way to turn her on." So he proceeded to stage a reenactment the next time he felt like sexing. The results were as predictable as his actions. Eventually they learned to explore and share their preferences, using them as a jazz pianist might use the entire keyboard and not just a limited repertoire with fixed arrangements. Oral sex was not abandoned, but took its place with the other notes of the music.

Ten minutes of spontaneous love *play* can surpass thirty minutes of (yawn) the same old thing, no matter how highly stimulating its potential.

Should you at some time spontaneously happen on some activity that causes her anxiety, discontinue it. Later it can be discussed and possibly tried again when she feels more relaxed about it.

THE VIRGIN

Mutual noncoital manipulation to orgasm has traditionally been recommended by Oriental bride books in order to condition the virgin properly and avoid too hasty or painful breaking of the hymen.

A virgin need not experience pain if she is properly stimulated and lubricated, particularly if she has already stretched her hymen. This can be done by exerting pressure on the sides of the vaginal entrance with a clean finger every day over a relatively short span of time. A hot bath beforehand *and a lubricant* (saliva or jelly) will help. When two or three fingers can be inserted she need not worry about pain. Should the hymen be too resistant it can be painlessly incised by a physician. That is preferable to having one's first coital experience associated with pain. Whether or not her hymen is intact (some girls are born without one), your initial attempts at penetration should be accompanied by generous use of saliva or jelly.

Whether owing to initial pain, which is then "forgotten," or other factors in their background, some women have unconscious fear of pain during coitus. They don't fully relax and let themselves go because they are on guard against being hurt. But if they are not aware of this, it is more difficult to deal with.

The phallus has long been associated symbolically with a knife, and vagina is the latin word for sheath. Knives and guns are common phallic symbols in dreams.

Where there is fear of pain, sometimes a woman will become aware that she relaxes when the man ejaculates, because when he stops thrusting, she doesn't have to fear being hurt. Reassurance by her lover that he will be gentle and careful not to hurt her can be helpful.

Any persistent pain during coitus should be carefully investigated by a *very thorough* physician. Too many take a cursory look and pass it off as psychological, according to Masters and Johnson.

Painful intercourse caused by a wide variety of reasons—from gang rape to medically undetected lesions of the genital tract or ligaments—can result in vaginismus, an involuntary spasm of the vagina, preventing any efforts of a man to penetrate, even with his fingers.

Vaginismus can also result from a severely antisexual upbringing reinforced by restrictive religious beliefs. This requires professional treatment of both emotional and physical factors. The physical aspect is treated by Masters and Johnson with graduated vaginal dilators to be inserted by the husband every day.

The Frigid Couple

Sometimes a man seeks help for his wife's "frigidity" and avoidance of sex, and after she loosens up and displays more sexual desire and enjoyment, then *he* begins to avoid sex or develops dysfunctions. As one therapist put it, "When you have a frigid wife, look for a frigid husband. That may be one of the reasons he picked her."

It is for reasons of this sort that Masters and Johnson would not treat the wife without her husband. They see all sexual dysfunction within a marriage as a couple problem, not his or hers. That is a much more realistic approach than labeling someone frigid, which is very rarely the case.

The key is desire; to help each other, to make love—to love.

> A ninety-year-old-woman
>   can be a
> Sex Goddess
> If she knows where
>   it's at
>   and stays in
> Touch with it

15

FEMALE ORGASM: WHAT YOU CAN DO FOR *YOURSELF*

LET US suppose that you and your lover have already begun to follow the suggestions in Chapter 14. He is now doing his part to remove any pressure on you to perform for him sexually.

You no longer have to live up to *his* expectations, but what about your *own* desire to perform for him according to *your* expectations of yourself? Do you have rather high standards for yourself in general? Are you a perfectionist? Do you feel you have to produce in order to hold his love?

These are important questions to ask yourself. It's easier to relieve pressure when you *know* that you are doing it to yourself, and why.

Do you feel insecure in your femininity because you don't climax during coitus but use other methods? The vaginal orgasm myth must then be laid to rest in your own mind as well as your lover's. Reread Chapter 14 if necessary, or Masters and Johnson's *Human Sexual Response* for a scientific report.

Why do we tend to feel sexually inadequate when we don't function the way that men (therefore we) think we should? In part this is because our society has raised us in terms of our "value" to men. The more attractive and pleasing we are to men, the greater our value; the more "successful" the men we attract or snag, the greater our value; the more we live up to his sexual desires or standards, the greater our value. Society taught us that being a woman meant being able to attract a man, marry him, hold him and bear his children. Period. We were given no *independent* identity. Sex-object, wife, mother, homemaker. Period. The better we function *in these areas only,* the greater our value, therefore our self-image.

Orgasm has become just another success symbol. The more importance *he* places on the way we function sexually, the more important it becomes to us and the more anxious we become. This anxiety can be masked and reside below our level of awareness, just as guilt about breaking our parents' sexual commandments is frequently repressed.

The stereotyped version of womanhood is a remnant of the era when anatomy truly equalled destiny. It was woman's only value. If she didn't marry, she either took the vows or became a harlot—roles based on sex or antisex. Even becoming a nun meant marrying God and church. "Womanliness" is denied to those who do not fulfill their biological function: A girl or a virgin who never marries is called an old maid or spinster.

If you never exercise your biological options at all, you are just as much a woman as someone with multiple children and orgasms. You were born female. That makes you a woman when you grow up, whether or not you ever experience sex, have an orgasm, or bear children.

The cultural emphasis on acting feminine does not work toward *your* benefit. Its perniciousness is simply more subtle than the double standard that allows boys to have fun while "good girls" have none.

You are a unique *human being first* and a woman second. If it is the other way around in a relationship, it will have a negative effect on your sex life as well.

(For some women I have met, sexuality has become onerous because in their minds it is linked with the role of housekeeper and childbearer, which has been depreciated by a society that values impersonal achievement and financial success. They therefore reject one set of false values for another. Still other women have grown up to feel that their only worth is in pleasing someone else. The sensual end result for both is unsatisfying.)

Your lover, however, is not to blame for the way society brought both of you up. He is as much a victim as you. He feels as inadequate as you, perhaps more (because of the heavy male stereotype). He is at least as afraid of you as you are of him (many sociologists say more). He has as much trouble trusting you (deeply, from his center) as you do him. He is vulnerable, but seldom admits it. If he is slave to his stereotype, he has given you power to de-ball him because he equates his (phony) masculine image with his balls. He must hold on tightly. Hence, a power struggle—you for dignity, he for his balls.

If You Have Never Had an Orgasm

Perhaps you have never experienced orgasm. You have the ability. All women do. What gets in the way is the part of your mind that replays the no-nos, don'ts and shoulds you absorbed in childhood.

One of those was probably a strong taboo against pleasuring yourself, so you learned to shut off the sensual/sexual feelings. Physical ways of doing that are by shallow breathing and freezing the movement of your pelvis further blocking sensations. The sexercises in Chapter 16 should be helpful, especially after you have dredged up the painful experiences that caused you to turn yourself off.

You will probably need to deal with feelings that there's something dirty about touching, being touched, and sexual feelings in the genital/pelvic area. Try to recall and relive incidents that closed you off from your primal sensuality. When you release such feelings (as with the ice cubes, Chapter 12) the energy previously used to push them down will be freed for better use. You can then get maximum benefits from the experiences in Chapter 2, *which must be the starting point for you.* When you do the self-stimulation, think erotic thoughts and pictures. If nothing else works, use a vibrator (all drug stores sell facial massagers) and once that becomes easy, *try manual stimulation* again. If you can't seem to get around to these experiences, face up to the fact that you are not as interested as you thought in releasing your sensual potential.

Until Masters and Johnson came along, female orgasms were depicted in literature "like expanding ripples" or "the opening and closing of sea anemones." This may have meaning to someone who *has* experienced orgasm, but otherwise it's like trying to describe a flower to someone who has never seen or touched one. The most thorough and specific description I have seen is in *Human Sexual Response*. Masters and Johnson considered objective physiological orgasmic expression as well as the women's subjective physical perceptions. The physiological aspects were found to be consistent for orgasms achieved *by any means,* with variations only in intensity.

Taking Responsibility for What Happens

When you masturbate, you actively do whatever is necessary to heighten your tension to the point where—like the peak of a yawn—there's no option but letting go. You take the responsibility for elevating tension by thrusting your pelvis forward and back (with emphasis on forward) maintaining the stimulation and keeping your mind on erotic things. If your mind wanders, so does the feeling, then you have to build up all over again. So you use fantasies or whatever else excites you—but you don't expect the fantasies to give you an orgasm without *your* active physical stimulation (it can happen but it's rare).

In masturbation fantasies are like a lover. Yet women often imagine a prince-charming lover who can awaken their bodies with a kiss and give them magical orgasms ever after. But an orgasm is not a *passive* response.

To awaken your potential you must assume responsibility for *your own* sexual pleasure and the means of achieving *your own* orgasm. *It is a very self-centered experience.* To repeat, you can only have an orgasm for yourself. He cannot do it for you. And any effort to have one for *him* is doomed to failure. It involves a learning process, during which your focus must be solely on *your sensual stimuli* and whatever increases it.

If you tighten your hips and buttocks at some point while masturbating, why should you not do the same during coitus? It's not a magic key he's giving you, although its expansion and erection may seem rather magical and (I hope) beautiful.

He can give you his penis to enjoy, but the extent to which you enjoy it is *your responsibility*. If we use the analogy of food, he can offer you a meal but he cannot salivate, taste, chew, swallow for you and make you enjoy it. If he were feeding it into your mouth, however, he could help or hinder your enjoyment. Suppose you were in the habit of chewing slowly and he fed you too quickly, so that you had no time to finish one mouthful before the next was at your lips. If you wanted to enjoy the food, you would ask him to slow down. If you were too shy to let him know, and had indigestion, would it be his fault?

In sexing *you are responsible* for acknowledging and acting on your desire; for letting him know what turns you on the most; for making sure that you are sufficiently excited *before* he enters; for discovering what angles, positions and muscle manipulations most heighten *your* pleasure and *for stating those preferences;* for maintaining and building your tension/pleasure until the tension becomes release in the form of an orgasm.

These responsibilities are not yours to carry alone. You and your lover share them. But I stress *your* responsibility for your own pleasure because so often the man assumes too much and the woman too little.

Fully responsive women can assert their own desires and needs. They surrender, but to their passion and an *active* drive for fulfillment. That sort of surrender is responsiveness and receptivity—*not passivity*. It is a total immersion, absorption, a giving oneself over completely with no reservations, as a baby does with whatever holds its interest. That baby is not wondering "What if . . ." or "Maybe I shouldn't" or "What will he think of me?"

The baby is not split and pulled in different directions. Her mind/body is totally involved.

During the period when I was not yet able to fully assert myself sexually, a friend told me about his relationship with a woman who asked him to slow down while they were sexing. This struck me as rather "ballsy" and I asked if it bothered him. "No," he said. "She just wanted to be sure she got hers."

"Well, I could never do that!" I said righteously, feeling as though it was presumptuous on her part; that she should either have been able to climax in his mode or have hers afterwards. To ask a man to adjust to *me* was unthinkable. Happily, I've come a long way!

Unwillingness to take responsibility for your sexual desire may be manifested in your sexual and masturbation fantasies. You conjure up situations in which you (or someone else, because you can't admit that *you* could do it even in fantasy) are *coerced* into a sexual situation. You/she didn't want to but you had *no choice.* (You are still being a "good girl" for your parents by clamping a lid on your sexual pleasure.)

As you accept the idea of taking responsibility for your desire, consciously try to change your sex fantasies to include *choice* on your part. At first it may not be a big change. For example, if you have been fantasizing a rape situation, you can use the same scene but pretend that you are an actress who has *chosen* to play this part. If a group of men are involved in your rape scene, you may eventually allow yourself to fantasize choosing to make love with several men at a time. (A "good girl" couldn't admit that idea turns her on, but a sensuous woman can, even though she may never actually do it.)

If as part of your fantasy you were *forced* to strip, try the fantasy of stripping by *choice,* and eventually get up the nerve to do a striptease for your lover. That's what you would really like. We all have some exhibitionism in us.

Another expression of guilt and avoidance of responsibility is the inability to admit and demonstrate an interest in sex without being seduced. This is frequently coupled with the feeling that precautions against pregnancy are too "cold-blooded." If you do not find yourself hot for your lover's body independent of his overtures, or if you ignore *your* desire and wait for him to move, try a reversal. Ask your lover to wait until you genuinely feel like seducing *him*.

Aiming for Pleasure, Not Orgasm

"How," you may ask, "am I supposed to take responsibility for my orgasm but not aim for it?"

Let's go back to our hike to the waterfall. If you're hiking along with your eye constantly on the waterfall, you're likely to trip over something in your path and never get there. But if you focus on what's happening, all you have to do is keep going and you'll get there.

Pleasure is the path. Your lover and your sensations are the scenery. Each step on the path brings you more scenery and those are your focus. All of your being is involved. Nothing else exists. You go higher and higher, still involved only in the scenery. It feels so exquisite, *you just want to go on forever.* Suddenly everything seems to stop—and then it's there, a beautiful waterfall. Full, satisfying, pulsating.

Now suppose that you're moving along merrily, digging the scene, which keeps getting better and better, and suddenly you realize the waterfall is just around the bend. "I'm close," you exult. Just then—thud! You trip and roll down the hill! Like falling in love, orgasm happens when you don't *expect* it. It gets to a point where it feels so good you really don't want to have the orgasm yet; you want to keep going as long as possible because the orgasm interrupts those feelings.

The trick is to focus *only* on enjoying each moment to the fullest and *not even think about having the orgasm* during coitus. You can have it afterwards and that too is good. *There is no second-class orgasm.*

As Lisa, one of my seminar participants, said about her orgasms, "Whatever happens, it's perfectly beautiful and satisfying to me." I was grateful to her for sharing that because Karen had just finished telling us that a week before she broke into uncontrollable sobs (like an orgasm) when her boyfriend ejaculated just as she felt she was about to arrive at the coital orgasm she had striven for so long. Later, when she was able to accept her extracoital orgasms as first-class instead of second-class, and stopped shooting for an orgasmic goal, that's when it happened—and easily ever after.

Your *responsibility* comes in finding ways of intensifying your sensations (I'll give you some) and keeping your focus on what is happening *here and now,* not thirty seconds ago or thirty seconds from now.

If your mind has a tendency to wander off the erotic path, open your eyes and enjoy looking at your lover: his eyes, his body, his penis moving in and out if you can see it. (You might place a mirror to reflect both of you.)

The only sort of mind-wandering that may help is a sex fantasy, or rerunning an exciting scene from a movie you saw. Whatever it is, it should be something that arouses *you,* even if it wasn't anything obviously sexual. Once you start climaxing regularly, you'll be able to use fantasies or not, as you please, without being dependent on them.

When you get distracted, it is an indication that not all your systems are Go.

Somewhere under the surface there is fear, anxiety, resentment, conflict about what you're doing—any one of these factors can be enough to turn you off. Sometimes the anxiety can be about something unrelated. If it's resentment, it might be about something that happened some time ago but you never had the nerve to say anything about it. And sometimes, let's face it, you're not *really* in the mood.

On the Brink

The first time you get really close to orgasm, the sensations may be so much more intense than anything you experienced before that you may react unconsciously to keep them from getting out of hand. After all, we've been taught, "Keep your head, and don't get carried away."

You may feel as though you're on fire or about to die. You may experience an involuntary bearing down or pushing-out feeling. Be encouraged. Don't be frightened or stop, even if you think you can't stand any more. It means you're extremely close to orgasm, *but don't think about that.*

The feeling that you're going to die can be a fear reaction with the prospect of letting go experienced as death. (Among timid mammals, giving in to the male in an insecure environment can mean death.) What dies momentarily during orgasm is the ego—your control. It's a death and rebirth. Some people have difficulty giving up that control. The primal love-in (Chapter 8) is excellent practice when you are the receiver.

Old Fears

Many of us have had frightening experiences with sexual overtones in childhood or adolescence. Much child molestation is unreported and often involves a relative. Many women have narrowly escaped being raped at some time in their lives. (These are not included in rape statistics, which are themselves incomplete because many are unreported.)

A young child exposed to the sights or sounds of sexing may think Mommy is being hurt unless it is explained that those are pleasure noises.

Fears do not dissolve miraculously. Reliving "long-forgotten" incidents that contributed to an unconscious fear can release their power over you.

It may take the buildup of trust in a devoted, sensitive lover or therapy to overcome some deep-seated fears.

Dis-Trust

Trust can be the missing link for a woman who does not fully let herself go. She may be unsure of her lover's emotional commitment, whether he will treat her well, whether he will desert her. This can be complicated by sexual guilt and the feeling that he *must* marry her (which unconsciously may be the only way she can justify their sexing).

Usually it is not marriage, per se, but the emotional security within the relationship that is crucial. Some women take longer than others to achieve that feeling of security.

When you expect to continue to feel well-loved and valued whether or not your sexual performance is particularly sparkling, you will not worry about "failing" your lover. Security engenders greater confidence, enjoyment and sexual adequacy, free of distracting anxieties.

The importance of security and *absence of fear* as a prerequisite for sexual readiness in the female is linked to the behavior of timid mammals by Dr. A. T. W. Simeons in his *Man's Presumptuous Brain.*

Dr. Simeons points out that natural selection eliminated those timid wild animals that continued to copulate in the presence of mortal danger. This incompatibility of sex and fear was passed on as an important survival trait and is fully preserved in human beings today, he says. In timid mammals the female is responsible for the couple's safety while the male is wooing, and it is *she* who decides when the male may mount. Once mounted, the male takes over the watch.

This instinctive animal fear, according to Dr. Simeons, is expressed in humans as shame, modesty or bashfulness. If this is indeed so, a woman's modesty may mask a sexual fear of which she is not fully aware. Certainly with a person whom she senses may threaten her well-being, her modesty may be entirely appropriate. In other situations the fear is irrational.

Recognizing Your New Orgasm

When you start having orgasms during coitus, you may not recognize them because at first they may be milder than the ones you had from other types of stimulation. For example, if you were accustomed to having very intense orgasms with vigorous body contractions in addition to the vaginal contractions, you may not at first experience the body contractions and therefore not identify what you had as an orgasm. You may then desire another one afterwards through more direct stimulation.

If your lover keeps thrusting during your climax, you may not clearly feel your vaginal contractions and not feel as though your orgasm really happened. If possible, it is best for him to stop at that point and it is up to you to signal him. (This is another example of simultaneous orgasm being inadvisable.)

MULTIPLE ORGASMS

If you want to try for another orgasm, don't wait until your contractions have completely died down before you start moving again. At this point the outer third of your vagina plus your inner labia should still be engorged, and you are as close to orgasm right afterwards as you were beforehand. Unless the first left you anesthetized, the next one will probably come easier, faster and may be more intense. This is because it is possible to have several orgasms before you actually reach the *peak* of your sexual excitement—and several more as you descend from the peak. Naturally the one you have at the peak will be the most intense.

Sometimes orgasms simply happen consecutively at the tail end of one another, without any further stimulation.

INTENSIFYING YOUR FEELINGS

Thrusting your pelvis forward, tightening your buttocks and hips as you do this, is a highly effective way of intensifying your sensations during coitus. Tightening your hip muscles alone is not as effective as drawing them tightly toward each other as though they were being tweezed together by a giant tweezer. It is difficult to keep them constantly tightened this way throughout the thrusting, so I suggest you tighten as you thrust forward to catch the inward stroke and release as he withdraws for the next stroke. As you thrust forward, breathe *out* hard, expelling as much air as possible.

An important aid to keeping your pelvis forward is one or more pillows under your hips. It increases the pressure against your clitoris and is just as effective under your lover's hips when you straddle him.

The position with you above is the most favorable initially. In addition to good clitoral contact it gives you complete control over the movements and rhythm, while your lover can lie still and relax, thus assuring he will not climax sooner than you would like. In that position he can also stimulate your mons and clitoris.

In the preferred female superior position your weight is mainly on your shins and knees and you lean forward on your hands. Your knees would be on a line with his armpits or nipples. A half-inch further forward or back can make a great difference in your sensations, so that thorough inch-by-inch experimentation is in order. Lying down above him may also be worth trying. You may prefer that he lie still or sometimes you may like him to thrust his hips up to meet you on your way down—but *you* must set the rhythm to suit yourself.

When you are on your back (with one or more pillows under your hips) and your lover is above you, supporting his weight on his hands, some clitoral pressure can be attained if he moves up (toward your head) as much as possible and you brace one foot on the bed, bending the knee slightly while the other leg is raised up in the air, with knee bent. The foot braced on the bed gives you leverage for thrusting your pelvis forward while you tighten your hips with each inward stroke.

The latter (male superior) position requires good control and stamina on the part of the man. If you tend to worry about overtiring him, you might have an understanding between you that he will not do the superman number and will change position when he wearies. Since he will be moving actively in this position *you must guide him to the rhythm best for you.* Worrying about how long he will last is only important if you are aiming for orgasm. Otherwise it doesn't matter unless he comes very quickly before you get a chance to really enjoy yourself. (In that case consult Chapter 17.)

Another position to try is lying on your back (pillow under hips) with legs tightly closed or crossed after he enters.

Even if you had been almost at the point of orgasm before he entered you (which is highly advisable), do not expect to have sensations immediately upon insertion. Often this is not the case, because of the interrupted stimulation and the adjustment to a different, more diffused type of stimulation. So if you feel nothing, don't panic. Relax your mind and tighten your muscles, enjoy the feeling of warm fullness inside you, the sight of your lover and whatever stimulation (in addition to genital) is available. If you focus on your senses and enjoy whatever you can, eventually the feelings will come. After all, if you don't get a great deal of erotic sensation the second you start masturbating, why should you expect more when your lover enters?

Occasionally you may not be quite lubricated enough for comfort when your lover attempts intromission—particularly if there has not been much love play that was stimulating to you. If you are sufficiently excited but habitually on the dry side, discuss it with your gynecologist and have him check your estrogen level. Other reasons can be psychological tension. In any case, saliva on the penis (you can put some on your finger and apply it to the section still outside) can make intromission pleasant. A *small* amount of vaginal jelly can also be helpful.

One of the most effective ways to intensify your pleasure is through practicing the sexercises, particularly the contractions of the pubococcygeus muscle. This muscle is weak *in the majority of women,* no matter how good the rest of their muscle tone.

To check on yours, insert a finger in your vagina and try to bend it. If it meets with considerable resistance, fine. If not, your muscle is sagging and you need the exercise. A more exact way of determining that muscle tone is to find a doctor who will measure its strength when you contract by means of an instrument called a perineometer.

If your urine leaks, you can be certain that you need this exercise very badly. If you do the exercise conscientiously, it can firm up your vagina and increase coital sensations as well as stop the leaking.

Contracting the muscle pulls on the clitoral hood, stimulating the clitoris. When contracted during sexing, its advantage is obvious.

Genitals Are to Like

The way you feel about your vulva and vagina are closely connected with your sexual pleasure. If you like and enjoy your genitals there is a better chance that sexing will be pleasurable for you.

Start actively enjoying your vulva, the sight and feel of it. Learn to enjoy the odor of your vaginal secretions. Taste your joy juice. It's clean, healthy, and delicious to your lover. As long as you keep reasonably clean, you don't have to feel apologetic about it, douche it away or disguise its scent and flavor. It does *not* offend. You can be secure that to a sexually healthy man, your genital odors are a certain turn-on.

His genital odors will be a turn-on for you if you get rid of the notion that any body odors are bad. Find out when you like his odors the most—two hours after his bath (right afterwards may not offer much to sniff), or is it more like twelve?

Make friends with his penis; play with it and enjoy watching it

swell. *That swelling is caused by your lover's warm feelings for you.* It is
not divorced from his heart and mind.

Extend to his penis the same affection you have for your lover.

Faking It

The pressure to perform and a feeling of hopelessness about
living up to his and your expectations can lead to faking an
orgasm. You feel that you will be less a woman in his eyes (and
your own) if you don't perform according to popular expectations. You may (perhaps correctly) feel he will lose interest in
you. In that case you are merely a sex-*object* to him and will have
lost nothing; better to find out sooner than later. (But you're
afraid to take the chance of finding out what you *really* are to
him? Ask yourself whether it is worth being untrue to *yourself.*)

It is important to accept yourself as you are, that you are not a
lesser woman for not having an orgasm. To stop faking and be
yourself are important steps toward increasing your genuine
sexual pleasure. The more you can accept yourself as you *are,* the
less you will have to depend on your lover's opinion of you. It will
free you to concentrate on your *own* pleasure, not what *he* thinks
or wants.

Sexual Politics

The sexual revolution faces a major pitfall common to all
revolutions. Chances are that those who revolt have been raised
within the value system of the power structure against which they
rebel.

Intellectual ideals and slogans are usually not enough to
change the deep, often unconscious values with which people are
reared. Thus, revolutions may founder because the "revolution-
aries" have taken on (or not discarded) the *values* of their former
oppressors. You then have a new group of oppressors and
repressed.

For example: If the women's liberation struggle (much of

which is revolutionary in nature) had as its aim to show that anything men do, we will do as well or better, a logical extension would be to prove that women can wage wars just as well as men.

The sexual revolution began with the idea that women are *and have a right to be just as sexual as men.* Down with the double standard! Free love! That's fine up to a point. The point stops at *what standards* we are using.

The male side of the double standard has in many cases proven just as oppressive and repressive as the female. Many a male has been stereotyped into impotence by the established cultural standard that he should always be ready for sex. *Instead of being laughed out of existence,* that standard has merely been extended to women (with corresponding results.)

Always Ready?

Now women are also expected to be ready at the first pass, especially those members of the hip culture who have somehow confused the ideals of sexual freedom and love for humankind, with being in a constant state of sexual readiness.

Why *should* you be ready and panting every time anyone lays a hand on your breast or clit? That would make you a machine, not a woman. That is not freedom. It gives you the worst of both worlds. You don't ordinarily go out and actively choose the men with whom you wish to sex. They choose you. If you refuse, you're not "hip," you're labeled "uptight" or "frigid."

Throughout the rest of the animal kingdom, which cannot be accused of being uptight about sex under natural conditions, you find innumerable examples of females being highly selective about when and whom they allow to mate with them. Rape is found only among homo sapiens.

Selectivity *is* natural, normal and *sensual.*

Our minds can lie to us and tell us we want something that we really don't (because we *think* we should and the others do it) but *the body does not lie.*

Sexual freedom is the right to your feelings and the right to choose on that basis, without social pressure.

Sexual freedom is not having to apologize for saying no.

Sexual freedom is being able to make the same advances as men do without frightening off 95 percent of them in the process.

We don't have it yet.

Handling the Orgasm Watcher

I have already discussed the insecurity that prompts a man to inquire anxiously, "Did you come?" When the same man does this to you habitually, even though he knows you well enough to recognize your orgasm and knows that you come most of the time, it's understandable that his continued questioning could become irritating. I encourage the man in such a couple to examine his motives and ask both of them to come to a mutually acceptable alternative.

In one case Fay agreed to let Bob know if she needs or wants an orgasm afterwards, and not hide that from him. Bob, on his part agreed to cease worrying her about it. They kept their agreement and Fay's sexual interest, which had lagged behind her husband's, picked up considerably as they explored further into their primal sensuality.

When yours is a fairly new relationship and he doesn't know you well enough yet, it is perfectly understandable for him to inquire, if he simply wants to be sure that you too are satisfied. If you are annoyed by his question, you are simply telegraphing your own insecurity in that area. You may think your orgasm should be quite obvious to him, when it really isn't at all. There is so much subjective variety even in one woman's orgasms, and the differences among women are even greater.

Even when he knows you well enough to recognize your orgasm, he may on some occasion be so involved with his own that he misses yours. Certainly it is possible for a woman on occasion not to be sure about a man's orgasm even when they have been married for years. Ordinarily it's pretty hard to miss, but on occasion it may be less intense than usual or you may be too involved with yours.

So if he cares enough to ask, don't be annoyed; relax and enjoy it.

If your answer is no, leave it at that. Don't try to explain because that's putting yourself on the defensive and you have no reason to be apologetic. Along with your no, it would be gratifying for him to get the message, one way or another, that you enjoyed the sexing—if you did. It must be genuine. Anything else will be more transparent than you think.

If part of the reason you didn't come was because of something he did (for instance, changing rhythm) or didn't do, let him know *another* time that this takes you down, *without blaming or fault-finding* you *messages*. Use *I* messages, such as, "I find that when the feelings are very good, if they just continue that way without any change in rhythm or movements, I'll have a great orgasm, but any change takes me way down." A *you* message would be "when *you* change rhythm you make me lose the orgasm." It accuses him of short-changing her one orgasm, whereas the *I* message merely gives helpful information.

The Play's the Thing

Orgasm is not the show—it's the applause at the end. If you're merely playing for a good hand, the show will flop.

So forget the curtain calls and enjoy the play. . . .

> Bare buttocks nestle 'gainst warm rock,
>   Nude body shivers
>   to wind's soft caress
>   Nipples reach
>   toward hot sun
>   Breasts rise
>   like swelling waves

Body in tune
>   with the quiet . . .
>   breaking waves . . .
>   moist rocks . . .
>   verdant trees . . .
>   ocean melting into sky . . .
Legs open to leaping spray . . .

16

S-E-X-ERCISES

THESE sexercises are designed to directly benefit key areas of your body in terms of sexual functioning. However, the better the muscle tone and flexibility throughout your mind/body, the more you benefit sensually. Therefore, I also highly recommend Yoga, dance classes, body movement or any sensible physical fitness program.

Consistency is important. Even a few minutes daily is better than nothing; try to establish a set time each day.

Breathing and the Life Force

Healthy breathing flows like a wave. It starts in the abdomen (which rises as you inhale) and expands up into the thorax. Exhalation runs down from the neck, deflates the chest and continues in a wave of letting-go through the abdomen into the pelvis. *The flowing sensation travels smoothly down the body into the genitals.* This is the life force.

In many people the wave is cut off in the middle. The abdomen is a common place for this to happen, thus cutting off the flow into the genitals. The lungs do not deflate completely, holding onto a reserve of air, which prevents letting go, surrendering to the body.

When they think of deep breathing, most people envision taking a vigorous gulp of air that puffs out the chest like a West Point cadet's. But that is actually *shallow* breathing because it does not expand the lower sections of the lungs. In addition to inhaling with only the chest, shallow breathers hold onto that air for dear life, as though they might not get another breath. They are usually unaware that when they exhale, they are holding back this reserve of air. If they tried to let it all out, they would be unable at first to do it in *one* unbroken exhalation.

When tense, frightened or anxious, we hold our breath.

In my instructions, when I ask you to breathe deeply, I do not mean for you to take a much bigger breath than usual. Rather, I mean for you to *exhale* more deeply and completely, and start inhaling from your abdomen instead of your chest. When inhaling, concentrate on letting (and feeling) your ribs expand sideways like an accordion—beginning with the lower ones and expanding upwards in a count of three or four. As you exhale to the same count, your upper ribs contract first and the lower ones last.

True deep breathing can be observed in emotionally healthy young children and at intervals in persons who are asleep. You will notice that rather than the chest doing most of the rising and falling, it is the abdomen that expands first during inhalation and contracts last during expiration. Singers, actors and public speakers know this as diaphragmatic breathing. Practitioners of Yoga know it as deep breathing.

Take an ordinary deep breath. Now let out your breath in one smooth exhalation until it feels as though you have let it all out. Then say "Ssaaa" and see how much was left. Now pull in your stomach and notice that still more escapes.

Notice also that when you make the effort to take a superbig breath, you make a sniffing noise. This is produced by the automatic contraction of the nostrils, says Indra Devi, author of *Yoga for Americans*. In Yoga deep breathing, she says, the nostrils remain inactive. You inhale by slightly contracting the muscles of the pharyngeal area at the back of your mouth that connects with your nose. If you open your mouth and look in the mirror you will see a domelike wall at the back. Underneath it is the pharyngeal space, through which Yoga practitioners suck in the air and upon which they exert a slight pressure as they exhale. It is all done with the mouth closed, in one smooth, rhythmical flow—effortless and relaxed.

Both in Yoga and for our purposes, the major emphasis is on the exhalation rather than the inhalation. You may notice, also, that when your body involuntarily begins to breathe heavily during or after physical exertion, the accent is on exhaling.

As Reich pointed out in *The Function of the Orgasm*, children learn to hold their breath in order to shut off feelings that are unacceptable to the adults around them. Shallow exhalation inhibits feelings; fuller expiration releases them.

(Deep breathing is so beneficial, it can replace tranquilizers or sleeping pills!)

Rather than ask you to think about your breathing during sexing, the primal sexercise integrates breathing with sexual pelvic movements and, if practiced regularly for a few months, should become part of your sexing without thought or effort on your part.

Since the breathing is the trickiest part of it, I will ask you to start with that and combine it with the rest when you are accustomed to exhaling fully. Hopefully you will also be in touch with the letting-go orgasm reflex. This is an involuntary forward movement of the pelvis as deep exhalation reaches its nadir. It happens normally during healthy breathing, alternating with a slight backward movement during inhalation. These movements are intensified during sexing. When pelvic movements are restricted by chronic tension in that area, the person's orgastic potency is reduced.*

---

* Alexander Lowen, M.D., 1965 lecture series presented by The Institute for Bio-Energetic Analysis. Lowen worked with Reich and is a leader of the neo-Reichean movement.

Exercise

Lie down on your back, knees bent, eyes closed. Let your body feel heavier and heavier. Feel yourself sink deeply into the bed. Become aware of your body and the feeling of air, clothes or bedding against your skin. Relax your eyes, face, jaw.

Now become aware of your breathing. Put one hand on your abdomen and the other on any part of your upper torso that you feel may tense up as you inhale. Common places are the throat and upper chest.

Inhale as you do normally and notice any area of tension. It may be easier to spot with your hand. Without forcing, let your breath get deeper and longer by itself.

Breathe out as fully as possible in one *continuous* exhalation. Do you feel the wave stop anywhere? Place a hand on the place where the exhalation stopped, press down slightly at the end of your exhalation and suggest to yourself that you let go. Do you notice a difference in aliveness above and below the place where your breathing is blocked?

As you exhale, feel a flow within your body reaching all the way into your genitals. *Allow* it to go lower and lower. When it reaches your genitals, there will be a *slight* forward movement of the pelvis. This movement is completely natural and involuntary. Do not think about it, expect it or try to will it. It may take a while before it happens.

When you think you have exhaled completely, exhale some more. If necessary take your hands and push down on your diaphragm. Try to exhale more completely, all in one piece. You can also envision your breath moving down through your genitals, thighs, and out your feet. If after a while your pelvis does not move forward ever so slightly at the end of your exhalation, try putting the fingertips of both hands in the middle of the upper abdomen between the umbilicus and sternum (or let your lover do it). Breathe deeply, and during exhalation press the abdomen in gradually and *gently*. This may result in abdominal contractions. These in turn, according to Reich, may induce the forward pelvic movement that he named the orgasm reflex.

Another way of inducing the reflex is to breathe out as much as possible and then say "ssaaa" to get out the remaining air.

If you were told to move your pelvis forward, you would ordinarily tense certain pelvic and thigh muscles to accomplish this voluntarily. In the involuntary orgasm reflex there is a *relaxation* and letting go of muscle tension that allows the pelvis to swing naturally into place. You may also feel a relaxation in your knees as this happens.

Some people may experience an involuntary vibration or trembling of the flesh during exhalation at some point in a practice session. It can last for several seconds or minutes and is a *positive* happening. It represents the sudden release of dammed up energy from tense muscles and tissues that have now let go. After a while you may also find that your pelvis starts moving back and forth involuntarily and rapidly as it might at the approach of orgasm.

The gentle abdominal pressure described can be applied by one lover for another in working together on breathing. Place one of your hands under the nape of his or her neck and the other on the upper abdomen. As the breathing moves lower, the hand can be moved lower on the abdomen, encouraging the flow into the pelvis. The pressure should be slight, applied just at the end of the exhalation and released (without breaking contact) during inhalation. You can also do this for yourself, of course. Practice this deep breathing every day. A little more detail for helping each other can be found in George Downing's *The Massage Book*, the most beautiful of its kind I have yet seen. (It is published by Random House Bookworks and conveys the loving spirit and body awareness experienced by so many of us at Esalen Institute.)

The primal sexercise involves breathing, muscle contractions and pelvic movements. Until you have gained some familiarity with the first two, practice them separately. After several daily sessions, all may be combined.

The Magic Muscles

The inner muscle that you contract in your basic sexercise is the deep pelvic muscle mentioned in Chapter 14, the pubococcygeus muscle.

When a man contracts this muscle during intercourse, it momentarily lengthens and widens his penis, an enjoyable sensation for both lovers.

When a woman contracts it, this tightens her vagina, increases her sensations during thrusting, exerts traction on the clitoris and can help her reach orgasm. (Taut pubococcygeus muscle tone also makes childbirth easier and prevents sagging of internal muscles in later years.)

Most of us learned to use this muscle when we discovered how to keep from wetting the bed and started toilet training. The anterior portion of the muscle can be used to postpone urination; the posterior section does the same for the bowels.

It is the anterior portion that we use in our sexercises and to get in touch with the muscle we begin by shutting off our flow of urine, then releasing and letting it flow hard again, and shutting it off once more. At first this should be done several times whenever urinating; later you can do it without urinating. If you cannot shut off your flow you need this sexercise very badly. Diminish the flow as best you can and after a month or two of practice you will succeed.

It is important, when doing the muscle tightening, also to concentrate on the total *relaxation* of the muscle when you let go. For the man, this conscious relaxation can retard orgasm by relaxing the smooth muscles in the prostatic urethra which must contract in order for ejaculation to take place. For the woman who involuntarily tenses up during sexing, the ability to consciously relax the muscle opens the door to greater arousal. Fifty contractions *and relaxations* daily are plenty for men, but nine out of ten women need more.

The Female Sexercise

Interrupting or slowing the flow of urine in the ordinary way is not always sufficient to assure that you are using the correct muscles. Your knees should be as wide apart as possible, and at least one counseling institute recommends squatting the first time or so to make sure that you are not using the superficial sphincters instead of the pubococcygeus muscle. You can squat on the toilet seat or the floor, with a container beneath.

Once you know what to do you can practice your contractions just about any time or place: in your car while stopped at a light, while waiting in line at the market, as a passenger in a vehicle, while washing dishes, waiting for a bus, elevator, dentist, doctor, etc. No one can tell what you're doing. You need never again twiddle your thumbs while you wait!

The best plan, however, is to set aside a few minutes at a regular time at least twice daily. For some the contractions are easier before getting up in the morning.

Each practice session should consist of the following variations:

1. Contract for three seconds and release for three. *As you contract, count to three and with each count pull a little tighter.* Count as you relax and let go even more with each count. If you find this quite difficult, start with only five contractions at a time and increase five daily until you hit fifty. For the first several weeks do a few whenever you urinate.

2. Contract for a count of three and then *push out* for three seconds. Begin with a minimum of five and work up to fifty. (If you don't know what I mean by "push out," review Experience G, Chapter 3.)

3. Do as many as you can as fast as you can (eventually one or more per second for a total of 200 per day. With the rest, that's a grand total of 300.)

Utilize the fact that the mind and body are one and put all of yourself into the act. As you contract, imagine that you are gripping your favorite phallus, giving it a good, tight love squeeze. Think sexy. (But not while you're stopped at a red light or you'll hold up traffic.)

When your contractions are not too difficult, add the breathing—exhale fully and vigorously as you contract.

If your muscle is very weak or was traumatized during childbirth, you may find the contractions hard work at first. However, in a very short time they will get much easier until they are almost effortless.

You may feel the benefits during sexing in as little as three weeks. However, continue the exercises for at least eight to ten weeks as outlined. Then, if you have been conscientious about your 300 daily, and you have a regular sex life with orgasms (the contractions involve the same muscle), you can cut down to fifty a day for the rest of your life. However, if you still cannot shut off a heavy flow of urine with the muscle, 300 a day should be continued until you can.

When you first begin practicing your contractions, ask your lover to hold still after he enters and see if he can feel you contracting. If not, you have a lot of work to do. After you have reached the 300 mark, see how much of a difference he can feel when you contract.

Primal Sexercise

Once you are moderately comfortable with your contractions and your deep breathing, you are ready for the primal sexercise.

When you are first learning it, stand with your back, head and hips against the wall, or lie down on the floor. With your hand, feel the space between the small of your back and the wall. Now *simultaneously* do the following:

1. Exhale deeply.

2. Pull your abdomen in and up toward your ribs. There should now be less space between your hand and the wall. When done correctly, this pulls your pelvis slightly forward.

3. Swing your pelvis as far forward as possible. As the

movement is completed there should be no space between the small of your back and the wall or floor.

4. Contract your pubococcygeus muscle. (All this is done in one circular movement—your buttocks move down, pelvis forward and abdomen up—while you exhale and tighten your pubococcygeus muscle.)

5. Relax your muscles and let your pelvis drop back, arching as you inhale. *Concentrate on relaxing your pubococcygeus muscles as fully as possible.*

Tightening the muscle builds excitement. Relax it to prolong pleasure and delay orgasm. Women can also use the relaxation and slight pushing out feeling to build toward orgasm.

Eventually you should be able to do the primal sexercise at the rate of one or more per second up to 200 daily. This counts as part of the daily regimen of 300 pubococcygeus contractions for women.

Once you have mastered the primal sexercise, you can do it in almost any position—sitting, standing, lying on your back, stomach, side—or while dancing to music that encourages hip movement, especially forward and backward.

Practice to music, face to face with your lover. . . .

The Cat

Another variation that will increase flexibility of movement is to hold onto the back of a chair, step backward until your arms are stretched straight forward and your spine is at right angles to your legs. Your head is parallel to and between your arms. If you do your primal sexercise in that position, your back will arch up like a bristling cat's while your head drops below arm level. When you release, arch your back the other way as far as possible, pushing your buttocks out and bringing your head up above arm level. Begin with four and work up to eight times. The same sexercise can be done on hands and knees.

The Lift

Lie down on your back, bend and open your knees, planting your feet as far apart as possible. Now lift up your hips, as high as possible, and do your primal sexercise. Relax, lower hips and repeat two or three times, gradually working up to eight.

The Scissor
(for women mainly)

On your back, bend your legs and bring them up toward your chest, ankles crossed. Imagine you are entwining and gripping your lover with your thighs and legs. Then do your primal. Work up to eight.

The ability to wrap her legs around her lover and exert enough pressure to raise the pelvis up and down against his can be important to a woman's pleasure and satisfaction. This requires good thigh adductors—the muscles that move your legs toward each other, as when swimming with the frog kick. Wide-legged knee bends, trying to pull the thighs together as you squat, will also exercise those muscles. Here's one you can do together:

Thigh Workout with Lover

Seated on facing chairs, she places her knees inside his and tries to push them apart as he squeezes his thighs and knees together. Then they reverse positions, with his knees inside hers. Start with only *one or two* the first time and increase *very gradually*.

Back Strength for Staying on Top

Lie on your stomach with arms stretched in front of you and toes pointed. Simultaneously lift your right leg and left arm as high as they will go without twisting your body. Lower slowly. Keep the knee straight and reach toward the wall (or whatever's behind your feet) with your toe, while you stretch toward the opposite wall with your hand. Then raise left leg and right arm, alternating two to eight times, depending on your physical condition. Variations include raising both arms together, or both legs together, and finally, raising and stretching both arms and both legs simultaneously. Rest at intervals by turning over and pulling knees to chest.

Then you can do some good old pushups—a marvelous sexercise.

Swing Those Hips

Music and a partner will also enhance this sexercise:

Slowly at first, make a large circle with your hips. Push them as far as they will go in each direction, trying to make the circle larger each time. As this becomes easier, speed up your movements and add your primal to the forward swing. Change directions from clockwise to counterclockwise. Keep feet slightly apart and knees relaxed. Do not move the upper part of your body but keep the movement in the hips only. Make eight circles and change directions for the next eight.

If you have difficulty with this one, limber up as follows:

1. Swing your pelvis straight forward, then backward as far as possible. Start slowly and gradually increase the tempo as it becomes easier.

2. Swing your hips all the way to the left, then to the right. Keep your shoulders parallel, body facing forward. Move nothing but your hips. Keep your feet slightly apart, knees straight, and your arms straight out to the side parallel to your shoulders. At first you might do it in front of a mirror or with your back to a wall, to be sure you are not twisting the rest of your body.

When doing this with your lover stand face to face, hands palm to palm. Using opposite hips, try to touch hips at the extreme end of each swing.

Do a minimum of eight.

Yoga and the Sex Glands

The yoga exercise that most directly benefits the gonads, or sex glands, is called the reverse posture by Indra Devi. It is known, she says, as the restorer of youth and vitality.

This is assumed by lying on your back and raising your legs, buttocks and lower back up in the air towards the ceiling, at right angles to your head and shoulders. Your back is supported by both hands on your hips, with elbows about a foot apart on the floor and thumbs under your hipbone. Feet and legs should be relaxed. You can shake your feet gently to be sure they're relaxed. Do not bend your knees. While in this position, close your eyes and do Yoga deep breathing as described earlier in this chapter. At first hold the position for only a few seconds, and gradually increase to ten minutes.

This is called the shoulder stand in some yoga classes, and it is the beginning stage. The actual shoulder stand, however, places the body in a straight line from shoulder to toe. For this reason it affects the thyroid more than the gonads, which are mainly affected in the reverse posture.

If you do not feel that you can get into the reverse posture without some help at first, sit down on the floor with one side of your buttocks up against the wall, your legs parallel to it. Simultaneously swing your legs up the wall and lower your trunk to the floor at right angles to the wall. Your buttocks should be as close as possible to the wall with your legs at right angles, leaning straight against the wall and pointing toward the ceiling. (This is an extremely comfortable resting position, especially good for pregnant women or persons with varicose veins.)

Now bend your knees and, using your feet for leverage, raise your buttocks and back off the floor, supporting yourself with hands on hips as described for the reverse posture (or thumbs above hipbone, hands on small of back). Then walk your legs up the wall until they're straight. Breathe deeply. When you tire, bend your knees again and take turns raising and straightening one leg, then the other, aiming them toward your head. Then try the reverse posture.

Stretching Your Crotch

Seated on the floor, place your palms on the floor against your buttocks, fingers pointing directly back, away from your body. Your arms should be pressing against your back. Bend your knees, placing toe against toe as close to your body as possible and use your arms to push your back and buttocks forward. Pull your abdomen in and up. Now press your knees toward the floor. Hold several seconds and relax. Do eight times.

A variation is to put your hands on your ankles and push your knees down with your elbows. This is advisable if you are very tight in the crotch.

Stretching Head to Foot

Toe to toe, heel to heel, grab your toes and try to bring your head to your feet. *Do this gently, without forcing.* Begin with four and work up to thirty.

The Sensuous Tongue

A trained and talented tongue is one that can oscillate back and forth, up and down, the faster the better. Most of us can do this for a second or so. The idea is to practice several times daily (when you do your inner muscle contractions?) in order to extend the amount of time you can keep oscillating.

It will pay rich rewards in terms of ecstatic pleasure for your lover, who perhaps will also be inspired to develop an oscillating tongue. Practice to music with a fast beat.

Practicing together can be particularly pleasureful.

17

HIS ERECTION—WHAT YOU CAN AND CANNOT DO ABOUT IT

ONE of the most distressing and common human experiences takes place when two people engage in sex play, anticipate a happy denouement, the curtain opens on the big scene—and the leading man is struck dumb! His phallus has missed its cue.

He can recover from stage fright if his leading lady doesn't come unglued, if she wings it and gives him a chance to get himself together. However, if she decides that he's trying to make a fool of *her*, eyes him malevolently and hisses, *"Do something,"* she's liable to end up without her leading man.

Because of the masculine mystique, few people realize how common it is for a man to experience sexual stage fright, so they react as though it were something abnormal—which it is not when it happens now and then. That is not impotence. The very feeling that this *should not* happen is more likely to make it happen again.

As his lover, *your reaction* the first time his erection fails can be a major factor in whether or not he develops secondary impotence. How?

Imagine that so far you have managed to live up to a societal and personal expectation that you have an orgasm every single time you sex, but one night you're feeling under the weather and you don't have one. Your lover is very concerned and makes tremendous efforts to rectify the situation. In addition to your own disappointment, you pick up *his*, plus the feeling that something has gone wrong with you. You have heard that as they get older, women's ability to climax is impaired (not true) and you start worrying about losing your femininity. The harder your lover works at arousing you, the more you feel that you *must* respond *for him*. The orgasm becomes something you *must* have to prove to yourself and to him that you are *all right*, a real woman. So you huff and puff and try your best—and fail.

Later it occurs to you that the whole thing just happened because you weren't feeling well and had taken some medication, but there's a nagging doubt in your mind, perhaps it wasn't *only* that. *Meanwhile your lover is taking your lack of orgasm to mean that he no longer turns you on and you don't love him any more.* You try to reassure him, but you realize the only way is to go back to having orgasms the way you did before. "I'll do it this time," you tell yourself, when next you start making love. But between his expectations and your own you can't enjoy it the way you used to, so you fall short of the goal.

The Castration Threat

You can see, I think, how this could become a vicious circle. Substitute his erection for your orgasm and you can get pretty close to the dilemma of a man whose lover overreacts to a perfectly *normal*, human fallibility, and how her insecurity/anxiety can ease him into a sexual coma. Much as he would like to please you—and he would—he cannot *will* an erection for you any more than you can will your orgasm for him (although you have the "advantage" of being able to fake it). *He, however, is entirely vulnerable to possible scorn, abuse, ridicule or anger.*

A woman who reacts with even the mildest disdain is (whether she knows it or not) playing the role of a castrating woman who can visibly diminish a man's potency. The fear of this power that a woman (beginning with Mom) has over a man is a significant factor in the generalized male fear of women, the need to control them, to feel superior, and to concoct symbolic images of the witch, the devouring woman, Medea, et al.

Unfortunately, when we are angry (at a previous lover, perhaps) and have not directed it toward the person involved, it is all too easy for such unexpressed hostility to leak out before we realize what we are doing; a new lover's disappointing performance may touch off the buried pain of a past rejection. It is something to be consciously on guard against if you harbor unresolved anger toward someone else. (And just because a woman has no penis does not mean that a man can't just as effectively castrate her psychologically—and frequently does—so she does—and he does . . . ad infinitum).

On some level every man is aware of the tremendous power you can wield over his sexuality and he fears it. You can indeed offer him ecstasy or agony. Power requires responsibility if destructiveness is to be avoided. Such responsibility consists mostly of keeping that power judiciously in check through humanism and sensitivity.

Treat your power as though it were precious radium which must be used sparingly *and only to heal.*

Your lover is aware that nature has bestowed upon you a few gratuitous gifts: The responsibility for insertion not being yours, sexing is possible for you even if you're not fully aroused; you can do this as long and as often as you *like*, and you are capable of many orgasms in succession. He cannot match you when you are functioning at the full female potential.

This can be a threat to him if his self-esteem is tied up with the masculinity-virility myth.

Any sexual advantage is something neither to be ignored nor flaunted, but to be accepted and included in your consideration of him as a human being.

You would not want him to think less of you as a human being because you don't climax occasionally or are indisposed with menstrual cramps; certainly he is no less a man because he

occasionally does not get an erection or loses it at an inconven-
ient time.

It would be as inconsiderate of you to *expect* that he come up
with another erection immediately after ejaculating as it would
be for him to *expect* you to have one orgasm more than you
already had. If you want more sexing, you can try to arouse him
after waiting forty to sixty minutes. If you want an orgasm
sooner, get it another way. How?

Getting Yours

Let him know you would like one, either verbally or by simply
placing his hand on your mons or vulva (getting him started in
the rhythm and pressure you like if necessary).

An alternative is to throw one leg over his so that the top of his
thigh is pressing against your mons and vulva. If there's not
enough pressure, bending his knee slightly will help and flexing
his thigh muscle really gives you something to press against—
which is exactly what you do. In other words, if you were lying
on his left, your head on his left shoulder, you would put your left
leg across his left leg (in between his legs). Without removing
your head from his shoulder (or chest), you can thrust your pelvis
forward and bear down on the top of his thigh, pressing your
mons, clitoral area and vulva against the hardest part of his
thigh.

It may help to put some lubricant on his thigh or on your
genitals, but it may not be necessary if you're already quite
excited. This method allows him to be a participant, while
making no demands upon him. (You may wish to use it after
giving him a love-in.) Another way is to hand him a vibrator and
show him where to hold it.

The last alternative is, of course, to do it yourself and there's
nothing wrong with that, either.

If you didn't have an orgasm during sexing, he'll probably be
more than happy to give you a hand—or tongue. If you did, and

he knows it, but you ordinarily like more than one—it would be best to wait until you are sexcommunicating about your preferences (do it *soon*) and then mention your desire for several.

PUTTING HIM IN THE MOOD

Let him know how much you care about him, verbally and nonverbally. (This may be the time for a loving massage.)

Rub up against him and kiss him passionately. Use your tongue. Undulate and press your body against his genital area. Slip his hand under your clothes. Slip yours under his. Let him know *he's* exciting *you*. Remark how warm it's suddenly become. Unbutton, unzip or remove something to help you "cool off." He may pick up the cue and slowly undress you as you continue making love. You, of course, do the same for him.

Or, if he's been responding and has a hard-on, ask him if he's hot and then undress him—slowly—continuing the lovemaking as you go.

Or, he may enjoy a bit of fellatio play standing up with his clothes still on.

If things aren't moving that fast, ask him to dance with you—or dance for him in something sensuous. Or do a slow striptease. (Revealing your genitals is quite a universal aphrodisiac).

If you just finished sexing and you want to arouse him again, unless you know from experience that you can be direct, it's best to be subtle and inspire him to think it's *his* idea to do it again. Otherwise he may feel called upon to give a command performance. So don't go grabbing for his genitals just yet, although in a little while you can put a friendly, undemanding hand upon his penis while you tell him how beautiful it is.

But first, kiss him and tell him how great the sexing was; how he drove you crazy (going into detail about the things that drove you wild can be very arousing). Then run your hands and fingers

all over him and tell him how you love the feel of his body and
can't keep your hands off him.

(Caution: Say nothing that you don't really feel.)

Tell him what turns you on; *show* him what positions you'd
like to try "sometime."

Have you ever tried some of those yoga exercises in the nude?
That can be a mind-blower.

Once he has a full erection and shows signs of wanting to do
something about it, anything goes. For a special treat, give him
the primal lick (Chapter 8).

P.S. If he doesn't respond to your initial feelers, withdraw
gracefully, without ill feelings. It's no reflection on you. He's just
shot his wad for now.

All this will work just fine if your love life is on a pretty even
keel. But in the life of every couple that's been together long
enough there comes a slump. Maybe just a little one. Or
sometimes a big one. Then some extra effort is required on both
parts. (Check the variety chapter.) But before you go on to those
activities, you may have to pave the way and reassure him of
your love.

Making his favorite dish is an old standby—because it sends a
good message. Or you could bake him a cake that says, "I love
you." Be flirtatious. Make love with your eyes. Spruce up your
appearance. Leave him love notes of the sort suggested in the
love-in. Or write him a love poem.

Now, writing a love poem is much easier to do when things are
up than when they're in a slump. What I do is this. Since I can't
sit down and decide to write a poem—*it* tells *me* when to stop and
listen—when I *am* inspired I don't immediately show it to him. I
wait for a special occasion or some time when I want to give our
loving an extra boost—and it will. Then I slip it onto his pillow,
or produce it at the right moment. (I try to make it a time when
our son's not likely to come pounding at the door.)

Remember, you don't have to be Emily Dickinson or Eliza-
beth B. Browning. Just write down your *feelings*. (Occasionally I

see a funny or beautiful card and save that for the proper occasion.)

Do anything and everything you know or suspect is provocative for him—including as many senses as possible.

Subtlety can keep him from feeling put upon or, if he's just not ready, that he has failed you. Anything that leads to a lack of confidence on his part is a setup for impotence.

Sex, Love and Insecurity

As the message gets through, louder and clearer, that sex is something woman is not only allowed, but *supposed* to enjoy, she feels more free to assert her desire. Unfortunately what may sometimes seem like desire for sex is actually something else.

Because of social conditioning, it is not uncommon for a woman to feel that she is loved only when she is sexually desired. Then she is reassured that she is indeed lovable: Her breath and body smell sweet and fresh, her sheets are not dingy, she doesn't have the frizzies or dishpan hands, she's got the skin he loves to touch, sparkling white teeth and bedroom eyes (provided her eyelashes hang in there).

Sexing gives her reassurance for a little while. So she wants it as often as possible.

That may work out very nicely when the relationship is young, but eventually when the urgency and novelty of new love slows down, he may prefer a more pedestrian (but no less loving) gait. It can get to be a drag when you're constantly *expected* to perform.

At first he might get a kick out of telling the fellows how he comes home to find his bride so eager that dinner gets cold while they make love. But after a year or two he'd rather have a hot meal, some of the time anyway.

So one night he wants to cool it—the sex, not the dinner. But she panics. He always wanted it before. Something must be wrong. She wants to know if he is sick, or angry, or upset, or *what*. When all these have been eliminated her initial reaction is confirmed: "He doesn't love me like he did."

Many a male has taken his first steps toward impotence in trying to force a performance for a wife who complains, "Don't I please you any more?" In the case of one couple, the wife insisted on sexing every night because otherwise she couldn't fall asleep! Even worse than being a sex-object is being a sleeping pill.

In the situation where one spouse desires sex more often than the other, extra doses of demonstrative love and affection can help keep him or her from feeling rejected.

The First Time

Have you ever had the kind of nightmare where you tried to run or scream and couldn't?

Were you ever left speechless? You want dreadfully to say something but your tongue fails you.

Pause a moment and relive those feelings.

To do so can give you some idea of what it is like for a man when his phallus fails him. And the extent of your ability to empathize with his feelings can deeply affect your relationship. Compassion and understanding are called for, and are essentials in a healthy sensual life. Fear and scorn are the enemies.

Perhaps you've been lucky and have never been faced with an occasion when a lover couldn't get an erection. Within a sexually active lifetime, you're bound to, eventually. How you handle it is important. The fact that it happened is, in itself, exceedingly unimportant—about on the level of someone who ordinarily sleeps well but can't get to sleep one night. If you were both normal, healthy people, it would be of little concern to you, and he'd sleep like a rock the next night.

Does that mean that you should flutter about, jabbering how it's *perfectly* all right and normal and *not to worry* because *you don't mind at all.* No. NO. *NO!* There's no point in pretending that it's *perfectly fine* with you, when it's understandable that you'd be somewhat disappointed. There's no point in pretending *anything*. Especially since it won't work. But neither does that mean you should show him *how* disappointed you are, especially since that can be overcome by your empathy for his feelings.

You don't need to do somersaults, make miracles or create a sexual spectacular for him. When in doubt about what to do, say nothing and *touch*—not to turn him on, just to give him your warm feelings.

Very few, if any, words are required. And then it's not so much what you say as how you say it. It's easier for me to tell you what *not* to say or do. That's because an appropriate response is one that comes from an appropriate attitude, genuinely expressed.

Given that you haven't had a fight or a cold-war power struggle and you haven't just dented his bright red Maserati, you must first of all know that his lack of erection is no index of his feelings for you, or how much you turn him on. (On the contrary, a man with potency anxiety frequently fails with the woman about whom he cares the most, precisely because he is more concerned about what she thinks of him. So in a sense it can be a compliment, not an insult.)

His lapse is neither your responsibility nor a measure of your womanliness.

If it's never or seldom happened before, more than likely he's had too much to drink (the most common reason), is overtired or there's some other simple, physical reason that will go away with some sleep and relaxation (except in the case of tranquilizers which can cause impotence).

An appropriate attitude, verbal or nonverbal, is a mental shrug of the shoulders: "Oh, well, that was one drink too many. Let's just cuddle up and go to sleep."

Show him that he is infinitely more important to you than his erection. If you turn your back on him and go to sleep—or toss and turn—he has every reason to believe you're upset. But if you do some cuddling, give him some undemanding love, then fall peacefully asleep in his arms, he will be reassured.

Impotence

If it turns out that he does have an impotence problem, that may be solved if you care enough about him to work it out together. For most normal cases involving loss of confidence after one failure and subsequent *fear of failure* (which is self-fulfilling) this can be resolved with comparative ease when the situation is such that he *can't fail* because he is not *expected* to produce an erection.

What to Do

Be most careful to avoid, by word or action, anything that might cast the slightest doubt on his lovemaking, or the size of his genitals. This means that you must rid *yourself* of doubts and have full confidence in him—this will give him confidence. It is not so much what you say that counts, but your attitude, a lack of anxiety that is communicated nonverbally.

Above all, tell and show him every way you know how deeply you feel about him, how much you appreciate his qualities as a human being. Verbalize your admiration for the things he does, the way he handles situations, etc. *Minimize* criticism.

Let him know how much you enjoy any touching and lovemaking that takes place.

Although you may get him in the mood by the way you move and dress, by talking about things that are sexually arousing to him, dancing, looking at erotica, arranging a sensuous meal, etc., *be subtle*. Let him initiate the love play, if possible. When it's *his* idea, he feels less pressure and demand upon him.

Focusing

Sensate Focus (proper sensual focusing) and freedom from

anxiety will overcome impotence and orgasmic dysfunction alike.

It is impossible to focus properly while tracking one's perform-ance. Therefore, the cure, as the sex clinics practice it, consists of getting his mind *off* his erection and *on* your mutual pleasure. That done, *his body will respond naturally and effortlessly*. Demanding, cajoling or overt seduction will not work.

This means that the priorities in his mind (and possibly yours) must be reversed. He must be helped to realize that for you (and him) the most important aspect of your lovemaking is the eros, caring and affection expressed in caressing, holding, touching—not how or even if you have an orgasm or he, an erection. Instead of focusing on arousing *him*, remember that it's exciting for a man to know that you want to be touched and stimulated by him, i.e., if *you* bring your breast or vulva to his hand or mouth.

MINI-MINIMOON

Although it is particularly important in the case of any sexual dysfunction to follow the directions completely for all experi-ments and explorations, the minimoon is handled differently for overcoming impotence. It should be done in an abbreviated manner at least three times (preferably on succeeding days) and should last no longer than is pleasurable for both of you, even if that's only a half-hour. All parts of each other's bodies should be explored as described in Chapter 4, EXCEPT THE GENITALS. On the fourth session the genitals can be stimulated with a lubricant, each of you showing the other what is most pleasurable. There should be no coitus and no expectation of erection or orgasm.

This mini-minimoon, including genital stimulation, should replace any efforts at coitus, whenever and as often as you both desire. It is the most important step in the "cure."

An ideal time to begin the sequence of mini-minis is during a vacation or extended weekend when you are both fairly relaxed. At some point include the explorations for helping each other connect. The sessions can be gradually lengthened, and various explorations for lovers may be included or done separately.

During an exploration, any activity that makes him too uncomfortable or anxious should be discontinued, discussed later and possibly tried again some other time. It may be the very thing he needs the most.

If he has been getting erections pretty regularly during the mini-minis, the next step is to lie quietly together after he has achieved an erection, until it subsides, then start over again so that he can *gain confidence in his ability to regain an erection* after it has receded. That accomplished, you can kneel above him, play with his penis and when it's erect insert it yourself, *calmly and confidently*. You don't want to fumble around or push it in hurriedly as though you're afraid he won't last. Stay seated quietly on him, moving *slowly* and *undemandingly* back and forth, following the angle of his penis.

You can simultaneously stimulate him in other ways—play with his testicles, his nipples, kiss him.

If you have learned to use your inner muscles (see sexercises, Chapter 16), you can sit perfectly still once he's in you and do some squeezing and undulating that will be highly pleasurable for him. It should be clearly understood that nothing more is expected at this stage. Any time the erection subsides, you can raise up and manipulate the penis to erection as you did before.

After he has been in you for a few minutes you can be still and let *him* move slowly and gently, focusing on his sensations *with no other goal in mind*.

Nonphysical Factors Are the Most Important

Avoid sexual activity when either of you is tired, tense or under stress from work or anything else. Try not to leave it till late at night *after* other activities have tired you. Also avoid it after a rich, heavy meal. Feed him a high-protein, low-calorie meal before sexing.

When making love, do not focus on his penis or check to see if it's erect. Focus on expressing your love in as many *other* ways as occur to you before you get around to the genitals. (I assume that you've memorized his inventory and his reactions during the minimoons.) Let your fingers cover his body, and do the same with your mouth. Apply everything you've learned from the minimoon and primal love-in chapters.

Talk to his penis lovingly as you play with it. Let him know how beautiful it is to you. Kiss and fondle it accordingly.

Practice your sensuous (oscillating) tongue technique to use on his genitals and other erogenous zones. (See Sexercises.)

Use erotic language. If you don't already know what sexual expressions arouse him, ask—and use them! Tell him also what excites *you*.

Fellatio Play

His desire to have you place his penis in your mouth as part of lovemaking is perfectly natural; most men enjoy it tremendously, unless you are prone to baring your teeth. That is not usually a problem on the down-stroke, but as you come back up, the counter friction may pull your lips away from your teeth unless you resist that tendency. Experiment and practice your technique by inserting both your thumbs in your mouth (one *on top* of the other, not side by side) and then withdrawing them. Do you feel your teeth on your thumbs as you pull them out? Now try it again, keeping your lips over your teeth, which should be drawn as far back as possible.

If you have reservations about this, read the section on genital loving in Chapter 12.

Perhaps you've no objection to oral-genital contact but are afraid of having him ejaculate into your mouth.

It used to scare me. I imagined great globs of mucus fluid spurting down my throat, with me gagging and sputtering as I dashed for the bathroom! The consistency bothered me, too. I envisioned it feeling sort of slimy, like soft-boiled egg white, which I abhor as a result of having it forced down my throat as a child. And this ejaculate would be "forced down." Or so I thought. *None of this could be further from the truth.*

As an initiation before deciding whether to go further some other time, I recommend putting a dab of semen on your finger and tasting it. It's not whipped cream, but it's far from unpleasant. Hurdle number one.

As for choking on it—surprise! You don't even get to taste it because the half-teaspoonful of semen (or full teaspoon if he hasn't ejaculated for four or five days) is combined with your own saliva and you feel almost cheated because you hardly know it's there.

The semen itself is *not harmful to swallow*, being clean and pure water; minerals; nitrogenous substances like protein; lipids; fructose (sugar); organic acids; vitamins (like C, choline, inositol), and enzymes. It's a low-calorie dessert. (And need I reassure anyone that it's impossible for sperm to swim from the intestines to the reproductive organs?)

Ordinarily, if you have objections to fellating him to orgasm, a lover will obligingly withdraw before the point of no return. (For most couples fellatio is merely one part of their foreplay and is only occasionally continued to orgasm.) If he has potency anxieties, however, it would be preferable not to restrict him from ejaculating during fellatio play. And there are men who respond better to fellatio than to manual stimulation.

Be sure to get into a comfortable position for the greatest mutual enjoyment. He may, for example, find it most exciting when he is standing. In that case you might prepare a low stool or some pillows to kneel on. Or you can sit on the side of the bed while he stands in front of you. Or you may prefer the sixty-nine position. See that you don't depress the penis much below its natural angle when it is erect, since that can be painful. If he is not circumcised, draw back his foreskin as far as possible to give him maximum sensation.

DIVING FOR PLEASURE

When you slide down toward the base of the penis and back up, keep your tongue pressing against the corpus spongiosum, which looks like a vein running from the frenum to the base. This increases the pleasure and brings your tongue right up against the highly sensitive frenum. Imagine that you're trying to suck out all the juice, starting as far down on the base as you can reach and sliding very, *very* slowly toward the head, where the pressure should lighten slightly because that's usually the most sensitive area.

CIRCLE GAME

Allowing your moist tongue to protrude between your moist lips, run your relaxed lips (and tongue) around and around the head of his penis circling clockwise and then counterclockwise. For the ultimate touch, oscillate your tongue as you do this.

THE PUMP

As you move your head up and down and side to side, circularly, the penis head can also be slowly and *gently* sucked, then pumped in and out of your mouth several times. More vigorous suction can alternate with relaxation: suck—relax—suck—relax. . . .

While your mouth is busy, let your fingers roam over his scrotum, perineum, anus and any other voluptuous places you can reach. To increase erotic sensation you can pull the skin of his penis taut by gripping the shaft and pulling firmly toward its base.

Ask him to teach you what is most pleasurable for *him*, because everyone is different—for instance the shaft of the penis is usually not terribly sensitive, but can vary considerably, and occasionally someone is more sensitive near the base of the penis than the head. That is why, although my recommendations are generally effective, you must consult your lover if you wish to give him optimum stimulation.

For example, some men, but not all, respond with an erection to heavy pressure with a finger around midpoint on the perineum (between balls and anus) and may also receive added enjoyment from such pressure at the point of orgasm.

Play with many different kinds of stimulation. If he likes a vibrator, use that in addition to soft, sensuous objects.

When you know the things that turn him on the most, plan a primal love-in for him.

Other Potency Problems

Premature ejaculation is the most common form of male sexual dysfunction, affecting and frustrating many millions of men. Some experts define it as inability to postpone ejaculation longer than thirty seconds, others say a minute, and still others, three minutes after the penis has entered the vagina.

Masters and Johnson, who have developed the most effective method thus far for curing premature ejaculation, do not define the problem according to a rigid time limit. They see it as a problem when at least 50 percent of the time, a man cannot postpone ejaculation until the woman has an orgasm, provided her inability to achieve orgasm is due *solely* to his lack of control.

Therefore, if a woman habitually climaxed after seven to ten minutes of thrusting, her lover's habitual ejaculation in six minutes would be premature unless he or she were able to keep going, afterwards.

Fortunately this seems to be the easiest of all sex problems to cure, according to research with Masters and Johnson's squeeze technique. This requires your active participation in the form of learning how to squeeze his penis just before he reaches the ejaculatory point of no return. The technique is described and illustrated in the *Yes Book of Sex—You Can Last Longer*, designed by the National Sex Forum, which is affiliated with San Francisco's Glide Memorial Methodist Church. A second choice would be the paperback, *Understanding Human Sexual Inadequacy* by Belliveau and Richter.

Ejaculatory Dysfunction

The opposite problem from premature ejaculation is the inability to ejaculate *within the vagina* no matter how long or active the thrusting. Sometimes it is a recent problem or it may have existed since his very first sexual encounter. Whatever the duration, the problem is psychological in origin and can be the result of a mental trauma such as being severely punished for masturbating. Sometimes it is due to a fear of getting the woman pregnant.

An effective cure includes dealing with the psychological components. In terms of physical methodology, Masters and Johnson's first step is to have the woman stimulate the man to orgasm manually. Once this is accomplished, the next step is to manually bring him close to orgasm and then, kneeling above him, for the woman to insert his penis and move actively in his rhythm to elicit orgasm. If this does not succeed, she goes back to manual stimulation and then inserts it again. If he ejaculates as he enters and just a few drops of semen get into the vagina, it can break the pattern.

There are some men who are able to ejaculate some of the time but other times cannot. This is not a serious problem, for if he has ejaculated within you once, he will be able to do it again if you and he relax about it.

You can help, but *you are not responsible for his erection or his orgasm,* only for your mutual pleasure.

Security is a copout
to life
To feel the earth beneath

        my feet
to breathe a full breath
to listen to my body,
        to my organism
that is my only security—
        one breath at a time

18

POTENCY: WHAT YOU CAN DO FOR YOURSELF

THE FIRST time is a shock. You've always been able to rise to the occasion and *now* of all the times to let you down! It's mutiny! Nothing works.

What's wrong?

There the trouble starts, with the idea that this *should not* have happened, therefore something is *wrong* with you. Your penis acts like it's dead and won't ever work again.

Impotence is the specter that paralyzes. As a term it is misused and misunderstood so that a man who fails even once may think, "My God, I'm impotent!" That's like saying, "I'll never be able to eat again," on one of those unhappy occasions when you can't keep food down. According to Masters and Johnson, a man is not considered impotent unless he fails to attain erection during 25 percent or more of *all* his opportunities.

But the masculine mystique told you that it only happens to some poor sexual loser, not to you because you're virile—a potent man. But now it has, so what does that make you? Even men who know that one lapse does not mean impotence can still fear (unnecessarily) that this is a warning sign that old age and impotence are creeping up.

If you are *not* controlled by the mystique, then you are the same *potent* man who was simply under par for one reason or another. You don't go around expecting it to happen (or it will), but you don't panic if it does, knowing that it happens to most men some time or other.

For many other men that scenario is the first act of a personal tragedy.

For Dave it started, as is common, with an overdose of a popular drug—alcohol. After one drink too many he found his body unable to follow through with the gleam in his lover's eye. She said nothing, but mentally raised her eyebrows. Her body language asked, "What's wrong with you?"

"I guess I drank too much," he said, but he wasn't entirely convinced. He and she both knew that at other times he'd drunk too much but that hadn't stopped him. (If Dave considered the many physical and emotional conditions that make the same drug affect the same person differently from one occasion to the next, it still wasn't enough to allay his unconscious fears.) Next day he was full of confidence—or so it seemed. "I'll show her," he thought. But mainly he was out to prove to *himself* that there was nothing wrong. With the command performance he set up for himself he didn't have a chance.

After his second failure, the idea that he was impotent really grabbed Dave in the gonads. He had bought the cultural myth that a real man should always be ready for sex. So whenever he tried, his manhood was on the block. With it came fear of his lover's rejection. Naturally he was scared stiff-less.

Dave now developed the habit common to persons with potency difficulties and other sexual dysfunctions as well: He put himself under tremendous pressure to perform—both for himself and for his lover—then monitored his performance.

He watched himself constantly, becoming a spectator (and director) at his own performance. It's as though part of him was split off, hovering about the room worrying, watching and evaluating like an ambitious parent monitoring his frightened child at an audition. Dave, however, was not aware of the extent of his pressure to perform and totally unaware of his spectator role.

Masters and Johnson found that the performer-spectator split was a major factor to be overcome in their treatment, and they were not easily dealt with when the person was unaware of them.

To reduce a patient's fears of poor performance they reassure him after a medical examination that there is no physical cause for his impotence. (It is estimated that only 5 percent of impotence stems from physical impairment. The remaining 95 percent are affected by *fear* of failure. However, on the occasion of the *initial* failure that set off the subsequent fear, a majority of the causes seem to be of physical origin such as overtiredness or drugs, with alcohol at the top of the list.)

The sex clinic patient is reassured that he need make no *effort* to do anything at all in order to get an erection; that in essence nobody can teach him how to have one because *that is something his body already knows*. Masters and Johnson then convince him that they will provide the conditions conducive for his mind/body to become sexually aroused and potent. They must give him this reassurance and confidence in order for him to accomplish the key activity in their cures—sensate focus.

Suppose for a moment that you were brought up to believe that eight hours sleep *every* night was essential in order for you to function properly and maintain a good self-image. Then one night, for the first time, you spend hours tossing and turning, unable to sleep because of something at your job or in your personal life. You've heard of insomnia and considered it a neurotic affliction, having taken pride in being a sound sleeper.

You desperately resort to counting sheep and when that doesn't work you think, "My God, I've got insomnia!" You feel terrible the next day and work hard at convincing yourself that tonight you'll sleep like a rock. Somebody at work gives you suggestions for getting to sleep, and so armed, you approach the bed. You really are tired, but you go through a prescribed routine for relaxing your body, all the while monitoring your sleepiness. Your body is ready, but your cortex is watching and waiting. You get a pleasant, sinking feeling, then it nudges you, opens its big mouth and says, "I think I'm falling asleep." Oh, well, back to the sheep.

Your anxiety now mounts and the next night you try to will yourself to sleep and fail again. "This is terrible," you think, "my work is suffering and everything's falling apart!"

Substitute erection for sleep, impotence for insomnia, and you have the dynamics.

If the labels "impotent" and "insomniac" didn't exist, a person could not think, "I must be impotent." He could simply think of what happened as a unique *experience* rather than a *condition*. Impotence and insomnia are emotionally charged concepts. Applying the *label* to oneself reinforces the malfunction. The body, being one with the mind, carries out the mental diagnosis.

What You Can Do

You only have a potency *problem* if you *think* you have one. What you define as a problem is an illusion—or delusion. Ideas of gloom and doom can become *self*-fulfilling prophecies.

Think back to the first time it happened. Had you been physically or mentally fatigued, drinking, overeating, taking tranquilizers, barbiturates or some other drug that affects potency? * Perhaps you had been ejaculating so frequently that your semen had not yet been replenished. Or you were really not in the mood, but felt you *should* please your lover, who was.

George, for instance, wilted up against a sick, hard-to-get game player who muttered at the crucial moment, "Well, you finally got what you wanted."

If you recall a reason, either physical or psychological, the odds are very high that any ensuing dysfunction was not due to an illness or to a hormone deficiency that some men develop in a male kind of climacteric. (Hormone treatment can take care of

---

* Dr. Fellman, professor of genital-urinary surgery at University of Michigan Medical School, found many cases of impotence among men taking large doses of guanethedine for high blood pressure.

that.) A regular sex life is likely to keep the hormones flowing adequately. However, mental or physical stress can disturb normal functioning of glands and various body secretions.

Cigarette smoking has been listed by Dr. Donald Hastings among drugs and chemicals that reduce potency. In 1970 the results of further research in this area were reported by Brazilian doctors Fish, Albuquerque and Brito, who stated at a press conference:

> People who do not smoke show a more intensive sex life and so do those who give up smoking. . . . It really does cause a reduction in sexual activity in persons aged between twenty-five and forty since the nicotine poisons the central nervous system and affects the whole body.

If you have the slightest suspicion that any potency difficulties are caused by an ongoing physical problem, ease your mind by having a thorough medical examination *and tell your doctor why you want it.* Then he'll test you for diabetes or any other potency-impairing illness.

Unless there has been a physical or surgical trauma secondary impotence can be reversed in most cases whether a man is thirty or eighty.

REEXAMINING YOUR FEARS AND FANTASIES
Aging and Potency

Aging does not cause impotence. But some aspects of aging can frighten a man into impotence if he does not understand that what is happening is normal.

If you're in competition with yourself (as perfectionists are) and *expect* of yourself certain sexual abilities in your forties, fifties or sixties that you had in your teens or twenties, you will feel inadequate if you fail.

When you were eighteen you could be angry, tired, or loaded

and it could have little effect on your erection. (Note I didn't say "scared"—that would blow it at any age.)

You might not have had much control over your ejaculation and ended up quick on the trigger, but you were so perpetually horny that getting it down was likely to be more of a problem than getting it up.

So now you're older and the hormones aren't propelling you along like a tidal wave. You can't get another erection as soon after ejaculating as you used to. (If you're over sixty, it may take twelve to twenty-four hours.) And you don't have as urgent a physical need for frequent release because your seminal fluid doesn't build up as fast.

Does that mean you're less virile than a multiejaculatory youth? If frequency of erection and ejaculation were the mark of a man, then a teenager would be more of a man than a forty-year-old. Yet the contrary is true. If anything the mature man can be *more* potent: He has better ability to postpone ejaculation as he gets older and more experienced. All his experience, maturity and increased sensitivity (you have it if you're into this book) make him a better lover by far than he was at twenty.

If you don't allow soft living, alcohol, tobacco or pill-popping to deteriorate you physically, you can reach your human *prime* of life at forty and maintain it at least a score of years—and more. (That goes for women as well, of course.)

Frequently, as people reach their forties, the inevitability of death becomes a reality and they grasp desperately for proof of youth. Whether or not they verbalize it to themselves, they decide to "enjoy life while they still can." And what is more symbolic of life than the sex act?

Sex in pursuit of youth, to "get it while you can," to make up for time lost developing successful roles in society—sex for these reasons is doing the right thing for the wrong reasons. Compulsive is not spontaneous. "Forced" sex requires more and more stimulus for arousal and eventually reaches the point when nothing works. Then a person thinks, "It's a sign of old age creeping up." But it's only a sign that your mind is trying to will your body to perform. That kind of split is contrary to nature, which is you.

Janov points out in *The Primal Scream* that tension can be mentally eroticized and labeled "sex:"

> As evidence for this I cite the fact that the majority of patients who lose their tension in the first few weeks of therapy also lose their sex drive for a while. In some cases, it disappears completely for a period of weeks. . . .
>
> Before therapy, I had all kinds of suppressed feelings which I let out through sex [one of his patients reported]. I thought I was sexy. I could do it all the time. Now I know that my high sex urge was all those other feelings trying to get out in any way they could. I shot them out of the end of my penis. It was no wonder that orgasm often was painful for me. I used to think that it was natural for the climax to be painful. I climaxed early in sex because the pressure of all these other hidden feelings were pushing for release faster than I could control them.

A moderate or gradual decrease in frequency of the sex urge is *not* a sign of creeping impotence. *You can be fully potent into your nineties* (probably all of your life) if your mind/body is reasonably healthy. Far from weakening the heart, a *regular* sex life strengthens it.

An active sex life continued—even if frequency is somewhat diminished—into your older years is your best potency and health insurance. It keeps the sex glands active (but if they start dragging, they can be nudged medically). If you can accept some changes in desire or occasional erective failure with good grace, sex can spice the quality of your entire life.

In Masters and Johnson's research group aged fifty-one to eighty-nine, those who had relatively high levels of sexual activity reported similar levels from their formative years, no matter whether it involved another person or masturbation. That does not mean if your activity was low or nonexistent at some period in your life that you cannot be just as potent as the

Masters and Johnson group when you get older and have the opportunity.

Even if for one reason or another men in their seventies or eighties have had to suspend their active sex lives for many months or years, they have still been able to return to potent sexual activity, barring physical disability. During such a period when a man is not functioning sexually with a partner, Dr. Reuben strongly recommends that men in their older years masturbate to avoid the possibility at advanced ages of not being able to regain their potency after a prolonged hiatus.

However the dictum, "Use it or lose it," is not inexorable. If you are bedridden for a long period, you may have trouble walking when you get up, but if you keep at it, the other part of nature's law works to your benefit: The more you use it the stronger it gets. More primally sensuous Eastern cultures know this and make it a custom to use masturbation for increasing their sexual abilities.

The Too-Frequent Ejaculation Myth

Many men have fears that too frequent ejaculation (by any means) will have the opposite effect of weakening them physically or mentally. This is directly traceable to the masturbation/ insanity myth that has been laid to rest scientifically, but not emotionally, in cultures with a history of sexual repression.

Some men also act as though they think their semen is rationed: Life allots them a certain number of ejaculations and once the limit is reached—impotence comes knocking at the door. Others seem to feel the cutoff is at a certain age. So when they approach whatever they unconsciously think is the cutoff, they get compulsive about squeezing as much action as possible out of their remaining years. Both attitudes are self-defeating. Grasping at sex eventually has the same effect as grasping tightly at a beautiful flower.

As Dr. Simeons points out, "Sex is absolutely self-limiting and cannot be indulged in to excess as far as the organic function is concerned, nor is there a shred of clinical evidence to suggest that its indulgence to the limits of capability is in any way harmful to the body or the mind." * The same is true of masturbation and the only thing that is harmful is the guilt and fear of "entirely fictitious consequences," he says.

The Myth of Size

As we learn about many things, bigger does not equal better. This is certainly true of the male genitals. For a woman it's not the size but what you do with it that counts. Her vagina will *expand to fit* any but perhaps the most unusually large penis.

A problem is more likely to arise in the case of a rather short vaginal barrel and a long penis, rather than the reverse, and then only in exceptionally deep positions. If you recall that most of the vaginal congestion and sensation occurs in the outer third of the vagina, there is no particular advantage to a long penis.

If there is a preference, it is sometimes for the thicker penis, especially in the case of women who are stretched after childbirth. However, the Kegel exercise can take care of that problem.

Furthermore, a penis that looks small in its flaccid state can expand considerably when erect, equalling or surpassing one that looks larger when flaccid. Neither is penis-size related to the height of a man, *and is most assuredly no measure of his maleness.*

Take the Pressure Off

In this enlightened time taboos are being removed and information disseminated that should help take the pressure off the man who is concerned about whether he can manage to get his penis erect enough for coitus. (It is even possible to use one's hands to insert a flaccid penis which, once in, can then become erect.)

* *Man's Presumptuous Brain*, E. P. Dutton and Co., Inc., 1962.

The taboos against mutual oral and manual stimulation to orgasm have now been relegated to nineteenth-century history. And research shows (as already indicated) that it is the woman's clitoris, not the vagina, that corresponds to the glans of a man's penis in sensitivity and functions as an orgasmic receptor-transformer. It is for this reason that women have had such a difficult time achieving orgasm from penile-vaginal stimulation alone.

Therefore, for an orgasm alone she does not need your penis, which can be less effective in satisfying her than your tongue or finger. Most efficient, in terms of stamina, agility, and sensitivity, is your finger. The only advantage the tongue has is natural lubrication.

At a party one evening I met a man suffering from multiple sclerosis, which had left him impotent. He wasn't there long before he received a phone call and left. My hostess later told me it was one of his girlfriends, and that attractive young women were constantly seeking him out. He had a reputation as a sensuous lover—and it was all done with hands and tongue.

The fact that a man, for whatever reason, cannot get or maintain an erection makes him no less a man, no less a human being, and in all ways but one, no less a lover. That is a complaint I have with the second Masters and Johnson book. The title, *Human Sexual Inadequacy*, reinforces the concept that if one does not *achieve* society's highest, competitive standards, then one is inadequate.

That is nonsense!

Certainly at one time in the ancient history of homo sapiens the sexual potency of each person was essential to survival of the species and perhaps that is why it came about that to be impotent or barren was a cause for grief and shame. It was passed down from one generation to the next along with other myths, mores, religions, secular edicts and attitudes that may have been life-preserving in origin. Now they are obsolete.

In sex for procreation, it was the *duty* of the husband to ejaculate into his wife's vagina, to impregnate her. In many cultures his failure to do so has been the woman's only grounds for divorce.

In sex for pleasure it does not matter—for the man or the woman—where or whether a man ejaculates.

In the case of the man with multiple sclerosis, he told women right out that he was impotent—but they came to him just the same.

So the first step in taking the pressure off is to *know* that there is no physical basis to your problem, that the culprit is fear itself causing *you* to watch and judge yourself.

The second step is to realize that you are no less a man and lover—that you can make love to and satisfy a woman without having an erection—as in the primal love-in.

Talking *the Pressure Off*

The third step is to find (if you haven't already) a woman who really cares for you. Forget about making out. *Once the right kind of feelings are there on her part,* level with her about your fears. If she has any heart, it'll open up to you. (And who wants someone without heart?) Women like and often *prefer* men who can admit their own imperfections and talk about their problems. They'll open up and want to know how they can help—and they can!

Carl had a minor problem. All his life he had never been able to get an erection the first night he spent with a woman. Finally he met a woman whose openness about showing that she liked him gave him the courage to say, "I've never been able to do much on the first night, but would it be all right if we just slept together?"

"Sure," she said, and meant it. They ended up doing a lot more than sleeping together.

The ability to risk and put yourself on the line by leveling *is an act of potency.* You're more than halfway there; whatever happens, you're ahead.

Confrontation Is Potent. Avoidance Is Impotent.

Don had a series of potency problems following a divorce. Now he was dating a girl who felt really right for him and he was afraid of blowing it, so he stayed away from sex. Finally he got up the nerve and approached it this way:

"I find you very exciting as a person, and I want you sexually as well, but I'm scared. I've had a number of incidents when I couldn't get an erection and my confidence just went down the drain. How would you feel if we were just loving and close without expecting anything more?" The attitude was right, so it worked.

Admitting that you're fallible can be difficult, especially when you've spent so much effort creating the opposite image, according to the blueprints handed you by a society that says, *"Follow the directions, and no mistakes!"* Throwing away the blueprints, being yourself—human and fallible—is infinitely more rewarding.

"But what if she rejects me?" you want to know.

That is one of the possibilities. I won't deny that some women do treat men as sex-objects. Nevertheless, they are still in the minority. If *your* interest in women has been mainly sexual, you are likely to feel that this is their main interest in you, as well; therefore, you must perform to avoid rejection. In that case your attitude toward women is central to your problem, and needs some overhaul.

Fortunately, most women are still more interested in finding someone they can love than finding a good sex partner. It is only when a woman is not interested in love or has not found it with you that she may give sexual performance first priority.

If you don't level with her and then do not get an erection, she may still reject you. And that rejection will be worse than if you had ascertained the extent of her interest beforehand.

Though rare, an invitation at first encounter may occasionally be more than lust; you have to size that up for yourself. If it's a stud she wants, your penis will sense it even if your cortex doesn't.

If that's all she wants, she will reject you and although she's no loss, you're better off not playing her game (unless you function well with someone you don't give a hoot about and get uptight with the one you do care for). Usually, the better you know a woman, the better you can judge whether you can open up to her.

If she seems to care for *you* (not the places you take her); if she's *not* judgmental, supercritical, moralistic or prudish; if she *is* warm, affectionate, giving; chances are fairly good that she'll respond well when you open up. Again, how you do it is all important. The wrong way is:

"Doris, there's something I think you should know. I'm impotent." It sounds like an announcement that you're dying of syphilis. Impotence sounds like an incurable disease, although nothing could be further from the truth. There's no point saddling yourself with that sort of negative label.

Neither do I mean for you to pretend a confidence you don't have. What I mean is the difference between saying "I'm an invalid" or "I've had this recurring illness for the past six months." The latter indicates that you still consider yourself a basically healthy man who has had a bout of illness but expects to get well. The former means you've given up.

A loving woman, if she has not kept abreast of the strides in sexual therapy, would tend to feel hopeless at the statement, "I'm impotent." Actually there is greater reason for optimism now than ever before, even if the problem is longstanding and chronic. Sex clinics can be highly effective when your motivation is right.

When she cares about you and knows that she *can* help you overcome the problem, the prognosis is good—*providing that you are willing to let yourself care for her as well.* The latter is not an uncommon problem for some bachelors, especially when they're afraid of getting trapped into marriage. They don't realize that men also need to feel affection and tenderness.

Phil had fantasies of Donna's vagina as a trap that would capture his penis in order to get pregnant and force him into marriage. Needless to say he couldn't keep his erection. He was trying to will his body to do something his mind feared.

Fear and stress inhibit sexual functions, secretions, hormonal and total body balance.

Suspend Expectations

The key to taking the pressure off is to *suspend your expectations.* Otherwise you may reject what is happening *now* in preference for something you *think* would be better. To suspend expectations allows you to find *what is happening* quite sufficient and *satisfying in itself.*

If you look back at some of your great sensual experiences, the one thing they will all have in common is that you didn't *expect* them. What happened was a spontaneous, delightful surprise.

Abandon yourself to the *experience* as you would float on water. Let *it* carry you.

Do your primal explorations with this attitude and *no coitus.* Let everything else be sufficient for you. Begin with the first experiences, *allowing* your*self* to *feel* whatever pleasure (or pain) ensues.

Allow yourself to regress to *your infant* (primal) *sensuality.*

When doing a partnered exploration stay in the here and now. This is especially vital and good practice for being totally there during sexing. The past is then; the future is *not yet.* The minute you think, "I hope I can keep it up," or "This is great, I'm doing pretty well," you're split into spectator and performer. *Thinking* is not in order—only feeling. Don't concern yourself with how long you maintain the erection and desire. If you are just enjoying yourself with no goal anxiety, you will not have cause to worry. *Now* focus on your pleasure. It will add to hers.

As I've said, her orgasm need not be a cause for concern. You can help her have one later, if necessary. And simultaneous orgasms are not worth bothering about, ever.

If you catch your mind wandering, *keep your eyes open* to increase your sensory stimulation. Learn to get pleasure by giving it.

Notice how much pleasure your lover is getting out of what's happening. Tune in to the changes in her breasts, face and skin as she becomes aroused. See how excited she gets as she plays with you. (She too gets pleasure from giving it.) *Focus on her,* not on your erection.

For Ron, what worked was getting totally involved in kissing his lover, focusing above his belt instead of below.

George reported that he was enjoying the sex play tremendously, but noticed he still wasn't getting an erection. Then he reminded himself, "We don't have to do that tonight," and it blossomed.

Suppose you were just about to leave for a movie and the babysitter called in sick, so you had to stay in. You would like to see it, but there'll be other opportunities and other movies, so it's no tragedy. And if you don't get an erection on one occasion, there's always tomorrow, or the next day.

If your sexual appetite is low, don't try sexing in order to please or placate her; abstain when you're tired. Don't stuff yourself on a dinner date. You'll get more oral pleasure from sexing.

An Exception

In some instances it can help to seize an opportunity. When a man has been experiencing a chronic potency problem with no erection at any time during sex play, he can regain confidence in his potency if he should awaken one morning (or during the night) with an erection and, dispensing with foreplay, enter, thrust vigorously and ejaculate as soon as possible so that he will have experienced an entire sexual cycle. This possibility should first be discussed with the woman, so that she is receptive should the opportunity arise. This should be followed up as soon as possible with nondemanding explorations.

Naming the Fear

The best way to overcome a potency problem is to eliminate the fear—fear of not being able to live up to perfectionistic sexual standards; fear of being considered less than a man and without worth.

I have discussed the major aspects of overcoming this fear: removing the shoulds and expectations of performance; ridding yourself of the masculine stereotype; allowing yourself to be human, therefore fallible; focusing solely on your sensations here and now.

You can do this when you and your lover accept the *fact* that she can be well loved and orgasmically satiated without coitus, the *love* play being at least as important, to most women. This way you can stimulate her to orgasm after orgasm, something that is often not possible to do even with the most potent penis.

If you do suffer distress at even an occasional erective failure, it is necessary to become aware of the inner dialogue that causes *you* to react this way when another man can accept it as he might an occasional lapse in his tennis game. (You might overreact to that as well, because of perfectionist, highly competitive standards.)

Examples of inner dialogue might include, "What's *wrong* with me! Can't I do anything right? What sort of a *man* am I when I can't even get it up! This is awful. I'm no good for anything." These are all completely irrational statements and will not hold up once they are brought into the light of full consciousness and examined.

Failures are human and normal. To accept this is essential, as is the fact that although you cannot match your sex hormone level as a teen-aged boy, you are certainly much more of a man today.

Competition

Another aspect is the need to compete with your own past

performance; with claims (usually exaggerated) of other men; even with your lover.

Competitiveness is a scourge—useful only in making money to pay for the heart attacks and other diseases it causes. Declining to compete will benefit you in all ways. Your buddy says he can get a hard on again right after ejaculating—and you don't. He's probably lying, but whether he does or not, there's no reason to expect it from yourself, or worry about it.

The culturally imposed idea that the man must always be ready for sex too often produces neurotic males who are overanxious about passing muster.

Are You a Stereotype?

The real you is not a stereotype. The real you doesn't have to prove he *is* a man. Nevertheless, you were subjected to so many inputs that told you to put a mask over the real you that the socialized layer of your mind (which isn't as smart as it thinks it is) may have obliged by creating such a mask—which it *calls* you. But the real you knows better and has its own way of conveying messages which remind you, on some level, that Mr. Masculinity is a phony. It takes a tremendous amount of energy to suppress your inner voice and wear that heavy mask.

The mask-voice frequently tells you to do things when you really don't feel like it. Sometimes the energy required to overcome that reluctance is lacking. The mask fails in its efforts to manipulate you.

In the chapter on stereotypes we discussed how the need for proving your masculinity can cause you to demand orgasmic performance from your lover. The same need can drive you to manipulate your *own* performance as well.

"I must perform in order to be loved" is the inner dialogue. But underneath you feel that kind of love doesn't count because it's only the mask she loves. "The real me is not lovable because my parents didn't accept me—they wanted the mask!"

When a person responds by manipulating his performance,

making himself a machine to be turned on, steered and operated on demand, it results in less feeling for himself and his lover. The less feeling he has, the less genuine sexual desire and ability. He may be most efficient at first, but he may eventually become secondarily impotent, because he has made a technical thing out of sex. He has omitted the sharing of feelings, fantasies, his inner self—all of which give meaning and intensity to sensations and make him a lover instead of a sexual athlete.

When you let your *emotions* flow and give of your self, experiencing *here and now,* for its own sake, potency is *inevitable*—because that *is* potency.

Potency is not a hard-on; it is a state of feeling.

The real you will seldom have a problem with potency—only the stereotype mask.

The Madonna-Prostitute Syndrome

Female stereotypes are carried to their illogical extreme in the madonna-whore dichotomy. This is a complex that usually requires psychotherapeutic help to overcome, although in most cases the man is too repressed to know that he needs help.

Janov touches on one of the symptoms in *The Primal Scream*: "Too often, the neurotic boy relates to parts (the sexual parts) of a girl; he cannot treat her as a whole person. This split has been called the madonna-prostitute complex—and good girls are bodyless (nonsexual), and bad girls are only sexual."

As he grows up, such a boy incorporates the strong moralistic parental attitudes that sexuality is dirty; therefore, sexual women are evil, no good. Good girls are an extension of mother, who is pure. (Upon finding out in what manner he was conceived, his reaction may be one of disbelief: "*My* mother would never do a thing like that! My father, yes, but my *mother,* never!")

That was about the level of Jack's feelings when he first heard about sex from a friend. Jack grew up in a devout Catholic family with strong inhibitions about the body and touching. The mention of sex was abhorrent, except in oblique, negative terms.

He married a "good" girl who was less inhibited but inexperienced. Whenever she showed strong sexual desires or tried to take the initiative, Jack was turned off. He insisted that she dress very conservatively, got her pregnant as soon as possible and started calling her "Mother." He manipulated her into the maternal role by loading her with domestic duties, decision-making, and demands that she look and behave nonsexual. He started out as a quick ejaculator (interspersed with erective failure when his wife was too sexual) and eventually slid into secondary impotence. He tried a prostitute but his conscience was too tyrannical to allow him to continue that outlet and he sought psychotherapy. Eventually he became open enough to benefit from primal sensuality techniques and became truly potent for the first time in his life.

Feminine Sexuality

A fully sexed woman is threatening to a man only if she feels he must keep pace with her and be a Boy Scout.

Although you may not always be prepared with an erection, *it need not keep you from giving her intimacy, good loving,* which, if her head is in the right place, she will value more than the particular method by which she attains orgasm. Lack of erection is no excuse for castigation or insult; and if she uses that to belittle you, *she* is the one who very likely needs help.

Avoid Monotony

Some men lose their potency after many years of monogamous marriage simply because they're enjoying it less. "The same old routine" just stops turning them on after a while. An exciting sex life includes surprises, innovations, *spontaneity.* Year after year of predictability can be deadly.

Couples invariably develop joint sex habits and routines but are usually afraid to talk about changing them lest they sound dissatisfied and hurt the other's feelings (image).

Swinging couples often say that one of the benefits is learning different ways of lovemaking from various partners, thus improving their marital sex. Sometimes they talk about their swinging experiences and use that as a way of letting each other know about new things that excite them. Knowing that they have competition inspires them to try harder to please each other, as perhaps they did when courting. One couple at a seminar said sex had gotten so poor before they became swingers that the husband got more pleasure out of masturbating. Over a fifteen-year marriage they had never learned to communicate, especially about sex. It is not necessary, however, to become swingers in order to break the routine and sexcommunicate (see Chapter 9).

Taking each other for granted is another important component of sexual monotony. Sex drops lower and lower on a growing list of priorities and responsibilities. The energy and creativity goes elsewhere.

"By the end of the day I'm too tired to think up anything new," is a common copout. Sex is no longer something they look forward to. It's a rerun.

Talking about and occasionally reevaluating your sex life is an invaluable aphrodisiac, provided you keep it constructive rather than critical (no grinding axes in the background). Use the explorations in communication (Chapter 9), with special attention to effecting a change of pace. It should be understood that the desire to change your sexual patterns is not necessarily an expression of dissatisfaction but rather a decision that varying your sex habits is at least as important for your life enhancement as seeing new places, buying new clothes, or redecorating your apartment (please start with the bedroom). A change of scenery is fun and rejuvenating.

After indulging in communication explorations you might logically reread the chapter on variety.

Do not skip explorations that don't sound sexual—on the contrary, do those first. Probably those that seem most distasteful to you are what you need the most. For example, if you suffer from secondary impotence and you read the instructions for the primal love-in (which is effective and mind-blowing), you may think it sounds great till she has you on the verge of orgasm, then pauses and backs you off.

The "ugh" reaction invariably comes from the man who is afraid he'll lose his erection at that point and won't get it back. But that's precisely what he needs, the confidence that it will come back, without effort. The love-in is structured for that to happen, and it will. Just don't fight it.

Treatment Plans

Should impotence be a real problem in your life, you can best overcome it if:

(a) you have a lover who will cooperate (and follow the suggestions in the previous chapter); and

(b) you follow this sequence

1. Experience A–G.

2. Exchange and discuss sensuality profiles and aggression-gentleness profiles.

3. *Schedule* weekly time for additional sexcommunication explorations.

4. Follow the instructions for mini-minimoons given in the previous chapter. Incorporate the use of Batacas (see pleasure blocks).

5. Plan sensuous meals.

6. Plan a primal love-in.

Tune in to the *spirit* and philosophy of primal sensuality. This is the key. Otherwise, when you do the above, you may simply be going through the motions.

There are some whose impotence is due not so much to the usual fear of failure and lack of confidence as to unresolved guilt or hostility toward a partner (frequently subconscious) or hostility toward someone else projected onto the partner. The primal ice cubes exploration can sometimes provide insight. Certainly with a good psychotherapist the psychic factors can be dredged up and the primal sensuality explorations will do the rest. There are a few sex clinics that offer psychological help together with counseling. (Don't let the word "clinic" fool you. They're very expensive.)

However, unless your problem is psychologically deep-seated, the program outlined should be effective.

Premature Ejaculation

It's the first time you're making out with a girl. You're excited, nervous (maybe a little guilty) and worried that someone might interrupt you before you finish. You didn't plan it that way, but you explode almost as soon as you penetrate. A certain type of conditioned reflex has been initiated. The body records it and remembers. If a similar scene is repeated in the first few sex experiences, the matrix is cast and you join an army of men labeled premature ejaculators. This is the opinion of sexologists. It makes sense.

The most effective deconditioning devised in the Western world for premature ejaculation is called the squeeze technique. There are other methods, however:

1. Relaxing your pubococcygeus muscles and buttocks.

2. Exhaling deeply with each forward movement of the pelvis, concentrating on moving as freely as possible, tilting your pelvis backward and arching your back before each thrust.

3. Learning to back off (pause or slow down) at the verge of orgasm (as in Experience D and the love-in). While backing off, there are things that minimize your stimulation and are usually nice for your lover, like pressing sideways (alternating sides) and slow, shallow thrusting, penetrating only your penis head.

4. Starting with slow movements or adopting her rhythm, which is probably not the most exciting for you.

5. Learning to enjoy and focus more fully in the *now*. That means being unconcerned about what will happen in the next minute. It means not watching or talking to yourself, not even to reassure yourself that it's all right. It means having the con-

fidence that there is no real cause for concern and that whatever happens is all right. You can't *think* that; it has to be *felt*.

Sometimes it's just a matter of inexperience. My young nephew Ron (who asked to be quoted by name) added the following based on his own experience with the problem:

"Do it a lot. Control comes with experience if you let it." And "I'm a night person, and I find I have infinite control right after I wake up, though the girl has to initiate it. (I don't feel like it that early in the day until I'm into it.) Maybe that would be reversed for a day person."

Least recommended methods are: using a thick condom; an anesthetic ointment; thinking nonsexual (but not unpleasant) thoughts.

Obviously these methods are meant to dull your sensations, something antithetical to the primal sensuality concept. Albert Ellis has suggested using them temporarily until the person gains confidence and experience in postponing ejaculation. I would go along with that only if:

It is not possible to use one of the other methods I recommended.

Delaying ejaculation is that important to you.

You can still enjoy sexing that way.

It would be best to approach it as a *temporary* learning tool and abandon it *soon*.

Remember, there is no rule that says you have to keep sexing any certain number of minutes. Some women also climax in several minutes or less, so if you both enjoy that, what's the problem? You might like to prolong the pleasure, but that's not a *problem*, just a nice thing to try.

Before you label yourself a premature ejaculator—ask the question, "Premature for whom?"

Ejaculatory Dysfunction

Like the occasional loss of erection, an occasional inability to ejaculate is no real cause for concern. In this situation the man has no problem maintaining an erection but is not able to ejaculate *during* coitus.

Should it become habitual, the cause is usually psychogenic. In this case the man is usually able to ejaculate through means other than vaginal-penile stimulation. *The taboo is the vagina.* There may be a subconscious feeling that the vagina is unclean relating to deeper attitudes toward women. This problem will respond to good professional counseling.

An occasional ejaculatory difficulty can be overcome by thoroughly relaxing your pubococcygeus muscle. (Yes, it works both ways.) At the same time adopt a relaxed, goal-free mental attitude—you don't *have to* ejaculate every time.

Rather than exhaust yourself *trying,* it might be best to stop entirely and rest (relax) a while, then start again if you're both in the mood. An alternative to complete cessation is letting your lover get on top and do the moving while you relax and enjoy it.

Priapism

To the premature ejaculator it may seem like a dream come true, but to the sufferer it can be a nightmare. Priapism is a condition in which a man maintains a constant erection (up to days on end) *without ability for release* or even sexual desire (except insofar as he thinks an orgasm will relieve him). *He definitely requires* medical treatment.

Summation

When you demystify your erection and feel reassured that it is easy when you experience adequate stimulation, you are then able to focus on the pleasurable stimulation instead of your erection. The kind and source of stimulation may be varied and indirect, such as losing yourself in the *pleasure* of stimulating your lover to orgasm (as in the primal love-in). But anything you do must be solely for its own pleasure. If you do it with the idea that perhaps you'll get an erection, forget it.

If you do get one and a voice inside you says, like an excited schoolboy, "Wow, look at that!" it's your spectator.

Allow yourself to feel pleasure, tenderness, love *and lust*. They complete each other.

Potency is the ability to plunge into your feelings and *risk*.

Potency is risk. So is life.

Plunge!

19

PRIMAL SENSUALITY

WE WERE born highly sensuous. That was our primal state.

Unfortunately most of us were weaned from it as children. The result of environmental turn-off is less sensory and emotional feeling.

There develops a dictatorship of mind over perception. Censorship is established over more and more sensory stimuli until some people can look at a card printed with "vulgar" words and simply not *see* them, while seeing neutral words perfectly.

Fortunately such dictatorship is not invincible. Paradise *can* be rediscovered. Many persons who have been involved in psychotherapy or some other form of self-discovery report that once they are more in touch with themselves, they see more clearly, colors are brighter and more exciting, things feel, taste, smell and look better.

Paradise is you.

In many books, the words sensuous or sensuality are used as euphemisms for sexuality. *But they are not the same.*

To focus on sensuality is to focus on humanity, not merely sexuality (which is a part of sensuality). Humanity involves experiencing ourselves and others as human beings *first* (not as man or woman, black or white). It is experiencing ourselves as *part of nature.* To be divorced from nature is to be divorced from one's primal sensuality, to function mechanically, like a sexual performer.

When we experience a oneness with nature we can feel a oneness with all other humans, who are also part of nature.

We are at peace with the world. We know that what happens to another happens to us.

We are whole, sensuous, loving.

Sensuality is
   the River of Life
It holds flashing
   waterfalls—Sexuality.
  To ride the Falls
one must first swim the River.